CM0074I5I6

Dear Amily June,

For Christmas 2010

All our Love

Daniel
Angie
Zephy
Xander

THE MIEGUNYAH PRESS

This is number sixty-five in
the second numbered series
of the Miegunyah Volumes
made possible by the
Miegunyah Fund
established by bequests under
the wills of Sir Russell and
Lady Grimwade.

'Miegunyah' was the home of
Mab and Russell Grimwade
from 1911 to 1955.

THE PURSUIT OF WONDER

HOW AUSTRALIA'S LANDSCAPE WAS EXPLORED,
NATURE DISCOVERED AND TOURISM UNLEASHED

JULIA HORNE

THE
MIEGUNYAH
PRESS

Material in this book that is quoted or paraphrased from
original sources retains imperial measurements
1 foot = 0.30 metres
1 mile = 1.61 kilometres

THE MIEGUNYAH PRESS
An imprint of Melbourne University Publishing Ltd
187 Grattan Street, Carlton, Victoria 3053, Australia
mup-info@unimelb.edu.au
www.mup.com.au

First published 2005
Text © Julia Horne 2005
Design and typography © Melbourne University Publishing Ltd 2005

The following images also appear with captions on the following pages: p. ii, see p. 162; pp. viii–1,
see p. 19; pp. 22–3, see p. 41; pp. 60–1, see p. 74; pp. 98–9, see p. 102; pp. 140–1, see p. 146;
pp. 174–5, see p. 181; pp. 198–9, see p. 224; pp. 226–7, see p. 237; pp. 252–3, see p. 264;
pp. 280–1, see p. 295.

This book is copyright. Apart from any use permitted under the Copyright Act 1968 and
subsequent amendments, no part may be reproduced, stored in a retrieval system or transmitted by
any means or process whatsoever without the prior written permission of the publishers.

National Library of Australia Cataloguing-in-Publication entry

Horne, Julia.
The pursuit of wonder : how Australia's landscape was
explored, nature discovered and tourism unleashed.

Bibliography.
Includes index.
ISBN 0 522 85166 5.

1. Travelers - Australia - History. 2. Australians -
Travel. 3. Tourism - Australia - History. 4. Culture and
tourism - Australia. 5. Australia - Description and travel.
I. Title.

910.994

CONTENTS

ACKNOWLEDGEMENTS

To D and M, who showed me Australia and taught me how to travel

Writing a book is often a solitary experience, yet in the wings there are casts of thousands. I thank them all. For illustrations, among many who helped me, I especially thank John Low from the Local Studies Section, Blue Mountains City Library; Elizabeth Ellis, Margot Riley and Robert Woodley from the Mitchell Library; Richard Ratajczak from Rare Books, and Geoff Barker from University Museums, the University of Sydney. Most of my original documentary sources are from state libraries, these wonderful treasure troves that would take lifetimes to explore fully. Some are also from the local studies sections of municipal libraries, which, through their building up of trust with local communities, have become the repository for valuable historical material. All these public institutions, along with the essential reference tool the *Australian Dictionary of Biography* (and its hundreds of volunteer authors) serve the national purpose of preserving and encouraging the study of our history.

I feel very privileged to have had so much support from Melbourne University Publishing. Thanks to Louise Adler who said she loved the topic, to Sybil Nolan for her critical appraisal and useful suggestions on the manuscript, to Tracy O'Shaughnessy who turned it into a Miegunyah Press publication, and to Catherine Cradwick for shepherding the book to completion. Thanks also to Carla Taines for her gentle and consultative approach to editing the final manuscript, and to Roderic Campbell for his indispensable assistance in shaping the masses of illustrations into some sort of order and for producing an intelligent index.

For useful references and comments on early proposals and subsequent drafts, special thanks to Michele Field, Patricia Grimshaw, John McQuilton, Ros Pesman, Jill Roe, Peter Spearritt and Richard White; and to Stephen Garton, Donald and Myfanwy Horne, Beverley Kingston and Glenda Sluga, who have, over the years, been prepared to listen to my ideas and read drafts, all with an intelligent and critical eye. Finally, a very personal thanks to all my family, especially Stephen and Anna. This book is also for you.

WHAT THIS IS ALL ABOUT

In which the purpose of this book is explained

I n the 1860s and 1870s people were writing about the beauties of a wayside stop en route to the Victorian gold mines at Woods Point: 'the singularity and grandeur of the scenery, the new forms and luxuriance of the foliage, and the brilliant green that meets the eye on every side, suggest a feeling of tropical magnificence'. By the 1870s, Fernshaw had become a small saw-milling village. Within its forest of tall, straight mountain ash were gullies of tree ferns forming a feathery canopy of green, and beyond them, the distant mountain tops of the Great Dividing Range. The artists Louis Buvelot and Eugen von Guérard, the botanist Ellis Rowan and the photographer Nicholas Caire all documented the region, intent on capturing the delicacy of tall, slender tree ferns, the great height of the eucalypts and the suggestion of fascinating mountains beyond. The natural attractions of Fernshaw were an obvious drawcard to nineteenth-century tourists in Australia, fashionably interested in tree fern gullies and picturesque mountains, and by the 1870s, despite the long horse and coach journey from Melbourne, there was a small tourist trade to the area. Nowadays it is not easy to find this combination of magical tree ferns and giant mountain ashes. Many of the tree fern gullies in the Dandenongs and Mount Macedon have been destroyed either by the logging of previous generations, or by the landscaping accompanying the development of hill resorts. Today, where can one go to see this type of scenery so sought after in nineteenth-century Australia?

In my childhood on a family holiday in the area, long before I had heard of Fernshaw, we drove to Woods Point along a narrow, winding, precipitous mountain road. I spent most of the trip hoping we wouldn't career off the road down the steep slope or meet a logging truck head-to-head. Yet I must have had a few moments free of anxiety because I remember giant trees, like nothing I'd ever seen before, splendid in their towering above us. Perhaps there were still tree fern gullies in the

MOUNTAIN ASH AND TALL TREE FERNS. *By the 1870s Fernshaw in Victoria was recommended for these colonial favourites. (Samuel Calvert,* Holiday Rambles— Fernshaw and the Black Spur, *1874?)*

midst of the forest at Fernshaw, and I could return to seek them out and see for myself the celebrated dappled lighting effects produced by the canopy of interlacing fronds. Would the tree fern fronds also remind me, as they had many a nineteenth-century tourist, of pretty parasols or emerald-like jewels?

The helpful woman at Tourism Victoria could supply brochures for Mount Macedon and the Dandenongs—both places of interest to nineteenth-century tourists. But Fernshaw? 'What region?' I could only tell her that my information (an 1872 newspaper account) put it near Woods Point, Healesville and Marysville. 'Ah, the Yarra Valley region.' A long pause. 'Mmmm, I can't find it. Are you sure it's there?' Perhaps Fernshaw no longer existed as Fernshaw, its name changed as had happened to other nineteenth-century natural attractions. It seemed Tourism Victoria couldn't help me.

Back to the library and the work of dedicated compilers of documents of the past to find out what had happened to Fernshaw. And there it was in a painstakingly gathered, scrapbook collection of newspaper and other cuttings. In the mid-1880s the Victorian Metropolitan Water Supply Department had bought up Fernshaw, demolished the buildings and fenced off the surrounding land as a water catchment area. The Watts River was dammed, flooded the region, and became Melbourne's water supply, the Maroondah reservoir.[1] Not a name change, but obliteration, a reminder of natural beauty lost forever.

Yet, despite this unhappy discovery, I also found that in the concluding decades of the nineteenth century and in the face of increasing demands on the natural environment for water, pasture and minerals, many natural attractions were deliberately spared, although some the worse for wear. They survived largely because of an accepted belief that natural wonders did matter, that they were intrinsically valuable for a society's emotional health, that they were a necessary reminder of non-human forces and power and that they were an important spur to fruitful contemplation and the pursuit of knowledge. This complex relationship between people, culture and nature, how each shapes the other, is a central story in the history of colonial tourism and an important theme of this book. The purpose of this book is not to tell the story of the commercialisation of Australian travel and the development of a local tourist industry, which in any case is the major theme of Jim Davidson's and Peter Spearritt's *Holiday Business* (2000). As they convincingly argue, Australia only entered this world economy in the last few decades of the nineteenth century, specifically when Thomas Cook established a commercial interest in the possibilities of local touring. My book is largely concerned with the nineteenth century before the age of mass tourism. Its intention is to explore how the evolution of ideas about wonder in scenic Australia in the nineteenth century—produced by middle and upper-class explorers and tourists—had far-reaching social and cultural effects, and in its wake helped create not only a tourist industry, but also an enduring interest in the natural environment.

Interest in the tourist possibilities of Australia goes back more than two centuries, to the time when the term 'tourist' first emerged in the English language. From the second half of the eighteenth century, New Holland had aroused wide curiosity in England and other parts of the European world, for its natural attractions, its unusual scenery, animals, plants, rock formations. At the turn of the nineteenth century and for some time after, Australia, newly colonised by England, was an appealing destination for travellers keen to avoid the well-trodden path of the European grand tour and looking for novelty—perhaps collecting a botanical specimen unknown to the European imagination—or to publish accounts of their experiences in this New World. But later there also developed among the colonists an interest in finding out more about the country they had made their home. There were to be numerous accounts of Australian travels in colonial newspapers throughout the nineteenth century. By the 1890s, some writers were measuring a town's worth as much by its capacity to attract

THE PINNACLE OF MOUNT WELLINGTON.

ROCKY GULLIES AND MOUNTAIN VIEWS. *Mount Wellington, close to Hobart, was throughout the nineteenth century as much admired for the scenery on the way to its summit as it was for the view from the top. (Engraver unknown,* The Pinnacle of Mount Wellington, *1873?)*

tourists as by its natural resources, manufactures and industries. Districts were often praised for being 'a favourite resort for tourists'.[2]

By the end of the nineteenth century many scenic attractions were being recommended for travellers to see for themselves—magnificent views from mountain tops, such as Mount Buffalo in Victoria and Mount Kosciuszko in New South Wales and, if lucky, rainbows playing on slender waterfalls reminiscent of bridal veils. Then there were areas like Mount Wellington in Tasmania and the Dandenongs in Victoria where the ground was carpeted with ferns or the gullies filled with tree ferns hailed for their beauty. Lakes rimmed by mountains were highly valued (Lake St Clair in Tasmania and the Gippsland lakes in Victoria, for instance), as were fantastically shaped rocks or beautiful underground displays of shimmering or glistening limestone deposits, like those in New South Wales at Wellington and Jenolan Caves. South Australia was busy opening up access to Mount Gambier, Naracoorte Caves and Spencer Gulf, where tourists could see such wonders as an extraordinary blue lake, limestone caverns and the rocky vistas produced by glacial activity. South Australia also had its mountains, such as the Flinders Ranges and Mount Lofty, a summer resort beacon for well-to-do Adelaide residents escaping the sea-level summer heat. Western Australia attracted tourists to its south-western corner for native flora, tall trees and interesting caves. Tourists in Queensland sought the healing powers of nature in the ferny regions of what was to be known as Mount Tamborine, and from the rocky outcrops of the Glasshouse Mountains. The idea of the tropical north as a tourist paradise was beginning: North Queenslanders occasionally made up boating parties to view the brightly coloured fish and coral branches of nearby reefs, and the tourism potential of tropical rainforests, generally areas with a 'great spread of palms' and particularly the Barron Falls in far north Queensland, was being discussed.[3]

Yet why these particular natural features? Today when people visit natural attractions like Uluru, the Kimberley, the Great Barrier Reef or Kakadu, they do so partly out of a sense of duty to some of the 'greats' of Australia's natural attractions. They arrive with expectations of certain experiences (now often dependent on a sophisticated tourist infrastructure). Perhaps a helicopter ride over the massiveness of the Kimberley and a stop at a secluded gorge for a cooling swim. Or snorkelling on the Great Barrier Reef to view colourful fish, giant clams, and if in luck, to follow (at a respectful distance) a sea turtle doing the rounds. At Uluru, there is the chance to marvel, like thousands before them, at the great sandstone monolith rising out of the desert, which William Gosse in the 1870s described as 'certainly the most wonderful natural feature I have ever seen', or to follow the colours of the sandstone changing according to the time of day, or learn more about Aboriginal legends, rock art and bush food. In Kakadu, there are early morning boat trips on Yellow Water, sedately moving among the reeds and lily pads, watching an extraordinary variety of birds.

Many people will be moved by these sights. Some won't, puzzled at what meanings are to be gained from viewing a landscape or seeing fish or birds in their own environment. But those who are moved have crossed the line into wonder.

The pursuit of wonder was one of the driving forces of early tourists, reaching its zenith in the eighteenth and nineteenth centuries. The answer to the question of why particular natural features became favourite destinations for nineteenth-century tourists in Australia is in their appeal to certain nineteenth-century cultural interests and sensibilities, the wonder expected to be inspired by a view, a geological formation, a botanical specimen. Wonder as a response to the sight of natural attractions had not always been so defined. But for colonial tourists a sense of wonder at natural attractions was there because of what they had learned. As we shall see, nineteenth-century explorers and tourists writing in their journals, guided by upper middle-class cultural values and conventions and whether they were 'ladies' or 'gentlemen', selected certain areas, described them in certain terms, and

MAJESTIC WATERFALLS AND TROPICAL LUXURIANCE *in North Queensland became tourist destinations towards the end of the nineteenth century. The Barron Falls and their raging wet-season torrent were a short rail trip from Cairns. (Engraver unknown,* Picturesque Queensland—Cairns. The Barron Falls, *1888?)*

THE 'MOST WONDERFUL NATURAL FEATURE I HAVE EVER SEEN,' *wrote the explorer William Gosse, who named Ayers Rock during his 1873 expedition to Central Australia. Gosse drew this picture from a vantage point rarely used for later depictions of the rock. Renamed Uluru, it did not become a tourist favourite until twentieth-century transport improvements. (W. C. Gosse, [Ayers Rock (Uluru)], 1873.)*

even sketched them in particular ways. They passed on their 'discoveries' to later tourists who continued the process by finding their own. Time and again throughout the nineteenth century different scenes were made wonderful.

Is there such a thing as distinctively Australian natural scenery? Ask this of Australians aged over forty and many may quote these lines from twentieth-century Australian poet Dorothea Mackellar:

> I love a sunburnt country
> A land of sweeping plains,
> Of ragged mountain ranges,
> Of droughts and flooding rains.

Images of sun, sand and surf are also sure to feature, along with vibrant colour, bright blues, vivid oranges, bold ochres splashed around a canvas of sky, earth and sea. Uluru as a place for quintessential Australian scenery may be suggested by many, even those (most Australians) who have never been there.

Present-day attitudes would have been extraordinary to nineteenth-century tourists. From the huge amount of published and unpublished travel writing about Australia, as well as artworks, it would seem that our forebears felt that Australia was distinctive for its views from rocky outcrops looking out across deep ravines and into ancient, broad valleys, for its gullies decorated with tall tree ferns, for waterfalls with little volume but great height, and for caves filled with a variety of crystalline limestone shapes. In the nineteenth century pride was often expressed in these natural wonders, even if in people's imagination today places like the Dandenongs or Jenolan Caves may have lost the freshness of novelty.

There are difficulties in pinning down exactly what makes scenery distinctive. Like Australia, Africa has deserts and vibrant colours, North America has ancient broad valleys, New Zealand has tree fern gullies. Yet the notion of distinctiveness helps to define much tourist interest in natural attractions, and helps explain why people travel at all. In the twenty-first century such distinctiveness still signifies what might be interesting, spectacular or edifying, and perhaps an entry point into a state of wonder. Many nineteenth-century travel writers used the words 'novel' or 'novelty' as short-hand terms for 'distinctiveness'. For them, a 'novel scene' suggested such distinctiveness that existing descriptive vocabulary may not have captured its essence. Distinctiveness also defined Australia's difference from the Old World.

The Australian colonies were part of the British empire, with traditional institutions established in response to local circumstances, yet in an ancient and varied land that was increasingly valued as unspoiled. Travel through such a land could reveal whole new horizons of knowledge and turn existing wisdom upside down.

This book is a celebration of some of Australia's natural attractions. It takes up Bernard Smith's argument that European experience of the South Pacific and Australia, especially in attempts to articulate distinctiveness of its scenery, botany and local cultures, transformed European conceptions of the world, including aesthetic values and the natural sciences.[4] From the beginnings of colonisation there were people who liked much of what they saw. Their observations and remarks helped influence how others saw the natural environment. Tim Bonyhady's *The Colonial Earth*, a study of colonial attitudes towards the Australian environment, highlights the fact that from the early days of colonisation there were influential enthusiasts for colonial scenery.

There was also criticism. The travel-writing genre encouraged critique—scenery in Scotland, England, North America, anywhere, had its critics. A practical aspect of critique in Australia was allowing writers to query the usefulness of European terms in describing the scenery and the presumed superiority of English scenery. Early in his journal—on his outward journey to Bathurst in the 1820s—judge and literary critic Barron Field criticised features of the Blue Mountains that had been named by an early governor of New South Wales Lachlan Macquarie: 'The Prince Regent's Glen below it ... is not very romantic ... Pitt's Amphitheatre disappointed me. The hills are thrown together in a monotonous manner, and their clothing is very unpicturesque'. To Field, the landscape did not fit expectations aroused by 'glen' and 'amphitheatre'. But writers could change their judgements in day-by-day travel accounts, a literary technique often used in the late eighteenth and early nineteenth centuries to give immediacy to the experience. Twenty pages later in his account, Field described the return journey:

> Admired the view of Pitt's amphitheatre from this side of Blackheath much more than before. The sun was declining at the back of it, and the

Mount Lofty in South Australia *was a pleasant excursion from Adelaide, initially favoured by tourists for the region's fashionable rocky chasms, waterfalls and grand views, and later, for the smaller variety of ferns that grew in the shaded gullies. (George French Angas,* Lower Falls of Glen Stuart, *c. 1844.)*

shade softened its monotonous harsh bosom ... into misty blue or mountain grey ... Altogether the effect of this day's journey of a clear afternoon was much finer than I thought it, when I was outward bound on a sultry day.[5]

Aesthetic judgements in travel writing were usually made in terms of the sublime or the beautiful (and at times, both), concepts that were part of a broader cultural framework—the picturesque—that the eighteenth and nineteenth centuries used to judge landscape. This framework employed a range of descriptive terms, often superlatives, to establish the characteristics of a scene, but not all their nineteenth-century meanings have lasted. Tourists today might exclaim 'how grand' or 'how beautiful', but few would remark 'how sublime', or 'it was truly

LAKE SCENERY. *By the 1880s the Gippsland Lakes in Victoria could be reached by steamer, coach or train. They offered much-admired snow-capped mountains in winter and year-round picturesque lake and river scenery. To some they were comparable to the Scottish lochs. (C. Winter,* The Entrance to the Gipps Land Lakes, *1867?)*

awful' (unless they did not like what they saw). Yet in the nineteenth century such terms were used in praise, for instance, to indicate awe before grandeur. 'Sublime' was a useful word when a writer wished to suggest the all-powerfulness of nature as the central focus of a scene, while the notion of the beautiful included encouraging a sense of well-being. Assessments of beauty in scenery often depended on the prevailing light because of the effects on the viewer of colours and refracted or dappled light on elements that made up the landscape.[6]

The enthusiastic and influential responses of travellers to Australia's natural environment helped develop a colonial landscape aesthetic. Much of this interest was aroused by visual images—paintings, drawings, etchings and, later, photographs. But the greatest stimulus to this aesthetic appreciation was writing, in particular, published accounts, and much of the power of visual images derived from their placement in a written context.

A vast range of literature published in the nineteenth century helped invent scenic Australia. There were travelogues (including explorers' journals) designed for the imperial market, travel accounts (as articles or readers' correspondence) in colonial newspapers, tourist guidebooks, and pamphlets advertising tourist activities. All these contributed to notions of colonial touring and appreciation of natural attractions. Most such literature is an expression of attitudes about touring and about Australian landscapes rather than a list of facts. It was an integral part of the nineteenth-century touring experience because it 'surrounded and regulated' attractions people had come to see, and mapped out the established boundaries for future visitors to heed or not.[7]

In Australia from the late eighteenth century onwards, as the English established their presence, written accounts along with sketches and paintings created both knowledge and preconceptions about the land they desired to possess. As Bernard Smith has shown landscape painting that 'could first survey and describe, then evoke in new settlers an emotional engagement with the land' was important to Britain's imperialistic and expansionary aims in Australia.[8]

The English had only recently settled on this use for painting for imperial purposes. After the Jacobite uprising in 1745–46 the English ordered a detailed survey of the Scottish Highlands in an attempt to strengthen support for its presence there. Sketches and paintings of cities, castles, industrial life and natural scenery by the official draughtsman Paul Sandby were turned into engravings and prints in the last two decades of the eighteenth century and circulated in England. Their appeal led to an emotional acquisition of Scotland by England and later artists also sought the Scottish picturesque, eulogised in poetry especially that of Sir Walter Scott:

> The evening mists, with ceaseless change
> Now clothed the mountains' lofty range
> Now left their foreheads bare
> And round the skirts their mantle furl'd
> Or on the sable waters curl'd
> Or on the eddying breezes whirl'd
> Dispersed in middle air.

The Highlands were now desirable destinations, and tourists visited and viewed them, often quoting Scott's poetry in their travel diaries to evoke the effect such landscapes had on them.[9]

In Australia, explorers' accounts in the late eighteenth and early nineteenth centuries were usually part of a surveying process noting not only the economic prospects of the land, but also scientific and scenic novelty. How tourism makes use of the previously defined is particularly apparent in regards to the Blue Mountains, because, unlike most natural tourist attractions in Australia they were written about by explorers since the late eighteenth century and by tourists for much of the

'SOMETHING PECULIAR OF ITS KIND,' *wrote the Catholic priest and geologist Julian Tenison-Woods of the Great Barrier Reef. For much of the colonial period the two thousand kilometre stretch of the Great Barrier Reef was feared for its shipwrecks, but there was also interest in its opportunities for sightseeing. From Cooktown a two-hour boat party journey to a reef arrived at the turn of the tide. To see the 'full luxuriance', Tenison-Woods advised wearing hobnail boots and being 'prepared to wade up to one's neck in water and, if you want good specimens, to dive and swim in your clothes'. (Edwin Augustus Porcher,* Australia, Sandbank on the Great Barrier Reefs, *1843.)*

nineteenth. Many accounts survived and help trace the development of attitudes to celebrated locations from the time when the modern concept of a scenic attraction was emerging in Europe.

Historians have long noted the extensive accounts by men of their expeditions, explorations and tours, yet a cursory glance of bibliographies accompanying their studies reveals a great deficiency of women writers, although there were in fact a surprising number of them. It is useful to consider the influence of gender. There were conventions governing 'lady' and 'gentleman' tourists and these identities structured aspects of travel in ways they no longer do. At different periods particular aspects of travel were of greater interest to one sex than the other. Tourist writing from the second half of the nineteenth century evoked this gender divide to heighten the appeal of touring, and to designate difficulties and dangers.

The layers of meaning attached to notable Australian tourist attractions increased as tourist activity became the target of commercial interests. In the second half of the nineteenth century substantial local guidebooks were published, newspapers ran regular columns on 'the tourist', the railways conducted promotions about tourist destinations within the colonies, and hotel and boarding houses ran (modest) campaigns to encourage people to stay in one region for longer periods. Such publicity led to 'invention' of additional natural attractions as local tourist attractions to give tourists new opportunities. Increasingly, the possibility of rest in relaxing surroundings was combined with the edifying aspects of touring, gathering information or becoming knowledgeable about their surroundings. People invented tourism—the meaning (or attractiveness) of particular sights as well as their commercialisation, but then commercial tourism expanded the idea of the tourist, first, on the basis of social status and sex, and later in the nineteenth century, as customer, pleasure-seeker, holiday-maker.

Since commercial tourism in Australia was only beginning to emerge in its modern form at the end of the nineteenth century, the terms 'tourist' and 'touring' (or 'tour') had a different meaning throughout much of the nineteenth century. The term 'tourist', taken up by commercial interests in a push to increase a new and lucrative market, had developed a pejorative meaning in Britain by the 1850s, and was used to insult people's intelligence and individuality. Conversely, the word 'traveller' had more benign connotations: of someone who set out to travel the

AUSTRALIAN WILDFLOWERS AS COLLECTORS' ITEMS. *In the nineteenth century, King George's Sound in Western Australia was a regular anchorage for passenger ships. Local Aborigines often offered those who disembarked bunches of wildflowers, or negotiated to act as guides. The area developed a reputation for its abundance and variety of flowering plants and shrubs. (Robert Havell [engraver],* Panoramic View of King George's Sound, Part of the Colony of Swan River, *1834.)*

world, mix with the locals (not fellow tourists) and learn something from these new experiences.[10]

But up until the 1890s the term 'tourist' in colonial Australia did little more than describe someone setting out to see sights and places and to learn something more about the world they lived in. It was only at the end of the century that the term came to include pursuits such as rest and relaxation in the healthy atmosphere of mountain resorts (a development encouraged by the business acumen of boarding house 'proprietresses' seeking to persuade guests to stay longer). And, only in the early twentieth century in Australia, not long after organised touring had been taken up as a commercial activity locally, did the term begin to be derided. In Australia before the 1890s most commentators used the term 'tourist' as people today might use 'traveller', and most used the terms interchangeably (as they are used in this book).[11]

The term 'touring' (or 'tour') was the activity undertaken by tourists interested in seeing recommended sights and places, although it had also been used to describe early land explorations within the colony as in the military 'tour of duty' or 'tour of discovery'. Touring was a way of gathering information and also of learning about new things. Later, the terms 'touring' and 'tourist' came to be part of the wider phenomenon of democratised holidays and leisure.[12] But for most of the nineteenth century in the colonies, tourists were mostly the privileged with time and money.

Early tourists writing about Australian surroundings helped define not only sights that later became popular but also their noteworthy characteristics. Technological developments in transport—steamboats and trains (as in the twentieth century, motor cars and aeroplanes)—were certainly to improve travel conditions reducing time and costs, and thus, offering more people the opportunity to make a trip. But in the colonies trains did not so much initiate local tourist activity as contribute to and help develop existing tourist arrangements based as they had been on a network of coaches and coastal and river shipping.

Before the advent of cheap fares and accommodation there were new commercial ventures capitalising on already existing activity. Nineteenth-century touring in the colonies was imbued with significant cultural values including emotional acquisitions to the empire from learning about this 'new land', the gendering of activities, and a local desire to imagine the colony for its residents. What magic did stalagmites hold for the nineteenth-century tourist? Why were ferns and waterfalls such big attractions at the turn of the century? Why were so many observers inspired to describe the Blue Mountains as majestic mountains, when they can equally be seen as a series of grand canyons? Such questions take us into the territory of how culture defines scenery, but also how the environment shapes culture.

At its heart was a passion for wonder, an immense driving force that not only inspired people to leave the comfort of their homes to seek out the sights and experiences of nature, but also, upon their return, enthused many of them to recount their experiences for those who stayed behind. These accounts took many forms, from informal stories over tea or supper, to sketches and specimens collected as souvenirs, to published and unpublished travel journals, and the work of professional writers and artists. In all they reveal a profound nineteenth-century interest in Australian landscapes as both scenic and revelatory, and allow us to identify and explore these attitudes in the context of the past, and reflect on their present-day legacy.

MAKING TOURISM
AUSTRALIAN

*In which European ideas about travel, art
and the origins of tourism, and how they became
Australian, are examined*

Mid-August 1768, summer in England. The port of Plymouth was filled with naval ships and a few commercial vessels unloading cargo from domestic and foreign ports, and disembarking travellers from Europe, the Americas and the Far East. The better inns in England's ports could do well from the trade of travellers: not only arrivals from foreign ports, but also wealthy young Englishmen and their retinues of artists and servants ready for a lengthy grand tour of Europe, who often took up quarters in port towns, rather than wait for favourable sailing winds in uncomfortable ships' quarters. Part of this busy scene was one of the English Navy's latest acquisitions—the newly refitted *Endeavour* was at Plymouth making ready to set sail.

Two of its passengers, the naturalists Mr Banks and Dr Solander, were due to arrive from London, having been informed by its commander, Captain Cook, of the *Endeavour*'s imminent departure. Their baggage had already been loaded on board, their quarters prepared by Banks' servants. Their luggage was typical of wealthy tourists and filled many chests, but along with such traveller's essentials as umbrellas and oilskin coats was equipment to collect and preserve specimens of discoveries in lands hitherto almost unknown to European scientists. Also with them was a library of books and bundles of paper for recording and analysing their experiences. Banks had brought a skiff of his own since there would be no certainty of hiring one either en route or at their destination, the usual arrangement made by tourists, and employed several artists for the voyage, again not unusual for wealthy gentlemen tourists wanting to return with objects and drawings for display at their English estates. Like most travellers, Banks had a map, this one compiled by the

JOSEPH BANKS, GRAND TOURIST, *back from the south seas. Like many young gentlemen returning from their grand tours, Banks' family commissioned a portrait of him surrounded by souvenirs from his travels, including a portfolio of botanical drawings (bottom right). This 1773 mezzotint was after the 1771–72 portrait by Benjamin West. (John Raphael Smith [engraver],* Mr Banks, *c. 1773.)*

British hydrographer Alexander Dalrymple to illustrate his 1764 pamphlet on Pacific discoveries and the case for the existence of a large continent in the southern ocean.

At last a fair wind. The *Endeavour* weighed anchor and departed Plymouth mid-afternoon on 26 August to begin its journey to the South Pacific.[1] The reason for the voyage: the London-based Royal Society had persuaded King George III to back a scientific expedition to Tahiti to measure a rare astronomical phenomenon, the transit of Venus. On the King's command, his Admiralty took charge although the Royal Society continued its interest, providing scientific measuring instruments and recommending the astronomer Charles Green to oversee the observations in Tahiti. The Admiralty also had another purpose for the expedition. Captain James Cook had orders that the *Endeavour* was to proceed from Tahiti to search for a great southern continent.

Joseph Banks, who left Oxford before taking his degree, was a botanical enthusiast who liked unusual botanical excursions. Instead of taking the customary grand tour of European antiquities, in 1766 aged twenty-three he had sailed with HMS *Niger* to Newfoundland and Labrador, where he collected rocks, plants and animals. His election to the Royal Society in the same year was not a vote of confidence in his scholarly brilliance so much as recognition of the great family wealth he had inherited in 1764, his gentlemanly status, his botanical interests and, especially, his increasing association with important botanical scholars, including Daniel Solander, the Swedish-born protégé of the celebrated Carl Linnaeus, who was his companion—at £400 a year—on the journey. The young Joseph Banks was being groomed by his elders as a future patron of the sciences.

Several months before the departure of the *Endeavour*, the Royal Society suggested to the Admiralty that Banks accompany the expedition as a passenger, along with his staff of eight naturalists, artists and servants, not in an official capacity, but as a traveller wanting an experience of a lifetime and competent to observe the natural history of a new world. Banks retorted to suggestions he should undertake the more conventional European grand tour, 'Every blockhead does that, my Grand Tour shall be one round the whole globe'.[2]

The voyage to Tahiti took five months, but at ports of call on the way Banks and his men conducted botanical excursions. The English consul in Madeira provided permits, guides and horses to explore the countryside, and Cook stayed longer than necessary in the South Atlantic's Tierra del Fuego for the naturalists to begin their exploration of the southern hemisphere.

During calm days at sea, the crew lowered the skiff into the ocean. Banks and his party netted seaweed, fish and other marine life, and he used an unusual telescope to see to a great depth. Once in the South Atlantic there was an abundance of novelty to be sketched and examined: albatrosses, whales, seals, penguins, dolphins and petrels. Natural history books were consulted and where possible, everything observed and noted, even familiar sea birds, flying fish, sharks, crabs, jelly fish and insects.

In the late afternoons and during foul weather, the party retired to what had become the study centre, the great cabin, usually the preserve of the captain, now modified to accommodate Banks' needs. Specimens laid out by Banks' naturalists were scrupulously delineated by the natural history painter Sydney Parkinson who was sometimes helped by the landscape painter Alexander Buchan. Banks and Solander used this time to write up journal entries, in Banks' case, a day-by-day account, usually a record of natural history observations and, as opportunities arose, observations of local manners and customs. He also included emotion-inspired descriptions, a new technique in travellers' accounts, which counterbalanced objective observation with literary flourishes suggesting the effect of a scene on the observer's senses.

Months at sea without the distractions of a gentleman's life in London provided time for contemplation, and Banks used it productively, producing several long essays for inclusion in his journal: 'Manners and Customs of the South Sea Islands', an 'Account of New Zealand' and 'Some Account of that part of New Holland now called New South Wales'. By the end of the voyage, the journal consisted of more than a thousand sheets of paper which back in London would be bound into two volumes, yet like the writings of many travellers of the time, was never published,

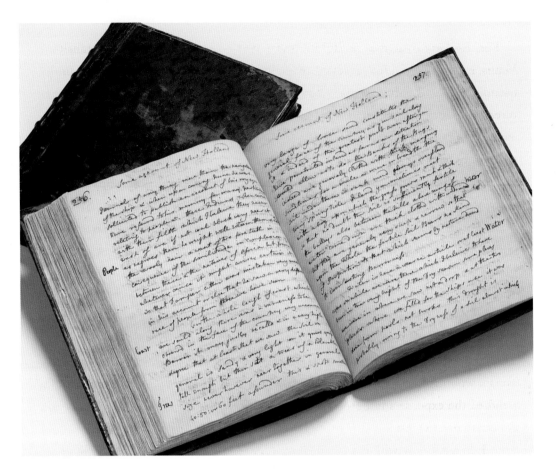

JOURNALS *were expected from late-eighteenth-century travellers, as much for their descriptions of the emotional effect of scenery as their factual observations. (Joseph Banks, The Endeavour Journal, August 1768 – July 1771.)*

although at least two hand-written copies were produced for private circulation, one by his sister who punctuated the text, corrected misspellings and added explanatory notes. Along with curio collections and sketches and paintings, journals were the expected outcomes of travel, reference tools for future contemplation intended to be not just descriptions of places visited but also an attempt to make sense of all that had been seen and experienced.

The *Endeavour* arrived in Tahiti seven weeks before the expected transit of Venus, in mid-April 1769, at least the second European ship to have done so in the island's recent history. Tahitians reached the ship by canoe, made friendly overtures, and Cook reciprocated with beads for coconuts, bread fruit, fish and native apples. The Englishmen went ashore to be met by hundreds of locals, not unfriendly but initially reserved, though they soon accompanied Cook, Banks and the other officers and gentlemen on a walk in the forest. Over the following days there were more exchanges of gifts, and the visitors began to be included in the island's daily activities, as they established camps and gathered food and water supplies for their expected three-month stay. Banks, who had little to do with the transit of Venus aspect of the voyage, spent his time botanising, journalising, and above all socialising, having formed various liaisons with the locals, of a friendly, informative and sometimes intimate nature.

Astronomical observations concluded, the *Endeavour* left Tahiti for a month-long tour of the archipelago, successful due to the navigation of the high priest Tupaia who had persuaded Banks to include him in the party. In his journal Banks weighed the expense and possible inconvenience of such an addition alongside the potential advantages:

> I do not know why I may not keep him as a curiosity, as well as some of my neighbours do lions and tygers [*sic*] at a larger expense than he will probably ever put me to; the amusement I shall have in his future conversation and the benefit he will be of to this ship, as well as what he may be if another should be sent into these seas, will I think fully repay me.[3]

The excursion probably would not have been possible without this knowledgeable guide negotiating their safe passage through hazardous waters, and the social and political realities of the island societies. The excursion certainly was made more interesting with his explanations of social and religious practices, and suggestions of places to visit.

In mid-August 1769, a year after departing Plymouth, the *Endeavour* began its seven-week search for a great southern continent, during which time Joseph Banks in consultation with Tupaia and other travelling companions, wrote his 104-page account of the 'Manners and Customs of the South Sea Islands'.

They failed in their search, and headed for New Zealand where they spent six months charting the islands. By 1770 Cook was moving up the uncharted east coast of New Holland. Cook later designated this territory 'New South Wales', starting from the newly named Botany Bay, an apparent tribute to the botanical discoveries, and which led eighteen years later to the establishment of a British colony some kilometres north at Port Jackson. On the return voyage to England via Batavia, just under a third of the ship's company died, including Tupaia. Back in England Banks and Solander were presented to the King, and Oxford University made them both doctors of civil law.

Joseph Banks set out on this journey at a turning-point in the history of travel, at the time, in fact, of the very origins of modern sight-seeing and its new breed of traveller. This new breed was generally interested in the natural sciences and brought a new emotional engagement with nature and natural scenery. Travellers offered in their diaries, journals, letters and paintings a scientific eye for detail, yet also an eye inspired by wonder, one that sought to observe the effect such sights had on the beholder. In late eighteenth-century terms, Joseph Banks was one of the first tourists to visit Australia.[4]

The term 'tourist' dates from the later part of the eighteenth century. It was used then to describe a traveller who toured sites of interest, with the journey itself as part of the purpose, the travel as well as the arriving being equally important. When in the early nineteenth century an English linguist recorded that 'a Traveller is nowadays called a Tour-*ist*' he was announcing not only the emergence of a new term, but also a recognition that the term 'traveller' could encompass the specific activity of touring. The two terms in British travel writing were interchangeable, at least until the second half of the nineteenth century. Travelling as a tourist in this period was a means of learning more about the world through empirical observation and emotional enlightenment, appraising the effect of a natural scene on the senses. The prime purpose of tourists' travels was to explore and ultimately try to understand the place of humankind in the earthly world, and travel in this sense came to be valued as a means to new knowledge.

By the time the British were colonising Australia, the idea of travel for edification was well established. Given the primary importance of exploration to the process of colonisation, it was not long before the colonisers were travelling, in fact undertaking tours often with official support through lands new to them, in order to collect data, make observations and learn something about the land and its people. Until well into the nineteenth century, as Eric Leed argues in his comprehensive history of European travel, exploration and tourist, travel had certain indistinguishable features, including the aim of describing or observing what was previously unknown (at least to Europeans). Travel was a means to learn of this 'new' world, the wonders of which could be discovered afresh by each new arrival. In this sense, the aims of those undertaking such travels were generally similar to those in England or elsewhere in Europe who toured districts to learn more about architectural styles or natural curiosities. In both, the reason for travelling was to view items of interest.[5]

Certainly, in Australia a major aim of much early colonial travel was to 'discover' (the term then used) land with economic potential. But, importantly, this went along with observing what lay along the route. In describing the country beyond the Blue Mountains the surveyor George William Evans proclaimed, 'no country can possibly have a more interesting aspect … I see no end to travelling'. In this sense (as is made clear in Evans' account of what he saw) travelling was the goal: there was 'no end to travelling' not because the land appeared to extend forever, but because there was so much to observe, to 'discover' in the immediate environment. Even when expeditions were unsuccessful in 'discovering' economically productive land, journals were still published to provide accounts of the journey and the Australian countryside and its 'curiosities'.

Notions of touring—the activity of observing places and sights on a journey—were important to much of this early travel (even when it was defined as exploration) and, inevitably, comparison was made with conditions in Europe. Watkin Tench, describing his expedition to the Nepean and Hawkesbury in 1791, wrote, 'instead of the cheering blaze, the welcome landlord and the long bill of fare, the traveller has now to collect his fuel, to erect his wigwam, to fetch water, and to broil his morsel of salt pork'. Despite differences in accommodation and board, overland travelling in Australia could be described in terms recognisable to a late eighteenth-century audience familiar with the notion of touring the English countryside. It was expected that such travelling might be informative and that the traveller should note the distinctive characteristics of a region.[6]

The comparison between early colonial expeditions and travellers touring to, say, the English Lake District or the Scottish Highlands, can, of course, only go so far. Tourists in England usually followed a made road, however rough, from which they could divert if they wished, and had probably read accounts, or poetry, associated with the districts they wanted to visit. In Australia the point of most early colonial expeditions was to find routes (such as those used by local Aborigines) through the terrain and to 'discover' what was distinctive about a region.

There is a danger of labouring these differences and imposing twentieth-century notions of tourists. The activities were essentially similar, aimed to gather information, to broaden experience, to see more of the world, to discover new and wonderful things, and intrepid travellers anywhere also faced the unexpected. It was a time when few people in Europe undertook such tours, and improvements in travel conditions had not yet been brought about by the new steam-powered technology. Indeed, it is misleading to see all touring in, say, the British Isles at this time as consciously following well-beaten paths since much late eighteenth-century touring in search of the picturesque in England, Wales and Scotland was significant in 'discovering' many of the natural features—such as Snowdon in Wales—that only later became popular tourist attractions.[7]

The contemporary terms for early colonial expeditions were 'excursion' and 'tour' rather than 'exploration'. Only from the mid-nineteenth century were leaders of these earlier tours of discovery identified as 'explorers', and their travels as 'explorations'. However, the term 'excursion' was not exclusive to exploration and was also used to account for travels over routes already established by the colonists that promised the opportunity to view interesting sights: in the 1820s the judge and literary critic Barron Field published his 'Journal of an Excursion Across the Blue

SKETCHBOOKS ALSO *recorded aspects of travel. The painter Oswald Brierly*
combined written observations with his sketches. (Oswald W.B. Brierly, Journal
of a Visit to Twofold Bay, Maneroo: and Districts Beyond the Snowy River,
Dec. 1842 to Jan. 1843.*)*

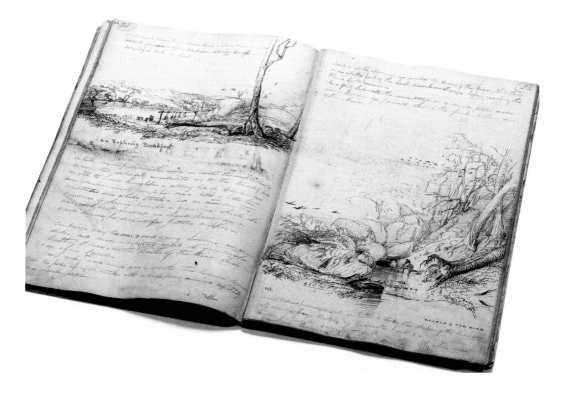

Mountains' and the colonist Mark Currie wrote of his 'Excursion to the Southward of Lake George'. The term 'tour' was also used both by those who are today called explorers, and sightseers travelling an already-established route. Gregory Blaxland, later to be known to Australian primary school children as an important explorer, entitled his account of the 1813 Blue Mountains crossing *A Journal of a Tour of Discovery Across the Blue Mountains in New South Wales*, and Governor Macquarie's 1815 account of his journey along the rough road following much the same route was called 'Tour over the Western or Blue Mountains'.

The term 'expedition' was also used in much the same way as both 'excursion' and 'tour': in the early 1800s Francis Barrallier wrote of his 'expedition into the interior of New South Wales' and in 1820 John Oxley published accounts of his travels as *Journals of Two Expeditions into the Interior of New South Wales*. About the 1830s the term 'expedition' became the preferred description of journeys seeking to 'discover' new colonial routes, and only from the 1850s did the word 'exploring' or 'exploration' begin to dominate the titles of such accounts.[8]

In this early colonial period of tours and excursions, maritime exploration was held in special esteem, particularly in England, proud of the role the English Navy had in the empire's expansion into the Pacific. In Australia it took time for exploration by land to achieve similar esteem, although there was early interest and general acclamation. Initially these 'tours of discovery' garnered public acclaim in the local press and from the publication of explorers' journals, and recognition by colonial governors and patronage by private individuals and scientific societies. By the second half of the nineteenth century, the explorers had been raised to the level of 'brave noble spirits, who ... [possess] a fortitude and patience which almost ranks them among "the noble army of martyrs"'—they had attained historical significance. From this period on, particularly around the 1888 centenary of European colonisation, there were published biographies of earlier land explorers, such as Hamilton Hume's *The Life of Edward John Eyre*, and histories of Australian explorations, such as George Frimm's *The Australian Explorers: Their Labours, Perils, and Achievements*. Although a few statues and memorials to nineteenth-century explorers were erected at the time of their travels, particularly if they died on the job, most were not put up until the twentieth century, which also saw an enormous creative output based on Australian exploration. The change in emphasis had something to do with feeding the beginnings of a national sentiment that looked for character and colour in Australian history, and found this in the conquest of difficult terrain by heroic explorers. But in the late eighteenth and first half of the nineteenth century, those who travelled over land to observe new surroundings were more likely to compare themselves with travellers/tourists in England, Wales and Scotland than with the then exalted maritime explorers.[9]

The origins of Australian sightseeing are in these early colonial excursions, tours and expeditions. Although the activities of early travellers might be more accurately identified as 'sight-identifying' rather than as 'sight-seeing', the process was essentially the same, seeking out sights worthwhile to view (alongside judgements about the productivity of the land). Their *worth* was often identified by reference to notions of the sublime, the beautiful and the picturesque and the important literary and artistic modes of expression in the eighteenth and nineteenth centuries to depict enlightening and interesting landscapes. This intellectual and cultural framework had developed in Europe as a consequence of increasing interest in and knowledge of the natural world, and soon came to be used by travellers in the appraisal of landscapes and natural features, a way of proclaiming them as wonderful and distinctive.

Scientific data collected on the voyages of discovery throughout the eighteenth and nineteenth centuries continued to challenge accepted theories about the natural world so profoundly that new literary, philosophical and artistic practices were developed to make sense of them and value wilderness. 'Nature' and 'natural' had been words generally used to refer to essential, unchanging aspects of human character. This classical usage continued throughout the eighteenth century, but there also developed a sense of 'nature' and 'natural' as going beyond human (usually meaning European) civilisation—'wilderness', for example. Wilderness, like mountains,

THE SUBLIME *was an important concept in colonial explanations of extraordinary natural phenomena. This picture is a print from* Australia Terra Cognita *(1855–56), a series of twenty-nine engravings the mining-engineer-turned-naturalist William Blandowski intended to illustrate a serious scientific account (not completed) of Australia's natural history. (W. Blandowski,* Pattowatto. Granite boulders (Perrys haystack) Looking N.W. 47 Miles N by W of Melbourne, *1855.)*

caves, ancient forests, was valued because its variety, imperfection and ability to change defied human control and even explanation. In Australia written exclamations such as 'never in my life was my soul struck with such awful admiration' was by then the sort of common literary device used to evoke the experience of wilderness as a characteristic of the 'sublime'. But the sublime as a measure of a natural attraction's emotional worth was relatively short-lived, not lasting much beyond the late nineteenth century, although the types of landscape once described as sublime continue to impress today.[10]

In 1756 the Irish political philosopher Edmund Burke published a treatise attempting to arrange ideas about the sublime and the beautiful into a system that identified and explained the effects of certain experiences on humans. He was not the first to publish such a tract: indeed, it was largely derived from the work of the English essayist Joseph Addison, who published his *Pleasures of the Imagination* in 1712. But Burke's system, *A Philosophical Enquiry into the Origin of our Ideas of the Sublime and Beautiful*, became influential in its application to descriptions of certain types of natural scenery throughout the English-speaking world, in much the same way as did Immanuel Kant's *Critique of Judgement* in the German-speaking world. Burke's system was an important resource for John Oxley, the surveyor-general of New South Wales, appointed by Governor Macquarie in 1812 on English orders to retain someone who could provide detailed descriptions of lands surveyed. Kant's system was central to the Austrian painter Eugen von Guérard in his appraisal of Australian landscapes.[11]

According to Burke, the 'sublime' engendered 'grand passions' and was a source of immense power. It induced an experience affecting the emotions so powerfully that most humans were unable to comprehend or explain their responses to it. A 'clear idea', he argued, is 'another name for a little idea'. There was nothing easily comprehensible about the sublime. The sublime indicated greatness and power—because the sublime physically and mentally challenged human capability. The feminist philosopher Christine Battersby argues that, in the eighteenth and early nineteenth centuries, seeking out and contemplating the sublime was certainly not seen as generally suited to women for whom such physical and intellectual 'power' was thought irrelevant, if not dangerous—it was a masculine activity.[12]

Burke's system was based on a list of physical occurrences seen as likely to produce strong emotions, and included terms for such emotions. It described the extremes of natural phenomena—the brightest light (as in lightning), the darkest prospect (as in a cave or a cloudy night), the loudest sound (as in thunder). It also included natural objects remarkable for their dimensions, such as tall mountains and deep ravines, which could command descriptions such as 'grand', 'rugged', 'magnificent', or which suggested 'infinity'. 'Suddenness', too, was part of the sublime, for instance when land dropped steeply, and for a great distance. He noted that 'darkness', and 'confused, uncertain images' had a 'greater power on the fancy to form the grander passions than those … which are more clear and determinate'. One of the main emotions resulting from a sublime experience was 'terror … the strangest emotion which the mind is capable of feeling'; in Burke's system the adjective 'terrible' described objects or scenes that produced a sense of terror, a profound mental and emotional experience. He pronounced great depth more sublime than great height because looking down a precipice was more likely to provoke terror than looking upwards. Other emotions produced by the sublime were 'astonishment', 'awe', 'admiration', 'reverence' and 'respect', all indicating an observer's recognition of the power of a sublime experience.

Whereas the sublime as a means of describing natural scenes was at its height in the eighteenth and nineteenth centuries, the beautiful and the picturesque continue to have meaning today. In the same essay in which Burke analysed the sublime, he also classified the characteristics of objects that excited 'the senses to see them as beautiful': perfect proportions, smoothness, gradual variation, delicacy, fragility, and gently coloured in hues such as light greens, soft blues, weak whites, pink red and violets, a type of beauty still valued today in the gently rolling hills clothed in green against blue skies, in the wonderful sunsets that colour clouds in pinks and crimsons.[13]

The picturesque as an aesthetic category was created by the English writers and essayists William Gilpin, Uvedale Price and Richard Payne Knight, of whose writing

THE PICTURESQUE. *Although in the eighteenth and nineteenth centuries 'the picturesque' came to be associated with conventionally beautiful English and European scenery, initially this literary and artistic framework was used by world travellers confronted by any noteworthy scenery. This painting by John Glover depicts the natural beauty and picturesque quality of the Lake District in England, conventions he continued to use as an artist in Australia. (John Glover,* Ullswater, Early Morning, *c. 1824.)*

Gilpin's *Observations Relative Chiefly to the Picturesque* was the more influential among tourists and artists in their search for the picturesque in nature, whereas Uvedale Price and Payne Knight explored its theoretical possibilities. Gilpin identified those places in Britain he judged to be picturesque for the interest they excited in the variety of nature, a scene with not just a stream, but a gently winding stream through a landscape of naturally clumped trees and grassy meadows, perhaps passing by a crumbling ruin covered in vines, set to a background of hills, sky and clouds.

Gilpin admired English scenery as quintessentially interesting, and for many Australians today, to talk of picturesque scenery is often a reference to the type of pretty countryside now seen as typically English. But in the late eighteenth and nineteenth centuries, tourists all over the world applied the term 'picturesque' to many natural scenes for their novelty and picture-like qualities, and even embraced what Bernard Smith called a 'growing interest in the exotic'.[14]

The notions of the sublime, the beautiful and the picturesque as applied to natural scenes evolved from a need to describe the previously 'unknown', and were used to express a sense of wonder and to characterise the distinctiveness and novelty of a scene. Their application to colonial travel was especially useful for describing natural attractions, such as scenery immediately recognisable, say, to an English audience. But they were also applied to that which bore no resemblance to anything ever before seen by Europeans.

From Frankland's Beaches at Lake St Clair in Tasmania, the view of the lake framed by distant mountain crags and sky is recognisable as the view the colonial artist William Charles Piguenit depicted in his painting *Lake St Clair, the Source of the River Derwent, Tasmania* (1887). But whereas in Piguenit's painting serene water, craggy peaks, threatening clouds and distant mist come together serendipitously for a nineteenth-century grand scene, in reality these elements are more disparate. Piguenit embellished his landscape with romantic sensibility.

There are two ways to appreciate fully the alpine nature of the Lake St Clair scenery, a five-hour walk to Narcissus Bay through a forest of indigenous pines and mountain eucalypts, stopping at various points on the foreshore for an extensive vista, or from the ferry that runs a pick-up service for those who have finished their overland walk from Cradle Mountain. Whatever way you choose the craggy tops of the surrounding mountain ranges tower above, although the effects can change according to the light and weather conditions, celestial in mist, forbidding in twilight, majestic against a bright blue sky. These are the sorts of characteristics that Piguenit was looking for. Now that I have been to Lake St Clair I wonder if his painting really does the scene justice.

W. C. Piguenit, Lake St Clair, the Source of the River Derwent, Tasmania, *1887.*

I came to Lake St Clair without formal preconceptions (although expecting great beauty and serenity, and incidentally found these words weren't good enough). But in nineteenth-century Australia most colonial travellers had definite ideas of what a lake should look like, and framed their expectations of lake scenery in terms of the best Europe (including England) had to offer based on writings by William Gilpin, Wordsworth and others. Whether or not colonial travellers had actually seen any of these lakes for themselves didn't really matter (although some travel writers among them had). They had 'learned' the European language of lakes and rivers.

To the colonial traveller, Tasmania provided ample examples of how they knew water beautified landscapes. Tasmania satisfied European expectations with its rivers winding gently through verdant hilly country, constituting picturesque and beautiful landscapes. Macquarie in the journal of his tour to Van Diemen's Land in 1811, praised the River Derwent (for its breadth, volume of water and hilly picturesque banks), the South Esk near Launceston (for 'meandering in a beautiful manner through the plains making the landscape complete') and the Cataract on the South Esk River (for 'foaming through this narrow gap in a most beautiful manner … [surrounded by] high rocky cliffs'). In *Geographical, Historical and Topographical Description of Van Diemen's Land*, George William Evans said of Tasmania's rivers: 'few are of great extent; but they all tend to enrich the soil through which they pass, and bestow a dignity and importance on this part of Australia'. As well as pointers to the economic possibilities of the land, rivers in Australia were also early objects of colonial aesthetic appreciation, signifying the possibilities of beauty in these new surroundings.

The Derwent, with Hobart and Mount Wellington juxtaposed at its basin, brought together noteworthy scenic elements to be extolled in comparison with European lake scenery. The well-travelled George Frankland wrote to a colleague in the Colonial Office that Hobart resembled 'a remote watering place in England, placed by the side of a Swiss lake. One of the grand features is the Mountain … behind the town', to him 'one of the most pleasing views that I have ever seen in any part of the world'. John Glover, already established as a landscape painter when he migrated to Van Diemen's Land in 1831, sent sixty-eight paintings to be exhibited in London in 1835. A critic in the London *Times* generally complimented these depictions of Tasmanian scenery: 'cultivated plains, stupendous mountain scenery and broad expanse of waters, delightful and noble. It bears … a resemblance of the views on the lakes of Cumberland, with the exception that the hills are more lofty, possess more of a primeval aspect.' The Derwent (named originally after Derwent Water in Cumberland) was to become Tasmania's most famous river, praised for its beauty and highly recommended to visitors.[15]

Once official exploration had reached the midlands of Tasmania, the inspiring scenery of the inland mountain lakes came to prominence. There is evidence there had been some previous awareness of their existence since one colonist, George

William Evans, concluded that 'the large lake on the top of the Western Mountains' is 'one of the great wonders of nature', and this was quoted in a review of his book in the English *Quarterly Review*.[16] Lake St Clair, in the region of Frenchman's Cap, was observed by colonial surveyors: William Sharland on his expedition in 1832, and George Frankland, who visited the lake on his 1835 expedition to find the head of the Derwent, and described the scene in great detail in his official report. He was clearly impressed by what he observed, and made 'drawings of the romantic scenery':

> we suddenly found ourselves on the edge of a most beautiful lake, in the heart of scenery of the most picturesque character … We again obtained a magnificent view of the greater portion of this beautiful sheet of water. … I will not dilate on the extreme beauty of the scenery as it might be considered out of place in an official Report, but I must confess that while narrating the circumstances of this journey, I feel inspired by the first discovery of such romantic Country, impressions which revive even in cold narrative. I believe that every man in the party felt more (or) less the calm influence of this scenery, and to all, this day's journey was a matter of recreation.[17]

The lake lapped the base of a 'lofty basaltic mountain', which he called Mount Olympus, and the view of the lake from its summit 'was beyond all description, the whole of Lake St Clair lay at our feet with its beautiful bays and golden beaches'. During the vice-regal excursion to Macquarie Harbour, Governor and Lady Franklin's party made a special detour to see Lake St Clair. Franklin was reported to have pronounced it 'the most beautiful he had ever beheld'. But access to the region continued to be difficult. The artist John Skinner Prout and his sketching group camped near Lake St Clair for about six days, viewing the lake from different angles in a boat and making many sketches, from which he fashioned a few paintings including *Mt Ida, Lake St Clair* (1845). The central region's reputation for abundant and beautiful lakes was promoted even among those who never ventured there. Louisa Meredith, the English travel writer who emigrated to the Australian colonies in 1839, wrote, 'embosomed in these dreary mountain wilds are several large and beautiful lakes, of whose lonely grandeur and picturesque scenery I have heard their explorers speak in terms of high admiration'. This sentiment was taken up in *Walch's Tasmanian Guide Book* (1871), drawing on written responses to questions sent out to people throughout Tasmania. The methodology, the authors noted, meant the guidebook was anything but exhaustive. But it is a useful gauge for what some Tasmanians considered the colony's best scenery and sights, even if they had never visited them themselves. Among the locations cited, Lake St Clair was 'much admired for its fine scenery', as were other nearby mountain lakes, all of which were highly recommended.[18]

Tasmanian lake and river scenery fitted European preconceptions of the picturesque and the beautiful, as did the Gippsland Lakes in eastern Victoria, which were easier to get to. Whereas in the 1880s it took four days to travel to Lake St Clair from Hobart, and then only by private transport since no public vehicles went near the lake itself, it was an easy train ride and steamer or coach ride to the Gippsland towns. Comparisons with European mountain and lake scenery were common. The Gippsland Lakes, with snow-capped mountains in view (at least in winter) and picturesque river scenery, were said to be similar to many notable Scottish lochs. Enterprising Gippsland locals operated services, such as the Lakes Navigation Company, allowing the lakes to be viewed not only from the water's edge, but from many angles including their very centre.[19]

Although this particular lake scenery most happily corresponded to European expectations, there was also interest in types of lake scenery that turned them upside down, of which there were a few magnificent examples in the Australian

TRAVELLERS AS CATALYST. *The artist George French Angas, who settled for a time in Australia, was an enthusiast for the 'grandeur and loveliness' of Australian scenery, and interested in local ethnography and natural history. He exhibited in the colonies and England and published illustrated portfolios which helped create and extend interest in Australia's natural wonders. (George French Angas, Self Portrait, 1849.)*

colonies. Just as Australian mountain scenery came to challenge conventional understandings of the sublime, Australian lakes also contributed to a new understanding of the beautiful, though in some cases, they were so unusual as to need aesthetic conventions of their own. European expectations of a beautiful water landscape depended on the combination of several scenic (and picturesque) elements, notably, verdure, undulations and gently shaped irregularities (either on the surrounding land or from the outline of the mass of water). Meandering streams, parklands at a lake's edge, rivers or lakes with a backdrop of mountains or hills, these landscapes were considered beautiful and might give rise to appropriate rapturous responses. But the scenic character of Australian lakes did not always fit easily into such categories.

South Australia's Mount Gambier lakes and the Coorong were first widely publicised in the 1840s by the English naturalist and painter George French Angas. Angas came to Australia, where he lived for almost two decades, 'actuated by an ardent admiration of the grandeur and loveliness of Nature in her wildest aspect'. His travels enabled him to make observations and produce sketches of Australian scenes which he brought together initially in exhibitions in Adelaide (the first of its kind there), Sydney and London, and then as publications: one, a two-volume account of his travels in Australia and New Zealand; another, a large folio of lithographs from watercolours he painted at the time.[20]

Angas expressed his enthusiasm for the unusual qualities of the lakes in Mount Gambier's crater and the potential for others to enjoy their beauty, which was limited only by access to the region. At Mount Gambier he found 'beautiful magic scenes presented themselves, displaying scenery of a character quite different from anything I ever before witnessed'. What his party saw was a 'vast hollow basin' filled with:

> black volcanic waters ... in calm repose ... The sudden view of the interior
> of the largest crater burst upon us, and called forth our rapturous admira-
> tion. It was indeed, a glorious and enchanting scene: a vast hollow basin ...
> shut out from the world by the walls of lava that surrounded it, and cov-
> ered with emerald verdure, burnished to a bright metallic green ...

George French Angas, Interior of the Principal Crater of Mount Gambier, *c. 1845.*

There were elements in the scene that were 'grand and stupendous', but the volcanic nature of the rocks surrounding the still, fresh water of the lake, the absence of snow-covered mountains, and the presence of intense colours reflected in the water, from the crater walls, created a 'most fascinating sight', a 'scene of fairy loveliness', rather than being picturesque or beautiful according to European expectations. It was this singularity of appearance, the combination of 'metallic brilliancy' and the 'black volcanic waters' that made the scene spectacular and, Angas wrote, 'truly Australian'. As a statement of its importance, he included in his folio of South Australian lithographs two of the lakes in Mount Gambier's crater, and two in other, nearby craters, a greater proportion than any other type of landscape.[21]

Later, in the 1850s, Julian Tenison-Woods, the Catholic priest in charge of a large parish that included Mount Gambier, and who became a well-published geologist, studied the Mount Gambier lakes for geological evidence of volcanic activity in Australia. Preceding his lengthy scientific discussion was a brief aesthetic

IMPROMPTU SKETCHES *were an aide-mémoire for the final artwork. Angas' sketch of the Coorong sand dunes corresponds with both his and Thomas Burr's 1840s written descriptions of their mountain-like appearance, although Angas chose not to depict this feature in his Coorong painting reproduced in* South Australia Illustrated. *(Above: George French Angas, [Sand Dunes, The Coorong], 1840s. Right: George French Angas,* Scene on the Coorong, *c. 1844.)*

description: '[The] crags [of the crater] hang over the water, whose already dark-blue tint is rendered still more gloomy by the reflection of their black and stony fronts. The whole appearance of the lake is wild and sombre in the extreme.' The 'black volcanic waters', noted by Angas, were now known to change colour according to the season, a deep blue in January and February, turning to grey by April.[22] There was nothing unusual about scenery arising out of volcanic activity being seen as sublime. But lake scenery? Sublime? Should it not really be picturesque and beautiful? That was the point of difference, and what recommended the Mount Gambier lakes, particularly the Blue Lake, as scenically distinctive.

It was even more difficult to apply the conventional definition of the concept 'beautiful' to the Coorong, a lagoon watered by Lake Alexandrina and stretching for almost 160 kilometres along the southern coast, separated from the sea by a

narrow peninsula. George French Angas described the Coorong as 'truly a wild and desolate place', distinguished by a 'profound stillness', 'a region of the most dreary and melancholy aspect'. As he looked over the lagoon to the ocean, Angas remarked that 'the utter and almost awful solitude was unbroken by any living thing … All was one vast blank—a sublime and terrible wilderness of nature.' These were words of praise in the conventional and confronting language of the sublime. Angas also observed various wildlife species including an abundance of birds, this specific aspect now widely promoted as a feature of the Coorong, and sought a human presence for the area in his many sketches of local Aborigines.

The Coorong fitted no notions of the beautiful or the picturesque. But Angas' reference to the sublime indicated that part of his interest lay in the challenge of making his readers understand the special characteristics of this natural attraction. Thomas Burr, then South Australia's deputy surveyor-general whose expedition Angas had accompanied, wrote in more pedestrian fashion in *Remarks on the Geology and Mineralogy of South Australia* (1846): 'amongst [the sand hills] the scenery is very beautiful, and may be termed mountain-scenery in miniature; in some places the sand-hills rise precipitately, in others gently; there are many glens and lofty summits, with undulating plains'.[23]

Angas also wrote of sandhills of 'immense height presenting the appearance of barren mountains'. The challenge was to find the right descriptive language to categorise this scene. To a nineteenth-century cultured European mind the very fact that sandhills could look like mountains was astonishing in itself. The description, with its use of European notions, served the purpose of establishing this scenery as especially distinctive. In 1857 Julian Tenison-Woods also went on an excursion to the Coorong. Interested in the geology of the southern coast, he wanted to examine the Coorong in the light of his geological theories. He and his party organised Aboriginal guides to lead them through the water to the sandhills separating the ocean from the lagoon. The crossing was perilous despite lower than usual water levels and he recommended others against attempting it, adding that he and his party survived only because of the guides' local knowledge. Over two decades later he published his account of the Coorong in the *Sydney Mail* reflecting that 'in every respect it deserves to be considered one of the wonders of nature in Australia'.[24]

The intellectual rationale of early colonial touring, observing sights as natural wonders and seeking out the distinctive, was part of an emerging western phenomenon that eventually led to the huge numbers of people worldwide who now set out on their own tours of discovery. The nature of colonial travel, the local circumstances, social customs and manners, helped ensure that these early ideas and experiences took on Australian shapes, and were often different to developments occurring in England.

Notions of tourists being a threat to civilised society, or so lacking in intelligence or manners as to be unable to derive the benefits of travel or become more informed about the world, rarely featured in public debate in nineteenth-century Australia. It was different in England. From the mid-nineteenth century there was a whole genre questioning the motives and intelligence of the English tourist. Such concerns grew out of a longer tradition of anxiety about the virtue of travel. In the eighteenth and nineteenth centuries the justification for the English gentleman's grand tour was that it would broaden the minds of young gentlemen, introduce them to classical thought (by visiting ancient Greek and Roman sites), help them gain foreign contacts and allow them to experiment with sex (an aim explicitly stated in many eighteenth-century books about gentlemen's foreign travel). Yet there was also debate, leaving aside intentions about what actually was achieved by such travel, with critics expressing concern that those who had been on the grand tour returned to England less willing to apply themselves seriously to business or study and altogether less tolerant of English society. These critics saw travel as having little value as a means of self-improvement; indeed, some believed that so degenerate was the behaviour of many returned from their grand tours that a risk was posed to the moral fibre of England's future leaders in business, politics and religion.[25]

By the turn of the nineteenth century and with increasing interest among the English upper classes in touring districts of England, Wales and Scotland to search for the sublime, the beautiful and the picturesque, there emerged another critical debate about the value of travel, this time expressed in terms of its threat to English rural life. William Wordsworth, one of the more vocal critics, identified tourists with an inevitable breakdown of rural society. Central to his fear was that rural districts would be swamped by large numbers of tourists taking advantage of new steam-powered transport, interested in little more than visiting what other tourists had seen, and caring little about the rural communities that resided in these districts or the disruption brought to bear upon them. The lower classes, he believed, 'the artisans and labourers, and the humbler classes of shopkeepers should not be tempted to visit particular spots which they had not been educated to appreciate'. Touring was only acceptable, according to Wordsworth, if it could be appreciated, and without the appropriate understanding that class and education provided touring became a mere mechanical process to see things that others had seen.

The notion that new steam technology provided the means for the lower orders to travel was of general political concern instigating major debates about possible outcomes. Of most concern was the possibility of social disorder, upper-class fears about how to control the 'common people': access to the new means of transport might provide opportunities to travel the country, perhaps leading to political menace with a mob preaching revolution. There were, of course, others who hailed the new transport as a peaceful means of changing society, of diminishing the importance of social rank in opening up to the masses one of the privileges of those in power—the ability to tour. Modern travel was either feared or praised for its democratic possibilities.[26]

Targeting a particular market for the organised tour first happened in England in the 1840s when Thomas Cook (to become the most famous of several similar entrepreneurs) began to organise rail excursions around parts of England, negotiating timetable connections and ticket and accommodation costs with district rail companies, steamship companies and local inns in order to offer a personally escorted tour without the usual difficulties associated with independent touring. Cook, a printer by trade and a temperance worker by moral code, initially investigated rail excursions as an appropriate leisure activity for the working classes whose morals, he believed, were seriously jeopardised by public drinking houses. He conducted a few such excursions, sometimes to religious meetings, sometimes to exhibitions, but although he was able to attract many members of the working class, his financial outlay was rarely recovered by ticket sales, because the real per unit cost was beyond the wage-earner's ability to pay. So he moved to catering for the middle classes who were attracted by the money savings of group travel and the experience of a tour guide who (it was expected) knew what to do and where to go, and by the 1850s, he had established a successful program of tours around England, to Scotland and a little later to the continent.[27] Thomas Cook and his kind (including English railway companies) were marketing the travel experience as a commercial commodity.

Since Thomas Cook had himself been so vocal about the mind-broadening effect of travel and, in particular, that it should not be denied to the lower orders, it was not surprising that his ventures should be criticised. His customers were described variously as 'Cook's Circus', 'Cook's Hordes', 'Cook's Vandals'; they were presented as a 'low, vulgar' mob, 'an irregular procession of incongruities' and even, on occasion, a 'swarm of intrusive insects'. Even though by then Cook was catering largely to the middle classes his tours symbolised what had been condemned over the last century: English tourists clustered together at some of the great European sights without (it was assumed) having spent time informing themselves of the significance of what they were seeing. But now there was another dimension. The new class of tourists was condemned because of social position. These tourists were a harbinger of social change and criticised because they were unfamiliar with the concepts inspired by earlier travel particularly as a consequence of forays into the New World. Without imagination, the skills of observation and description, modern tourists, some believed, could gain absolutely nothing from travel, because all they could do was blindly follow the trails of others.[28]

By contrast in Australia for most of the nineteenth century there was little debate about tourist behaviour. A tourist (or traveller) was noted as a type of person likely to be interested in particular natural and social phenomena and this in itself presumed certain sensibilities about a tour as a means of learning about the world. It was not often suggested that tourists were likely to be people undertaking travel primarily for unworthy purposes such as rising above their social position, and so— to purists at least—undermining the educational, intellectual and spiritual possibilities of the tour. The issue is not whether Australian tourists were worthier than their English counterparts, but why there was little comment about what some in England believed was the declining value of the tour.

One important difference was based in geography. The European tour (including a season in London) was still a mark of social distinction among Australians, particularly as it was beyond the financial reach of most. The tour was usually conducted at a respectably leisurely pace: first the sea voyage (about six weeks in the second half of the nineteenth century), then a lengthy period in London and perhaps a tour of the continent, followed by another long sea voyage home.[29] In England, however, the continental tour was no longer the particular preserve of the upper classes nor necessarily a sign of social position. In Australia there was little reason to comment on the erosion of a social privilege that was still thriving.

Nor did the development of transport technology, particularly steam trains, provoke special fears in the colonies about mobile masses and revolutionary tendencies. In a country colonised largely as a result of a population—including the lower classes—being prepared to travel often under extremely rough conditions the introduction of a relatively reliable form of transport was seen as making it easier to transform frontiers into outposts of English civilisation. The new means of transport might have been seen as helping maintain social order, both because travel time had been reduced drastically (making the cities and other large towns which were the centres of law enforcement seem closer) and because railways advancing into rural districts were seen as a potent symbol of progress desirably encouraging more people to settle there. 'The flaunting flag of progress is in the west unfurled, The mighty bush with iron rails is tethered to the world', according to Henry Lawson.[30]

There were barriers to the wholesale uptake of trains as tourist transport, and no early attempts to extend the benefits of travel as a worthwhile, morally uplifting experience for the working classes, as Thomas Cook had tried to do in England. The cost of even short tours was a major obstacle for the Australian working classes, and compared unfavourably with the costs of other forms of entertainment. For three shillings, or about one-fifteenth of the cost of a two-day trip to the Blue Mountains for two adults, a couple could catch a tram from the city to Coogee, a seaside suburb of Sydney, and spend all day at the aquarium with its numerous diversions included in the price of admission.[31] They could do this about once a month for over a year, before they had spent the cost of a two-day tour of the Blue Mountains.

Even a short visit to a region like the Blue Mountains dedicated to tourists was not cheap by many people's standards. Tours to districts further afield could be more expensive, not only because of extra transport costs, but also because accommodation, although usually of a lower standard than offered by more developed tourist regions, had little competition and thus was likely to command higher prices. Travel costs once on the road also had a habit of ballooning beyond expectations, as tourist information about incidental expenses was not always reliable. For example, a brief account of a trip to the Blue Mountains described a mother and her two adult daughters arriving ready to take 'delightful little excursions to places of interest' only to find train fares to other mountain destinations—the mode of conveyance to the sights recommended by the New South Wales Railway—were unexpectedly beyond their means, although fortunately, they were able to negotiate affordable rates for travel by horse and dray and so they saw something of the mountains' sights.[32]

There were calls to travel as a means of engendering colonial interest and pride in one's surroundings, without a flicker of concern that the middle classes, because of their position in the social hierarchy, would somehow damage the ideals of travel. Accounts of colonial tourist attractions in the major newspapers and journals, and celebratory centennial publications, emphasised the affordability of short tours—surely suggesting their likely readers were the middle classes, since the labouring classes could not easily afford such excursions. Accommodation charges in the Blue Mountains, for example, were said to be 'suited to almost any purse', to be within the 'reach of the well-to-do and the struggling family man alike'. The Blue Mountains, claimed one writer, could 'for a comparatively small expenditure of time and money … be enjoyed once or oftener every summer by persons who can boast of moderate incomes'. The upper classes were also a target, especially during the 1890s Depression when it was likely that many wealthy families would cut back expenses by postponing foreign tours. During the 1890s the New South Wales Railways (and likewise other colonial railways) in their campaign for more tourists addressed many of their advertising features to the 'businessman' and his family. Smaller entrepreneurs also got into the act, one proposal in a letter to the Railway Commission was to conduct tours to the Blue Mountains with the 'wants of all tourists' met by booking first-class carriages for the 'wealthier classes, and second class [for] the medium classes'.[33]

At the same time, local entrepreneurial interests had begun to identify and define tourist requirements: perhaps hiring out a horse and carriage transport between particular sights, or providing a knowledgeable local guide or taking advantage of the growing perception that mountain or sea air was healthy with suggestions that extended the tourist market to those concerned about their physical well-being. As the requirements of tourists began to be put into a commercial structure, the definition of the 'tourist' became wider in the cause of market possibilities. After all, what mattered was that people spent money, be they pleasure-seekers, holiday-makers, tourists, travellers or invalids in search of a cure.

Thomas Cook's particular enterprise—organising tour guidance and less expensive travel and accommodation by liaising with local and foreign contacts—was not a feature of tourist activities in Australia for some decades. From the 1860s onwards although colonial tourists began to be defined partly in terms of commercial opportunity they were not yet targeted by tour companies offering group tours, as was happening in England. Australian tourists were still largely independent of such predetermined travel arrangements, choosing to travel either with a party of friends or acquaintances, in a family group, with a companion or individually, but rarely with a guide (unless hired at the destination for particular activities such as caving or specialised sight-seeing).

Although local commercial services were available, not until the end of the nineteenth century were there centralised bureaus or tour companies that arranged all aspects of a tour. For much of the nineteenth century organising colonial tours required independent initiative to piece together an itinerary from information about rail routes, the cost of train fares and accommodation possibilities along the way. Even a tour to a destination solely for tourists, like the Fish River Caves in New South Wales, relied largely on word-of-mouth information about how to get there, how to organise a guide and accommodation; indeed, communications regarding intended tours to the caves were haphazard but this did not stop the caretaker, whose position was part-time, from giving tourists a piece of his mind if they arrived without prior notice.[34]

At this stage colonial railways, although having introduced well-priced excursion tickets, did not offer special tour packages at reduced rates. There was just not the population to sustain similar packages to those offered by the English tour operators which combined the costs of travel and accommodation, as well as organising travel bookings and guides for groups as large as five or six hundred. Such markets had to be created. Although by the late 1880s the railways hired out trains for special excursions or reserved (on one of their usual trains) an entire carriage for one party, it was up to the excursion organiser or party leader to make the travel and accommodation arrangements.[35] Individuals had to make their own travel plans, their own bookings and, if they wanted to travel with a large group, their own arrangements for this.

In the late 1880s Thomas Cook & Son had expanded to Australia, setting up offices in Melbourne and Sydney, and by 1893, in Adelaide, Brisbane and Hobart. Their initial motive was to compete for the increasing number of people wishing to travel to Europe, but they also aimed to attract a market for local excursions and soon offered organised tours of the colony. By 1895 the business had offices in five other major cities in Australia and New Zealand along with eighteen sub-agents authorised to issue tickets and hotel coupons. This expansion was part of the company policy from the 1870s to provide a system of hotel coupons and travel tickets that were exchangeable worldwide (which also meant a development of interest in the individual traveller and provision of tours for groups considerably smaller than some British excursions). Thomas Cook & Son organised deals with a number of colonial transport enterprises, including government railways, shipping and steamer companies. A consequence was reasonably priced packaged tours to the colonies' places of interest, available usually for three or more people. These were advertised in specially produced booklets such as *Excursions in New South Wales arranged by Thos. Cook & Son*, which provided details on the particular travel arrangements, including accommodation and meals.[36]

From then on other tourist bureaus began to open, and by 1900 according to *Sands* there were six in Sydney's main commercial district, some organising local package tours, a trend also noticeable in the metropolises of the other colonies. Rural tourist entrepreneurs took to this trend of setting up business as tourist agents. G. H. Cooper, the owner of Cooper's Tourist Agency, located in Pitt Street Sydney, had, since the late 1880s, owned and operated one of the better-appointed hotels in the upper Blue Mountains, Cooper's Grand Hotel at Mount Victoria, and operated a horse and carriage service to Jenolan Caves and around the Blue Mountains. From the 1900s state governments began operating tourist bureaus as centralised agencies that promoted local tourism by offering package deals.[37]

The term 'tourist' was defined by cultural and historical circumstances, and in Australia in the nineteenth century these generally did not include anything similar to the often savage critical debates then going on in England. In Australia, as the tourist became targeted by commercial interests, 'tourist' as a term became less definite, more flexible in meaning. There were tourists who were only interested in viewing sights of aesthetic interest and in touring places of botanical or social importance and the like, but there were also those who might combine rest and entertainment with their viewing and touring. A tradition of independent travel continued alongside the increasing numbers of people who sought the services of a tour company.

Changes in transport facilities, particularly the introduction of steam trains, reduced travel times and made it easier to travel long distances, providing greater reliability. The increased number of publications about particular districts meant better informed tourists. Attempts to make a district's features more accessible—the handrails and stairs through difficult cave passages or the iron ladders down sheer cliffs—meant sight-seeing was easier. Although a tour of colonial natural attractions in the 1880s and 1890s was, of course, very different from those undertaken by colonists in the early nineteenth century, or Banks' grand tour in the late eighteenth, in terms of purpose touring continued to have the particular meaning of travelling for serious observation and for opportunities to wonder at fresh surroundings.

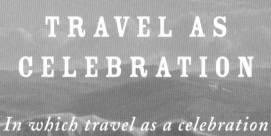

TRAVEL AS CELEBRATION

*In which travel as a celebration
of manhood, femininity and the power
of observation is explored*

In the late eighteenth and nineteenth centuries, travel for Europeans identified and celebrated particular social and cultural values. Charles Darwin described the 'pleasure of observing and reasoning', the act of rational observation, of holding landscape up to praise, the intelligent viewing for instance, of the waterfalls, tree fern gullies, mountains and forests of much colonial landscape art.[1] Celebration was also notable in traveller prototypes, the intrepid tourist, the lady traveller, the gentleman explorer, all manifesting certain virtues as a consequence of travel. The spirit of adventure, femininity and strength of character were highly valued in colonial middle-class culture, and travel could reinforce these ideals.

The idea of the lady traveller or of travel as a gentlemanly pursuit didn't continue much beyond the nineteenth century (although the spirit of adventure did). Nowadays, travel has new values to reinforce and celebrate, such as awareness of our impact as tourists on other cultures and the natural environment. We can still experience how travel celebrates distinctiveness—for instance, the Sydney Opera House as a symbol of Australian cosmopolitism, the Great Barrier Reef (and the need for its preservation) as an example of natural ecology. Although what is celebrated has changed, we still understand travel as the celebration of certain values and characteristics.

'The Blue Mountains have never yet been passed, so that beyond those tremendous barriers, the country yet remains unexplored and unknown', wrote the emancipist David Mann in the Present Picture of New South Wales 1811.

Of course, the Gundungurra and the Dharug people did know and had explored the mountains, their respective territories taking in sites of ceremony and art as well as valleys with plentiful game.[2] It is probable that colonists expected evidence of Aboriginal habitation, but David Mann had no interest in declaring an Aboriginal presence since the rhetorical power of his statement lay in its challenge to imperial might.

David Mann, a once-trusted member of Lord Somerset's household staff in England, had been transported to New South Wales in 1799 for fraud. Given an absolute pardon in 1802, he became principal clerk to the governor, dealt in livestock and was landlord of a weatherboard house in Sydney town, acquiring enough money to build a smart town residence for his wife and himself and hire a cook and servant. Although he did not acquire the horse and gig that were a sure sign of respectability, there is evidence to suggest he wished to improve himself socially.

In 1807, at the age of thirty-one, he wondered about undertaking an excursion to crack the secret of the mountains, imagining it lasting four to five days, aware of the Europeans who had tried to reach the other side of the range before returning with accounts of perilous chasms, mighty cliffs, and grave doubts about future success. Therein lay the attraction, the challenge to surmount these barriers and be the first colonist to gaze upon the pastoral paradise beyond. His party of five consisting of himself, another European and three Aboriginal men was recorded as climbing five 'stupendous acclivities', so steep as to send chills of terror through their bodies, and arriving at each new summit only to find more of the same. By the fourth day, according to the account his clothes so shredded as to barely cover him, with not an end in sight and with depleting supplies, Mann decided to return to Sydney.

We can't be absolutely certain Mann actually undertook this excursion, although the account was published in his book. His desire for so doing may well have been tied to the gentlemanly status such travels could bestow. Whether fact or fiction, the description of the journey helped fix in the public imagination the colonial desire to learn about what was beyond the mountains, and the need for men of exceptional bravery and determination to achieve such success. It is possible that his description was based on other people's journeys. There were several accounts of official expeditions circulating among colonists, and given his position in the governor's office, he may well have read them, familiarising himself with the language of travel and the celebration of male prowess even in the face of defeat. 'I think' he wrote, 'that after travelling a few miles over them, their appearance (although so amazingly grand) is sufficiently terrific to deter any man of common perseverance from proceeding in his design'.[3]

Colonial Australia is rich in examples of travel as a celebration of manhood. Many of the travellers who were publicly celebrated in Australia were white male explorers, who led journeys of colonial exploration through land already long discovered by its Aboriginal occupants. Since travel is part of the essence of colonialism and colonisation, a gentleman could make a career out of setting out on a tour of discovery. It was even theoretically possible for labourers to seek social advancement through such travel, although this was rare because it was expensive to launch a private expedition, and the usual practice was to appoint as expedition leaders men with professional experience.

Eric J. Leed's imaginative study places the beginnings of modern travel and tourism in medieval times with the distinction between travel performed of necessity, and other travel. It was a period when a predisposition to move on, in particular the idea of departure, came to be seen as manly, culminating in the character of the knight, who was defined by his mobility on a horse as much as by his weapons. Travel, Leed noted, had previously also been defined in masculine terms, particularly the 'heroic travel' of the ancient world enshrined in the stories of Alexander the Great and Julius Caesar (as well as in mythic accounts such as those about Odysseus and Heracles): perils encountered were overcome by masculine strength in deeds that lent to fame. The idea of 'departure' as a sign of masculinity did not then predominate. The period of 'discovery' and 'exploration' that began in the fifteenth century developed the idea of 'voluntary departure' as a statement of manhood. 'Departure' as a symbol of manhood, of freedom, was firmly established by the nineteenth century.[4]

Departing on a tour, such as that described by David Mann, in order to explore the land and make notable discoveries was well publicised as a male activity from the beginnings of the English colonisation of Australia. In some ways, departing on travels came to be a local male rite of passage, although only some achieved the ranks of official exploration parties. The process of public acclamation began almost as soon as these often publicly funded expeditions had been successful, or even if they failed and their leaders had died. Journals were edited, tidied up, stylistic flourishes and professionally drawn illustrations added and they were published, often only a few years after the actual journeys. William Bland, the editor of Hume and Hovell's journal, apologised for the six-year delay—he blamed a paper shortage in New South Wales—and his apology suggests that people wanted to read these accounts as soon after the event as possible.

Published accounts had similar storylines: initial expectations of triumph that day by day diminished, with the journey becoming life-threatening as it reached unfamiliar territory where rivers might flow the wrong way, or not flow at all, where explorers might become objects of interest or aggression by local Aboriginal people, and where there was no sure way of sending a distress signal if all hope seemed to have failed. The theme was how whites might overcome dangers of the unknown, but even the disastrous outcome of the Burke and Wills expedition, during which seven members perished on their return from the Gulf of Carpentaria, could be presented as public confirmation of the tough task that lay ahead for white civilisation in Australia. (And the search parties that set out to save Burke and Wills continued the process of colonial exploration.) In part, the accounts were adventure stories, the suspense not necessarily in actual life-threatening encounters (scaling steep mountainsides, facing bushfires, running out of food and water) but in the day-by-day account and the *possibility* that the next day (or even the next step) might present some new danger.

The number of nineteenth-century expeditions—some with a place in Australia's national memory, others with local interest—provided opportunities for a cross-section of white men to pit themselves against the dangers of starvation, lack of water and sometimes Aborigines (although this was not such a concern in the first few decades of the century). The index to the *Australian Dictionary of Biography* lists 144 men under the category 'explorer'. The number is deceptively small since it is made up mainly of those who made their names as expedition leaders or explorers, rather than the botanists or geologists, let alone the attendants, who constituted the actual exploration party. Only two of the twelve members of Oxley's party that set out to explore the western rivers in 1817–18 are listed as either explorer (Alan Cunningham) or surveyor (George William Evans). Only George Grey on his twelve-man expedition to the north-west of Western Australia in 1837 is listed as 'explorer'. Only four of the fifteen members of the Burke and Wills expedition in 1860–61 are categorised as 'explorers': Robert O'Hara Burke, William John Wills, Ludwig Becker and John King. No women are listed.

Opportunities for this male rite of passage may have been limited, yet they were available, and labourers as well as those with the gentlemanly skills of surveying, painting and collecting scientific and botanical data, and the ability to command took them up. Exploration usually was a 'gentleman's profession', and lesser positions, such as 'native guide', or labourers assisted the party in their endeavours. Parties usually numbered a dozen or so. Oxley, on his journeys to the western rivers in New South Wales, was accompanied by a second in command, two botanists, a mineralogist, a boat-builder, a boatman, a horse-shoer, a butcher, a horse leader, a harness-mender and two others, one of whom was Oxley's servant, their presence revealing the diversity of skills required. In the early years of British exploration in Australia, some parties also included convicts and Aboriginal guides, who might or might not have seen the journey as a rite of passage. The convicts were elbowed out by free immigrants and visitors, as the opportunity to pursue adventure became highly sought after. Tim Bonyhady's study of the Burke and Wills expedition estimates that more than seven hundred people applied for the nine positions of 'assistant', some doing so because they were unemployed and wanted work, but many offering to take less money to bask in the 'highest glory' of this 'national undertaking'.

Travel and adventure could also be among the aspirations of young and British middle and upper middle-class men who came to Australia to make money and seek experience before returning to Britain to marry and settle down. Allan Macpherson came to New South Wales in the 1840s and established several sheep runs before returning to Scotland to marry. His account of his days as a sheep station owner, published thirty years later, included fond memories of his feats exploring Mount Abundance. He told how he was inspired by his friend, the 'great explorer', Sir Thomas Mitchell, and noted that his own party had possibly come across the tracks of Leichhardt. Spending a period in Australia as a rite of passage could be seen as a means of gaining gentlemanly independence. Christopher Pemberton Hodgson, a young English gentleman who also came out to Australia to establish a sheep run and who was a member of Leichhardt's expedition to Port Essington for part of the way, explained somewhat wryly that 'many a fine fellow, educated at the finest establishments in England, nursed in every luxury, and endowed with the noblest principles, under false hopes raised by falser representations has been seduced from the endearments of home … to undergo a temporary exile preparatory to the gaining of an imaginary independence'.

As Kathleen Fitzpatrick has argued in her study of Australian explorers, the 'Pax Britannica' of the nineteenth century meant that a career in the military no longer guaranteed adventure. One outlet for these military men was to take up travel as a career, and she cites as examples Thomas Mitchell, Charles Sturt and George Grey. Other travellers came from the relatively new disciplines of natural history and botany, and for them public acclaim and success could ensure funding for further expeditions. If they had had enough adventure, they could be awarded a high-ranking position in a scientific society or a governing body, although this was never a guaranteed outcome, and there could be difficulties in readjusting to 'conventional colonial life'. Artists, too, could gain experience and serve scientific interests by accompanying exploration parties.

The possibility of fame or wealth was a particular attraction of travel. However, it was usually a gentlemanly concern for the 'public good' that was presented as the main impetus for people seeking to lead parties of exploration, with only a few explorers, like Mitchell and Sturt, actually admitting they were strongly motivated by the desire for fame. Yet public acclaim was a major factor in exploration, and success could have its rewards. Throughout the nineteenth century support for particular expeditions was vigorously debated in scientific societies and philosophical institutes, and in colonial parliaments once they were established; funding was sought from the public purse and by private subscription; newspapers reported all aspects of an expedition, from its proposal to its completion; explorers' journals were published as soon as available; sometimes public monuments were erected, especially after a tragic outcome. This public attention given to male explorers and their explorations celebrated travel as a desirable, if sometimes dangerous, activity in the gaining of knowledge.[5]

The 'grand tour' was an important part of a gentleman's education, seen as useful in establishing credentials in their chosen fields of interest, providing new experiences and furthering knowledge. With exploration presented as an activity for the general good, gentlemen who toured would sometimes cite this as a reason for their undertakings. James Holman, who spent seven months in New South Wales on his world tour, explained he had undertaken this 'long and arduous journey of investigation, with a view to contribute something, however slight, to those stores of information for which society is indebted to the exertions of practical travellers'. Thomas Bartlett, who toured Australia in the early 1840s, used the knowledge he gained from observing colonial agriculture and making contact with local experts to put forward a plan to improve English agriculture.

Touring was also undertaken for personal improvement, to boost prospects and perhaps ambition. James Froude explained that his son, recently graduated from Oxford, had been asked to accompany him to Australia on his 1880s tour in order, in Froude's words, 'to enlarge his knowledge of things'—before establishing himself in work. An important feature of the gentleman's tour, as Judith Adler argues in her study on the origins of sight-seeing, was to develop international contacts with other gentlemen in order to learn about the political, social and economic matters so that they might judge the poverty or prosperity of a region. This was certainly a theme in much nineteenth-century travel writing by men about Australia with a colony's 'prospects', its industries and products for 'trade', its imports, political situation, social relations and lifestyles of its inhabitants, all forming substantial sections of such accounts. This approach also enlarged knowledge in that it led to a greater understanding of political, social and economic principles.[6]

For men who had a bent towards natural history or geology, travel was a prerequisite for further, serious, study. For those training to be artists, at least in the eighteenth and first half of the nineteenth century, travel provided novel scenes and experiences that could influence a life's work. John Lewin came to Australia to pursue entomological studies; Augustus Earle travelled the world for thirteen years as an artist before returning to England, and Englishman John Gould arrived in Australia to study birds. Gentlemen who toured Australia often referred to its novelty as a reason for being there. Thomas Bartlett described Australia's 'unique character' as 'peculiarly interesting' and as having added a 'considerable amount of original information' to the world's 'stock of knowledge'. He recommended a tour of Australia to young naturalists as a sound career move: 'Boundless as is the country, unlimited is the learning which the student of natural history may glean from its otherwise barren soil. To the young naturalist who is ardent to distinguish himself in the science to which he has devoted himself, Australasia offers advantages possessed by no other country.' Christopher Pemberton Hodgson also recommended Australia as a destination for those interested in natural history. For the geologist, he suggested, Australia is 'a wonderful country … unfolding new mysteries everyday … leaving simple man to revel in the midst of wonder, uncertainty and amazement'.

Friedrich Gerstaecker, a German on his world tour, arrived in Australia in 1851 looking forward 'to travel a while among those singularities of the soil, that collection of natural curiosities, where the Almighty had made quadrupeds with birds-bills, and birds with hair'. Such natural curiosities were also recommended by the Rev. John Morison in his account of the colonies in the 1860s. He explained that 'geologists and mineralogists will find everything to their heart's content in Australia—if they might not, indeed, have to coin new words to add to their [already] very large vocabularies'.[7]

NATURAL HISTORY PUBLISHER *John Gould and his artist wife Elizabeth visited Australia in 1838–40 to look for Australian birds to include in their illustrated series of birds throughout the world. (T. H. Maguire, [Portrait of John Gould, Ornithologist], 1849.)*

Accounts of the colonial travel experience itself (not material about prospects for emigrants, settlers or investors) usually introduced elements of the adventure story, often making direct references to the bravery of explorers and the real possibility of getting lost in the bush. James Holman wrote that as he crossed Bass Strait from Hobart, through huge swells of water, he thought of the 'thrilling character' of the (European) maritime explorers who had faced such conditions for the first time, not knowing what to expect. (This adventure had a conventional happy ending with Holman reaching Sydney safely.) The Rev. John Morison warned of the dangers of bush travelling, explaining that Australia's geography—its steep mountains and wooded hills—hindered travelling in a straight line and establishing one's direction. Once lost, reorientation was difficult since, he explained, the physical features of the 'bush' were difficult for the uninitiated to distinguish. He recounted many stories about 'gentlemen travellers' lost in the bush. Joseph Phipps Townsend, in a lively account of his rambles around New South Wales, advised the 'wanderer in a pathless wilderness' to remember on which side of the tree moss grew.[8]

Many gentlemen travellers who published accounts of their tours may have sounded like 'know-alls', yet they all started from the position that their tours had taught them something they hadn't known. Even those like Thomas Bartlett, concerned that the then current images of Australia were misleading in their optimism and so set about undermining them, still managed to learn things he had not known and which were useful enough to apply to his activities back in England. In this sense, gentlemen who toured nineteenth-century Australia were entering the 'unknown', not necessarily into life-threatening situations, but into social, political, economic and physical environments that were, for many, beyond their previous experience.

Eugen von Guérard climbed to the summit of Mount Kosciuszko on 19 November 1862, his fiftieth birthday.[9] He had joined the Bavarian scientist Georg von Neumayer's expedition to north-eastern Victoria, where Neumayer, meteorologist, hydrographer, oceanographer and magnetician intended to conduct a survey of the mountain ranges. Guérard wanted to see the alpine country talked about for several decades in Victorian scientific circles, and was sure there would be scenery enough to make his sketching trip worthwhile. He had in mind a series of Australian alpine landscapes that might appeal to romantic sensibility and capture in oil, on large canvases, the 'details and effects' of Australian nature in all its grandeur. From sketching tours in Victoria, South Australia, Tasmania and New South Wales, he already had a growing portfolio of Australian waterfalls, tree fern gullies, mountains, lakes, rivers and rocky coastlines, and the Mount Kosciuszko region would provide yet another perspective on Australian scenery.

He was no amateur landscape artist. Trained initially in Rome in the classical landscape tradition of Rosa, Poussin and Claude, Guérard later at Düsseldorf attended one of the first European landscape schools teaching painting as '*naturgetreue Wiedergabe*' (a 'response true to nature'). Underlying this approach was the imperative for the artist not to paint from the imagination but to travel into the wilderness seeking the many effects of nature.

Georg von Neumayer's party of three had left Melbourne in mid-October for a leisurely tour in a specially designed horse-drawn wagon that was a work station by day and a comfortable tent by night. They stopped off at Wangaratta, Beechworth and Yackandandah before reaching Albury in late October where they rested before their ascent of the highest mountain range in Australia. At Albury, they discussed with the district surveyor a suitable route for collecting magnetic data, and acquired a map of the region and a guide. Their suggested route took them via three pastoral stations, residents at the first two informing them of the conditions of the mountain tracks to Mount Hope, which was to be their first truly steep ascent. At the station closest to Mount Kosciuszko, where they spent a couple of nights, they

E. von Guérard, Prof. G. N.'s Wagonzelt 18–19 October 1862 *[Tent Wagon], 1862.*

accepted the offer of a station manager to act as a local guide. They prepared their supplies for the two- to three-day return walk to the summit and decided to take one horse with them as far as could be managed.

The first day was very warm, and the need to thrash a path through the subalpine vegetation made such hot work that Neumayer, fearing heat exhaustion, called a halt early in the afternoon in order to revive his party with brandy and water. They finally reached the beginning of the alpine country in the late afternoon, set up their tents and spent a comfortable night despite a strong breeze that started up later in the evening.

The next morning's climb to the summit was not particularly difficult with the weather much cooler and, unlike the previous day, no dense timber to hack through. Neumayer and his assistant intended to spend the day taking measurements as part of his study of the effects of terrestrial magnetism. Guérard had time to sketch only three views before Neumayer urged his party to make for the next peak for more measurements, since the weather was judged unpredictable and the party wanted to fit in as much as they could. Over a quick lunch Guérard revealed that it was his birthday, so they all drank his health before clambering up the large boulders to the top. On this new summit the fresh mountain air, clarity of light and low-lying alpine vegetation all came together to focus the onlooker's view onto the craggy tops of surrounding mountains, but Guérard had time for only two sketches before Neumayer decided they should head back to camp post-haste: Guérard had noticed threatening storm clouds, and Neumayer's barometers suggested the approach of a terrible storm.

The storm engulfed them, and with howling gales, torrential rain and thick fog, progress was so slow that Guérard and Neumayer took over five hours to find their way back to the camp. Another member of the locally expanded expedition suffering from exposure had to be dragged back, and a fourth took over eight hours to find the camp, and then only because he spotted the campfire. Neumayer's assistant,

E. von Guérard, North-east View from the Northern Top of Mount Kosciusko, *1863.*

feared to have perished in the storm, was not reunited with the party for another seventeen days when they met him by chance on their return journey to Melbourne.

The significance of this story lies not in the adventure but in what it tells about nineteenth-century travel as celebration in that, despite difficulty and danger, certain landscapes were worth seeking out, were worth celebrating, as was rational observation of them. After Guérard returned to Melbourne with his small sketchbooks, he immediately set about producing a large, arresting oil painting of a view from the top of Mount Kosciuszko, which was to be displayed in a Melbourne shop window soon after it was finished, then shown in the colonial Exhibition of Science and Art (1863), before being chosen for the Intercolonial Exhibition in Melbourne in 1866, and printed as a lithograph in Guérard's large-format book *Australian Landscapes* (1867).

Contemporary reports praised this painting, certainly for its technical execution, and especially for the subject matter, a view of an Australian landscape to excite an audience's interest in their environment, perhaps to challenge preconceptions of Australian scenery, and to proclaim this mountain top a natural wonder. Guérard wrote of Mount Kosciuszko, 'This is the grandest, the loftiest, and the most imposing of all the Mountain Crags which constitute the Australian Alps'. Perhaps to quieten any scepticism about its magnificence, he quoted the Polish explorer and scientist Paul de Strzelecki, who had ascended the mountain over two decades before, and written, 'Mount Kosciuszko is one of those few elevations, the ascent of which, far from disappointing, presents the traveller with all that can remunerate fatigue'.[10]

Viewers of the painting saw Neumayer's party as tiny figures on piles of boulders looking across the snow drifts mingled with summer grasses, far in the distance towards other mountain tops, with rainstorm clouds beginning to threaten a clear pale blue sky. 'This picture alone is a complete rebuttal of the theory, if such a theory be now held by anyone', wrote one contemporary reviewer, 'that Australian scenery possesses no elements of the sublime'.

This painting, like many other contemporary landscape paintings, was taken to be a true representation, not some whimsical expression of fancy. It is possible today to locate the very same view, in the foreground a low-lying pile of boulders including a distinctive triangular rock and slab, in the middle Watson's Crags, and in the distance Mount Jagungal.[11] There is some artistic licence in the form of a large boulder pile in the foreground to the left—look for this on site in vain. The introduction of landscape features in the foreground of early- to mid-nineteenth-century landscape painting was a convention often used to give the painting shape and structure, and help frame its subject matter.

Paramount to visual and textual images was the power of rational observation, to look at the whole picture in order to find connections between natural phenomena, objects, both animate and inanimate. During his Australian stay Charles Darwin commented on how his voyage on the *Beagle* had developed his interest in rational observation:

> During the first two years [of the voyage] my old passion for shooting survived in nearly full force, and I shot myself all the birds and animals for my collection: but gradually I gave up my gun more and more, and finally altogether to my servant, as shooting interfered with my work, more especially with making out the geological structure of a country. I discovered, though unconsciously and insensibly, that the pleasure of observing and reasoning was a much higher one than that of skill and sport.[12]

Shooting provided the all-important specimens for reference back in England. But to make sense of the specimens and to be able to propose scientific theories required observation of the whole scene (rather than of only some components), made as daily jottings or sketches in notebooks, as watercolours in sketchbooks, and sometimes written up later as detailed journal entries or painted in oils on canvas.

Rational observation required time for reflection and contemplation, to make the connections between what travellers' eyes saw and to give them possible meanings. Time for reflection might occur anywhere—Darwin was lying on a sunny bank when reflecting on the strange character of Australian animals compared to the rest of the world. Its value increasingly recognised in the eighteenth and nineteenth centuries made a virtue of stopping to look out over natural scenery, letting the effects of nature, the combination of light, sky and anything else in view, figuratively wash over observers, cleansing them in preparation for inspiration. A young James Martin (later to become chief justice of New South Wales) explained that 'Australian scenery always delights the traveller, and wraps the prying naturalist in thoughtful meditation'.[13] Travel could help set the mind free to contemplate great thoughts, and Australia, with the freshness of natural scenery new to the colonists, developed a reputation as a destination where travellers could expect to be inspired.

Steep mountains, dark caves, wild dogs, bull ants, thirst, hunger, these were all reasons likely to diminish the pleasure of travel, and in the context of the times, with its heightened awareness of the distinction between feminine and masculine attributes, this was particularly so for women, or so it was often claimed. Yet alongside the desire to protect women from many adventures, there were also codes of behaviour that allowed women at least some space to move.

At 6 a.m. one March morning in 1886 three ladies, four gentlemen and Punch the black horse set off to walk the recently opened bridle track from Katoomba to Jenolan Caves. Excited at the prospect of their visit to the Blue Mountains, most famous of colonial natural wonders, the friends had arrived from Sydney the night before provisioned with food, clothing and two tents. They planned to spend one night camping out on their journey to the caves, four nights at Caves House, and then another night camping on their return.

The idea of three young ladies in a camping party had raised at least one eyebrow, but the member of the party was finally reassured when arrangements were made for suitable supervision.[14] The ladies themselves were concerned only about

THESE FOUR DRAWINGS *accompanied the lively account of a camping trip from Katoomba to Jenolan Caves that three women and four men undertook in 1886. Above:* Descending the Megalong Cleft. *Below:* Cox's River, Drinking. *Opposite above:* First Camp at Little River. *Opposite below:* Ascending a Hill. *(Artist unknown, 1886.)*

*of the Club undertook his & her respective share of
the work.*

The First Camp at Little River

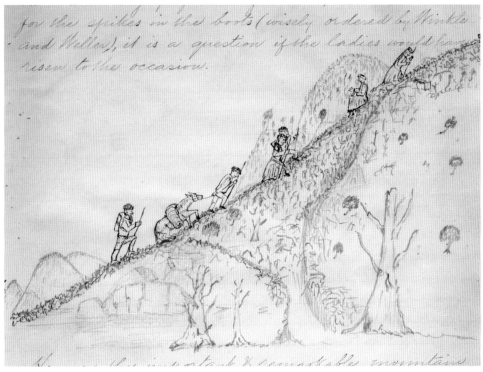

*for the spikes in the boots (wisely ordered by Winkle
and Weller), it is a question if the ladies would have
risen to the occasion.*

actually surviving the 84-kilometre round trip—a sentiment shared by the gentlemen about their own physical capabilities.

Anxiety had been fuelled by friends and family who had been clamouring to outdo one another with possible calamities: 'thunderstorms, rivers too high to ford, snakes, kangaroos, snowstorms, want of water, tight boots, teeth-aching, cold, heat, wild dogs, bull-dog ants, spiders, no tracks, blackfellows, crows, want of food, milk, butter'. The list went on, with the general feeling that the ladies should travel to the caves by coach while the gentlemen pursued the rigours of the outdoors.

The gentlemen took it for granted that they would protect the 'weaker sex': this was how one behaved, and they admired the determination of their feminine companions to undertake the trip, to see for themselves the far-famed scenery and experience the 'novelty of the venture'. Lured by the thought of fantastic scenery both gentlemen and ladies refused to be put off by the threat of wild dogs or crows.

And so preparations went ahead. Boots were forwarded to a reliable bootmaker to have grip pegs fitted to their soles. Preliminary walks were taken for endurance training. Accommodation was booked, tents organised, a packhorse arranged, billies and provisions assembled, articles of clothing chosen, a railway compartment booked. Finally departure.

Now, on an early autumn day, after several hours of walking, the party had halted at a creek for a late breakfast of billy tea, bread toasted on green twigs over the fire, potted meat and fish. The division of labour would have been approved in any respectable parlour. It was a feminine pursuit to supervise the breakfast spread and a masculine one to attend to the fire and organise comfortable seating for the ladies. They weren't in a parlour, though, so the gentlemen also kept a watchful eye out for bull ants. The conversation was cheerful with much comment on the lovely surroundings, the beautiful mountain air and its energising effect on the mind and body.

When they were on their way again, the day was hot, the ascent tiring, and the creeks dry, a matter of concern since they had expected to find water along the route at regular intervals. But the party made light of the situation: 'Oh for the Arcade' quipped one of the ladies as they talked about the delights of lemon squash.

They finally found a little water mid-afternoon, then continued to ascend until they reached the campsite on the bridle track where there was plentiful water from a small watercourse.

The gentlemen made a campfire, erected tents and collected ferns to make the bedding more comfortable. The ladies put the finishing touches to their canvas boudoir, brightened by shawls and small bouquets of native flowers, then arranged a 'rough tea spread' of toast and potted meat. The party, exhausted, drank their tea and ate their food in silence. The cool evening air revived them to delight in the twinkling stars, the crackling fire and the joy of being a party of friends on an adventure. Before they retired one member called the rest over to look at the effects of bright moonlight on the surrounding hills and valleys—'grand and awful: no power of man could describe that wonderful picture by night'. The day's walk may have been physically demanding yet it had provided many such moments of deep contemplation.

The next morning the ladies took themselves off to a suitably private waterhole for a bath. The party breakfasted together, packed up the camp leaving the tents and some supplies for their return journey, and began their trek planning to reach the caves by nightfall. The long, steep ascent was followed by a seemingly never-ending equally steep descent, almost the last straw for one of the ladies, although several of the gentlemen were also starting to tire. They all revived later in the day after refreshment at a pleasant halting place. The trek was beginning to raise concerns: a wrong turn was taken, and there was the possibility of having to stay out a night in the open without tents. But perseverance triumphed: they located the right bridle track and walked into Jenolan Caves by the light of the moon.

Later that evening they sat down to supper with Jeremiah Wilson, keeper of the caves who 'assured the ladies they were the first of their sex who had ever made the journey on foot'. Later, back in Sydney the gentlemen liked to tell the story of how on their return journey they met a local settler, a man, who upon seeing the party exclaimed, '"Be them the ladies that walked all the way from Katoomba?" Then he scanned them from head to foot and added, "Bedad, then, they don't look a bit the worst."'.[15]

'Lady traveller' or 'lady tourist' were the terms used in the nineteenth century to describe women who toured their own or another's culture. 'Lady' was a telling word, providing an immediately identifiable account of a woman's social position. The term 'tourist' also carried implications of cultural and class background. Joined together they suggested a perspective steeped in the *feminine* cultural education of the middle and upper classes. 'Lady tourists', although they hailed from the same class backgrounds as (gentlemen) 'tourists' and hence were likely to have a somewhat similar point of view, were distinct because of their femininity and its perceived different interests and manners.

The currency of the term 'lady tourist' suggested that throughout the nineteenth century it was generally acceptable for upper middle-class women to tour in the Australian colonies. From the late eighteenth century, upper middle-class women were describing journeys to New South Wales and even publishing their accounts, such as Mary Anne Parker with *A Voyage Round the World* and Eliza Kent's articles 'by a Lady' on her voyage from New South Wales to England. Of course, such early publications by women were not commonplace, and none (accounted for so far) had the depth and breadth of David Collins' *An Account of the English Colony* (1798), nor the appeal of women's accounts of their travels in Europe by such authors as Mary Wollstonecraft or Mariana Starke.

Within a few years of the beginnings of English colonisation in Australia, however, there were examples of how a lady might tour the colony. From then on not only did upper middle-class women tour, but further accounts of their experiences were published, forming a wonderfully rich source of material on feminine travel in Australia.[16] In this material we learn about gender relations in the colonies, and that travel for many women was a way of furthering their education at a time when they were denied formal instruction in either science or the humanities. However, the rigidity of the class system of the time must be remembered. As Beverley Kingston has pointed out, throughout the nineteenth century different descriptions, for instance, 'girl', 'woman' and 'lady' helped create and maintain class distinctions in Australia. A 'cultured' education was one distinction between a 'woman', and a 'lady', who belonged to the upper classes where such an education was feasible.[17] Touring widened the lady traveller's education and understanding beyond the domestic sphere, but it also created its own set of feminine conventions.

That is not to suggest unanimous support for the idea of ladies touring. Indeed, there were strong social undercurrents against it, which were particularly pronounced from the 1870s. English social reformers Rosamond and Florence Hill wrote how their sea voyage and expedition to the Australian colonies caused some concern among acquaintances in England since such a tour 'undertaken by ladies travelling alone, is still considered extraordinary'. The Hills added that their tour was generally tolerated since they were visiting South Australian relatives, although one of the ship's officers apparently proclaimed that 'no woman ought ever to go to sea'.

The attitude that a woman on tour was 'alone' even if accompanied by a female companion or a personal maid was noted by the middle-aged world traveller turned botanist, Marianne North, who visited Australia in the early 1880s. For the most part, Marianne North undertook sea voyages and land expeditions with a female companion, sometimes an unmarried woman like herself, often the wife of a gentleman occupied at home with his own concerns at the time of the tour. Otherwise, she accompanied married couples of her acquaintance who had asked her to join their expeditionary party. She rarely toured by herself, although she did occasionally take up residence in foreign lands alone, but even then, she always hired a maid. When she undertook a voyage with no companion, she compiled a list of respectable contacts she could call upon at her destinations, even if they were not always awaiting her arrival at the port or railway station.

Yet, in spite of her careful planning, the absence of a husband (or father or brother) marked her out for special comment. She noted the pleasure of friends in

England when she accompanied a married couple on a tour to Japan in the early 1870s since they believed 'it was so nice that I was not going alone this time, particularly for that long Pacific voyage'. This attitude was echoed by her sister, who prepared for posthumous publication Marianne North's autobiography—a detailed account of her world expeditions and botanical encounters. Her addendum to the book commented that 'few women, travelling absolutely alone, would have dared to face' all the hardships that Marianne North had faced.

Absolutely alone? This attitude was common in many accounts of women travelling the world. Very few, if any, were completely alone since most, like Marianne North, usually were at the very least accompanied by a maid. 'Alone' meant travel without someone else of one's own class, and, even then, lady travellers could be seen as alone if a gentleman, preferably a relation, were not in their party. A woman on tour accompanied by dozens of indigenous men—who carried the luggage, guided the conveyance, hunted for food—would still be described (or describe herself) as travelling alone.[18]

A predominant view defined women travelling without gentlemen escorts as in need of special help and advice—in order to survive the dangers outside their domestic locale. Books of travel advice that presumed a male audience often presented observational skills and classificatory systems useful for the gentleman's travel journal, and there is no book for male travellers comparable to Lilias Campbell Davidson's *Hints to Lady Travellers at Home and Abroad* (1889) or others of its type.[19] Although this book, published in England, encouraged women to travel and provided practical tips for inexperienced lady travellers, the immediate concern of Davidson was how women to maintain propriety and respectability. Women were under constant threat because they were outside the safety of the 'home': accidents could happen, swindles were likely, sexual harassment possible. Davidson presented accidents and swindles as at the very heart of travel, but dangerous for ladies whose protected existence had not provided them with the means to handle such difficulties. While travel could be made more difficult by a lady's cloistered past, a feminine demeanour and courteous manner would be a protection from unwanted male advances, and also a means of commanding help:

> Much has been said about the danger to women, especially young women, travelling alone, of annoyance from impertinence or obtrusive attentions from travellers of the other sex. I can only say, that in any such case which has ever come within my personal knowledge or observation, the woman has had only herself to blame. I am quite sure that no man, however audacious, will, at all events if he be sober, venture to treat with undue familiarity or rudeness, a woman however young, who distinctly shows him by her dignity of manner and conduct that any such liberty will be an insult. As a rule women travelling alone receive far more consideration and kindness from men of all classes than under any other circumstances whatever, and the greater independence of women, which permits even young girls in these days, to travel about entirely alone, unattended even by a maid, has very rarely inconvenient consequences.[20]

Behave as ladies and treat men as gentlemen, and they will be forced to behave as such. This view was reiterated in the accounts of lady travellers. Rosamond and Florence Hill writing about their Australian tour remarked how everyone they met was always helpful, even though they were 'two ladies, unmarried and unattended'. Of course, such helpfulness was part of Australian etiquette in the second half of the nineteenth century: courtesy demanded that gentlemen should see to the luggage of an unescorted lady, put her safely into a carriage and so on, and that lady travellers should assist the less experienced of their own sex.

Even when there was no assistance immediately forthcoming, a lone lady was not entirely helpless. When Fanny Rains, who described herself as a 'lone damsel [who] travelled the greater part of the way round the world, without even a maid', arrived late one night at Mount Victoria in the Blue Mountains, she was approached by a man unknown to her, who did not appear to have the status of a gentleman, but who offered to take her to her hotel. Natural caution had her question the station-master to ascertain that he was in fact the 'boots' of her hotel. Feminine caution and the ability to detect potentially difficult situations along with good humour could be part of the protective feminine armour. Women were advised that the 'discomforts of travelling should be borne cheerfully' and Marianne North claimed that 'her most useful friend in travelling alone' was 'a joke … helping me far more than any quantity of money (or men) could'.

The concern was not only because of social conventions, but also because of the perceived physical weakness of women compared with men, and cautions were even given to women travelling with their husbands, particularly when travel conditions might be hard going as was the case with almost all travel outside metropolitan centres before rural districts began to be linked by rail. Intending to travel from Sydney with her young daughter and husband to visit a sheep station in the Gwydir district of northern New South Wales in the 1850s, Emma Macpherson wrote how her Sydney acquaintances had suggested it unwise to undertake such a trip because of the 'inconveniences and hardships incidental to travelling'.

As well as safety, touring with a group of men and women could have other advantages that had nothing to do with women coming to harm, especially in opportunities to socialise under more sustained circumstances than the usual round of social gatherings such as 'at home' functions, picnics or dances. Rachel Henning described how in the 1860s a Bathurst doctor's wife organised a party of twenty-seven people, including 'young ladies', to visit Jenolan Caves (as it later became known) for a week. There at night they talked or read aloud around the campfire, and during the day explored the caves and went for walks around the campsite.

Touring with a male relative, or for that matter another woman, could also mean an increased range of social contacts. For gentlemen meeting people and the professional contacts so established was a major reason for undertaking tours, but not so for lady travellers who had to depend on chance or on seizing opportunities. Emma Macpherson's husband had already spent a few years establishing business interests and contacts in the colonies prior to her arrival in Sydney and she utilised these contacts to learn more about her location and its inhabitants. After her mother's death, Marianne North developed many local and international

CAMPING TRIPS *under appropriate supervision provided opportunities for young people to meet and socialise on a more intimate level than generally enjoyed. Pictured is the Pickwick Corresponding Club at their last camp on a trip to Jenolan Caves in 1886. (Photographer unknown,* Last Camp, *1886.)*

contacts as hostess to her British MP father Frederick North that were useful to her in later travels.

Even when a woman's travel was relevant to her work and interests and this was the purpose of it, such as Marianne North's journey to collect botanical material, the most important contacts arranged for arrival were seen in terms of etiquette and social companionship. Florence Davenport Hill had already published *Children of the State: The Training of Juvenile Paupers* when she went to Australia with her sister Rosamond, yet they depended not on her credentials but on family connections to gather material about the colonies, and to tour them extensively.[21] The help they received led to the publication of a very detailed travel account. The expectations that women travellers would have arranged social contacts at their ports of call, whether to call on acquaintances or more usually acquaintances of family or friends, was a part of travel etiquette and the only way they could be introduced into colonial society and pursue their interests in the colony.

Accompanied or not by a gentleman escort, a lady traveller describing her encounters with danger was a familiar literary device in nineteenth-century travel accounts. Indeed, it was often mandatory if the account were to be published. Travellers' accounts were generally published only if they fitted a particular mould, and one mode was travel difficulties. Since being a lady tourist was a travel difficulty in itself, add to it fierce storms at sea or, on land, attacks by bushrangers, rocky precipices, pitch-black caves, and interest was assured.[22]

Eliza Davies first toured Australia in the late 1830s and in her autobiography she wrote about the 'exploring expedition' up the Murray valley with the governor of South Australia, George Gawler, his daughter, Miss Julia, and Charles Sturt and Mrs Sturt. The account was filled with details about meeting 'savages', provisions running low and even the death of one of their party. She explained that in agreeing to her request to join the party, Gawler and Sturt believed that 'the policy of taking ladies with them, and bringing all back in safety, would insure [sic] a readier sale of land in England [since] Capitalists would not fear the savages when ladies had traversed the country in safety'.

Of course, part of the reason for defining a category of travel as suitable for a lady was to construct a masculine, particularly a gentlemanly dimension: gentlemen could traverse the unknown and face its dangers. Mrs Sturt, Miss Eliza and Miss Julia would be safe because their gentlemen escorts would ensure their protection, but in this case the presence of lady travellers was intended to indicate that Aboriginal people were harmless, and the land might be safely colonised.[23]

Writing about lady travellers was not always about representing the places through which colonial women travelled as now safe and domesticated: after all, women liked to show they had courage in adverse situations.[24] Danger was often presented as a general possibility, even if it did not arise during a specific journey. Before Jane Franklin set out in 1839 by ship from Van Diemen's Land to Melbourne, then overland to Sydney, her husband wrote to her sister that despite the possibility of being stranded by heavy rains and impassable rivers, he believed that she was not 'a person to be overcome by ordinary difficulties, and if the heavy rains keep off … none [will compare] to those she has experienced in her travels in Asia Minor and Egypt'. Jane Franklin's report of conditions, nonetheless, revealed how things might have gone wrong, but (unfortunately?) did not: the rivers were not in flood (yet might have been); 'the well-trained horses' coped with the difficulties of the land and never strayed too far from camp (as they might have done); the travellers' diet was 'simple in the extreme', but 'wholesome and sufficient'; they were not attacked by bushmen; and their carts did not stick in the mud (although this was a problem that struck most travellers).[25]

In writings by women, the land and its native inhabitants as a possible source of danger or misfortune was a dominant theme, yet so was the fact that they did not come to harm, either because danger had briefly subsided, or because of the great care taken with each step, or because men were present to protect them, or because (as in the case of Eliza Davies, who on one occasion seemed the object of unwelcome attention from a local Aboriginal man) they called up feminine charm or haughtiness—if that failed, they could try fleeing behind a rock and waiting until the coast was clear. Whereas men could use brute strength or a well-reasoned plan of attack to save themselves from danger—and this was a feature of men's travel accounts—women depended on methods acceptable to the conventions of feminine behaviour.

Women were allowed, if not expected, to show fear and anxiety, and flee and hide. Men were not. On a sea voyage, for example, women concerned for safety, even in mild swells—if strong enough to sway the boat—would take to their cabins, fearful of being swept overboard. The fear was legitimate, though rarely expressed by gentlemen passengers, who were equally aware of the danger, yet because of masculine conventions had to be ordered during bad storms—rather than take the initiative themselves—to stay below. Eliza Kent described how during her voyage from New South Wales to England in 1800–1801, an attempt to land for a day's excursion was abandoned since the venture 'was found impracticable for ladies, owing to the surf, which had nearly swamped the boat'. It is not easy to tell if women were actually fearful of sea voyages. Louisa Meredith felt 'dizzy with the mere remembrance' of a terrible storm with 'awful waves' during her voyage to New

BEING PREPARED. *Lady Franklin organised a carry-chair for an 1842 expedition with her husband the governor through Tasmania's central mountain region to the west coast, although the steep inclines and rocky condition of the track meant she rarely used it. (Maker unknown, Trafalgar-back carrying chair, c. 1840.)*

UNPREDICTABLE TRAVEL. *Fallen trees or flooded creeks often affected road conditions. (Above: John Andrew Bonar,* Goulburn River Crossing Place Flooded and a Horse Gibbing, *c. 1856. Below: Engraver unknown,* Getting Over a Difficulty—Corduroy Road, Beyond Fernshaw, *1881.)*

South Wales, but even so, her account was presented as an uncomfortably sublime experience, revealing the enormous power of the natural elements in contrast to humans, rather than dwelling on her own fear. Eliza Davies recognised sea storms as sublime, yet commented how she 'not only had no fear, but … apprehended no danger'. Lachlan Macquarie wrote of Mrs Macquarie's 'sea sickness' during their voyage over a turbulent Bass Strait, and noted that despite this 'she makes a most excellent brave sailor, never expressing the least fear or apprehension of danger'.

Accounts of ladies being ill on sea voyages were so often included in their travel accounts that illness appeared taken for granted as respectable, feminine behaviour. Not even Jane Franklin felt well enough to leave her cabin on the voyage between Van Diemen's Land and Melbourne. Louisa Meredith described the reaction of the 'lady passengers' to a heavy swell during the voyage across Bass Strait: all those on deck 'either vanished altogether, or assumed suspiciously recumbent attitudes'.

Illness (often unspecified) and fatigue characterised much of women's travel on land in Australia. For example, Lachlan Macquarie expressed concern about the tiring effect on Mrs Macquarie of their tour over the newly constructed road across the Blue Mountains to Bathurst; he feared that the six, sometimes seven, hours on horseback in 'such very hot sultry weather' with the added strain of walking up a 'high steep hill' would be too much for her. He added, however, that she 'bore it uncommonly well' and arrived in 'good health'. His protectiveness was understandable: his first wife had died of consumption in India, and Elizabeth had already had five miscarriages in as many years before the birth of their son the year before the journey.[26] Yet his concern for her frailty was a common nineteenth-century comment on women, and was often reflected in women's travel accounts.

So dominant is this image of feminine reaction to travel that it helped construct and maintain an image of travel in Australia as adventurous, and sometimes dangerously so. That is why the Australian situation doesn't entirely match claims made by Shirley Foster and Joanna Trollope in their separate accounts of British women travelling abroad. Trollope's account of women drawing self-esteem from their work in parts of the British empire argues that travel was an escape from the

Joseph Gould Medland, Cabin Scene. Time 9 a.m. Aboard the *William Jardine*.
Oct. 31 1844.

Victorian ideals of feminine frailty because much nineteenth-century travel required stamina. Foster speculates that frailty and ill health, although sometimes a motivation for women's travel, were really signs of their powerlessness in England since symptoms of illness often disappeared during their travels.[27] Regional boundaries, however, gave rise to different reactions.[28] Literary accounts of fragile English ladies might have them blossom with good health during a tour of Switzerland—that is what was expected—but many women tourists in Australia stressed the fatigue and problems associated with such difficult terrain and climate. The same terrain and possibilities of danger that challenged the manliness of gentlemen explorers and travellers helped to construct ladies as feminine. Illness and fatigue as a feminine response was entirely appropriate to a travelling armchair audience's expectation of Australia.

Men rarely admitted to general fatigue except in particularly gruelling circumstances. Accounts of feminine frailty did not prevent women from undertaking strenuous activity so much as define their reaction and the type of activity they engaged in as different from men's—and help invent Australia as a destination for the adventurous. Men might finally admit to weakness brought on by enormous difficulties. And this could make them more manly, and Australia a more daring destination. Kathleen Fitzpatrick notes that explorers described their physical condition, disease and all, adding to their heroic status. Ophthalmia, scurvy and starvation as well as irritations due to flies and heat were common difficulties. Lachlan Macquarie on his tour over the Blue Mountains only admitted to his fatigue after a very long day on horseback, having ridden for at least seven hours over at least 30 miles (50 kilometres) and in searing heat. Emma Macpherson described her husband as having 'tic douloureux' (facial neuralgia) on their inland tour. Anthony Trollope wrote that his Australian tour did not fatigue him 'bodily', but mentally he tired of the novelty, and blamed this on his advanced years. James Froude also blamed age for his fatigue. On his tour to view the giant trees at Fernshaw in Victoria, he wished he was forty years younger since, he wrote, 'age and its infirmities' were not recognised in Australia.[29]

Some women did not write about their fatigue at all. There were, of course, other conventions by which one expressed femininity. One such, which defined women as in need of certain physical comforts, was feminine expectations of their sleeping quarters. Women could put up with almost any discomfort on their tours—terrible roads, perilous mountainsides, delays, even the possible threat of bushrangers—yet the conditions under which they slept required particular attention. Women did not expect the comforts of their own homes, but they did expect certain standards of cleanliness, good ventilation and at least some personal space. Colonial sea vessels transporting people around the colonies caused most distress. Louisa Meredith explained that the sleeping arrangements on most of these vessels were, 'especially for ladies, inadequate in point of space, and totally bereft of ventilation'. Jane Franklin complained about the disagreeable smell during her voyage across to Melbourne, her cabin located as it was near where the horses were stabled. Fanny Rains, on her voyage up the coast to Sydney in the 1870s, explained how accommodation was so limited that eight ladies had to share the same cabin, which had no place for any personal items, not even a hook to hang her clothes on, the light was dim, the atmosphere stuffy, and she shared her berth with cockroaches and weevils. 'Possessed of a good stock of patience and philosophy', she wrote, she withstood these irritants.[30]

Accommodation while touring could also have problems, particularly in regard to the civility of the servants and the cleanliness of the establishment generally. Elizabeth Hawkins, who journeyed from Sydney to Bathurst in 1822, decided that 'a good barn in England would have been a palace' compared to the inn at Springwood, which was not only 'dirty, damp and cold', and filled with hundreds of crawling bugs, but the woman who ran the house—the convict wife of the corporal stationed there—was described as a 'most depraved character and well-known thief'. Later, another woman at another inn, who offered her a bucket of fresh milk, she found 'clean and civil'. Louisa Meredith, travelling over the Blue Mountains almost twenty years later, also commented on the standards of cleanliness and comforts of inns, despising one for its intolerable deficiencies, another for the dirtiness of its linen, and praising a third for its 'plain homely cleanliness'. Many years later, Fanny Rains expressed her disappointment with her room in a hotel at Mount Victoria: it was neither clean nor secure, the appointments were meagre, her window was hidden behind a dirty yellow blind, and the servant was not 'civil'. In men's travel accounts, descriptions of inns emphasised public rather than private spaces (such as their gardens, general appearance and, in one case at least— Trollope—a bathroom) or whether the writers had a good night's sleep.

It is not surprising that the conditions of bedrooms in inns and hotels and of ship's cabins—places where a woman prepared her toilette, dressed and rested— were subject to such scrutiny. After all, feminine upbringing stressed the importance of a person's customs, manners and morality as a way of assessing respectability. And sleeping quarters were of particular interest to ladies because women were expected to spend much time in them, not just sleeping, but occupying themselves with various tasks; thus (it was believed) the appearance and condition of a bed chamber symbolised the refinement, and respectability of an establishment.

For these reasons making camp on tour was often accepted by women as superior to other available accommodation (apart from, perhaps, the homes of respectable settlers). Camping out solved the problem of bad ventilation, and those touring could more easily control the cleanliness of a campsite and its utilities. Mrs Macquarie, who accompanied her husband on most of his official tours of the colony, often went ahead to oversee the household-side of the camp. The comfort

WOMEN TRAVELLERS OFTEN SUPERVISED CAMPSITES *when travelling with their husbands. Emma Macpherson sketched her family's campsite on the journey to the Gwydir district in New South Wales in the 1850s. A lithograph of the sketch was included in her published travel account. (Engraver unknown,* A Bush Encampment, *1860.)*

of ladies was seen as important, with many accounts of gentlemen preparing 'beds like down'—apparently made from piles of soft moss, fern or herbage—and placed in tents or other sheltered places designated as the ladies' quarters at sufficient distance for privacy. Gentlemen, on the other hand, usually slept in the open, by the campfire.[31]

In some ways women in the eighteenth and nineteenth centuries did not stray from the domestic hearth. Physically, of course, many did, particularly those of the upper classes, yet social convention demanded a sort of portable domestic hearth, a protective barrier against the evils of the world. Armed with a list of respectable contacts at one's destination, codes of ladylike behaviour drummed in from girlhood and good sense, a lady could more or less go where she liked. The masculine and feminine dimensions of touring gave rise to the presence of two types of travellers, the 'gentleman' and the 'lady'. Their travel accounts, with different emphases from each, was, for a period, a powerful means of maintaining the existing social order, and celebrating respectable values.

INVENTING THE
MOUNTAIN RESORT

*In which the Blue Mountains as a tourist resort
is introduced and its characteristics as
a new type of social institution examined*

Sydney Railway Station, late afternoon, mid-autumn, fin de siècle.* The train sighed, letting off a great cloud of steam, and with a long whistle heaved itself along the rails leaving the platform on its three-hour journey to Katoomba in the Blue Mountains.[1] Two sisters sat in a first-class carriage, reading matter, warm coats, shawls and other creature comforts within reach, their dress trunks and hat boxes in the luggage compartment. They had spent the last few months in Sydney with an aunt, and had found the lively ways of this big metropolis very different from the quieter refinements of Adelaide where they lived with their parents. The younger sister had won a scholarship to the University of Adelaide and now, her Arts degree awarded, was poised for the future. The elder, like most such young ladies, had not enrolled at the university, but had enjoyed with her sister its social world, and had attended lectures that interested her. Some may have seen the sisters as 'bookish', and they were in the sense that they were intelligent and enjoyed reading for its opening out of both real and imaginary worlds. To those within their social circle they were bright, young and adventurous. The trip to New South Wales was at their father's expense, a gesture of goodwill for their future, and a highly anticipated adventure.

The Sydney stay had included a round of social engagements arranged by their aunt: tennis, picnics, boating, afternoon teas, evening parties, even a dance, furniture pushed back in the big sitting room. But there was also their own program of visiting Sydney's edifying attractions—the art gallery, the public library and the city's well-known museums. They had been introduced to the sons and daughters of university professors, journalists and lawyers, whose parents were part of their aunt's social world. At one gathering the daughter of a journalist had insisted the two sisters join her family party in the Blue Mountains. The sisters, of course, knew about the Blue Mountains as a page from colonial history, the story of barriers insurmountable to European colonisation until Blaxland, Lawson and Wentworth

---

* This section of the chapter is a story, a composite picture, fictional, but based on many accounts published in the nineteenth-century travel journals, memoirs and other sources noted throughout the book. The names of people and places are accurate. For more details see note 1.

followed a ridge to the western side in 1813, thus solving the puzzle of access that had baffled a generation of colonists, and they were interested in seeing for themselves the mountain scenery, said to be one of the world's natural wonders with grand views of cliffs and valleys and opportunities to walk amid ferny dells.

'It will be great fun', the journalist's daughter had said. 'We've booked three rooms at the Hurlstone guesthouse in Katoomba. There's generally a good bunch of people there, and we'll be well looked after by the proprietress, who knows everything and everyone in the Blue Mountains. My brother and two of his friends will be joining us, so the two of you can share one room, I'll share the other with my mother, and the boys can have the third. Oh, do come! I'm sure your aunt can spare you for a week.'

The aunt found the arrangements satisfactory, and believed that a week of mountain air and strenuous exercise would certainly benefit her nieces. This she said publicly. Privately, she thought that a week with three eligible young gentlemen—properly supervised of course—was an excellent idea.

The sisters prepared for the excursion not only by packing appropriate clothing—sturdy boots, skirts and jackets suitable for walking, raincoats, warm wraps and mufflers, and evening wear—but also by learning a bit more about their destination. Over dinner one night an acquaintance of their aunt had spoken of the mid-nineteenth-century artist Eugen von Guérard who had visited the mountains in 1859 and produced several paintings of the scenery. The acquaintance had viewed one during a visit to Melbourne in 1862, a fine perspective of Wentworth Falls. That had been the first time he had ever seen the Blue Mountains either depicted or in true life, though he had heard about the plunging chasms and grand vistas. The painting had, however, opened up the scenery for him. The chasms and vistas of his imagination were minute compared to the depth and distance of rock and valley depicted by Guérard. Just contemplating the human figure on the edge of one cliff had made him feel decidedly uncomfortable, a pinching feeling in his lower body which he knew would have transformed into dizziness had he been on that edge. Some years later when he finally went to the Blue Mountains he sought

E. von Guérard, Weatherboard Creek Falls, Jamieson's Valley, New South Wales, *1862*.

out the setting of that painting, wondering whether Guérard had perhaps not over-stated the power of the view. But the scene was even grander than he had imagined, and what Guérard had depicted in paint was further enhanced by sound, smell and sensation. Certainly, he could not bring himself to go anywhere near the actual edge. The aunt's friend suggested the sisters look out for one of the art gallery's new acquisitions, a watercolour of the Grose Valley in the Blue Mountains by the fine landscape artist William Charles Piguenit. They had postponed their trip to the art gallery, but did borrow an informative guidebook which now lay open on one sister's lap at a reference to the great zig-zag railway, an engineering feat that had opened the mountains up to trains, although the zig zags on the Sydney side had now been replaced by a series of deep railway cuttings.

They arrived at Katoomba in the dark, the brisk cold air alerting them to their new altitude. A strange-looking man enquired whether the young ladies were looking for a place to stay, to which they replied they already had accommodation. But don't the Misses need someone to take them there? They thanked him kindly but assured him they were already accounted for, that their transport would be along shortly. He persisted, though, with a convoluted story about his mistress sending him to the station telling him not to return without some ladies, all of which the sisters tried politely to ignore thinking that he was a rogue until they realised that no one was left at the station apart from themselves, and that this man was the boots of their guesthouse sent to collect them.

The Hurlstone occupied adjacent houses at the end of Katoomba Street, within walking distance of the escarpment. A clean, well-kept guesthouse, the business had been established initially out of economic need when Rosanna Knight's tradesman husband died of a chill in 1888. The Knights had moved to Katoomba to take advantage of a buoyant building economy. After his death, and with many children to support, Rosanna Knight took a lease on a nearby boarding house where she could combine work and child-rearing under the same roof. The business was successful, and though the guest facilities were modest, her reputation as a respected Methodist helped ensure a loyal and growing following. The Hurlstone was her fourth guesthouse, larger than the previous residences, and allowed her to expand the business. She also saw her duty as providing employment opportunities for those suffering misfortunes as long as they could prove themselves honest, trustworthy and willing to work, even if their manners were sometimes gruff.

The sisters arrived, were shown to their room, simply furnished, large enough, though, with a good-sized dressing table and mirror, a chest of drawers, small wardrobe, washstand with a clean bowl, and two beds, each with a large quilt. Their room looked onto a garden, although it was so dark they couldn't see out. They were refreshing themselves after their journey when Mrs Knight knocked and entered to introduce herself. A composed woman with the calm authority that comes from years of dealing with children and paying guests and a pleasant manner,

THE RAILWAY TO THE BLUE MOUNTAINS *was first opened in 1867, terminating at Weatherboard (Wentworth Falls), and shortly after at Blackheath. The railway was a boon to commercial development of a tourist resort with a long-standing reputation for magnificent scenery. The township of Leura, complete with railway station, was established in the late nineteenth century. (Charles Kerry,* Leura Railway Station, *1890s.)*

she apologised for any mix-up at the railway station caused by the 'boy' whom she assured them was perfectly harmless. Their late arrival meant they had missed tea, although the cook would rustle them up something to eat as soon as they were ready. A light supper would also be served in the drawing room at 9.30 p.m., where most of the guests were now gathering. Breakfast was served in the dining room until 10.30 a.m., arrangements could be made for a light luncheon, either in the house or, if she was given notice, made up as a picnic hamper. On Sundays dinner was served after the late-morning church service. She told them that the rest of their party, as they knew, had already arrived, but for the convenience of the cook, she asked that they first go to the dining room. There were books and maps about the Blue Mountains in the drawing room, and she was happy to give advice about where to go for what. She hoped they found their rooms adequately furnished and should see her personally if anything was amiss. Copper pans would be brought around later to warm the beds. Finally, she explained to them the sanitation and bathing arrangements.

They made their way to the dining room, a functional area although the drapes and red cedar sideboard added a hint of elegance. Comfortable austerity, they decided. But austere the drawing room most certainly was not. The largest room of the house, it was here that Mrs Knight had revealed a talent for home decoration. The drapery, masses of cushions, soft lamp light, mantels crammed with glittering knick-knacks, and some guests in various free-floating garments and turban-style head-dresses at first suggested a Middle Eastern treasure trove, although this initial impression mellowed once the sisters recognised the Victoriana staples of a piano, card tables, shelves stacked with books, a cosy fireplace and proper armchairs. Obviously Mrs Knight intended her guests to spend most of their time in this room when not out and about. When the sisters entered the room most of the guests were in the middle of a parlour game which had required dressing up.

There were fifteen people altogether, the sisters' party of seven, another party of three young ladies and two gentlemen, two elderly women who were content enough amid the buzz of activity around them, and an elderly gentleman reading in the corner, apparently oblivious to the din. Introductions were made, turbans taken off, enquiries made of the sisters about their journey and a brief account given of the activities over the last day or so. The party of five had just returned from a three-day excursion to Jenolan Caves, a brief visit in fact since much of the time was spent getting there and back. The younger guests then turned their attention to tomorrow's activities, a long walk, they decided, to show the sisters some of the grand sights. By the time debate had subsided about where to walk, supper had been laid out, a generous spread of cheese tartlets, veal patties and anchovy toast, and soon after that, the guests began to retire to their bedrooms.

The week was a whirlwind of activity. Most days were spent exploring the surrounding countryside, not just with members of their own party, but also with some of the other younger guests staying at the Hurlstone. Some days they went on long walks along the edge of the sandstone escarpment, and, where they found paths, down into the valley to explore waterfalls, ferns and have their picnic lunch. The valleys around Leura were particularly well served with fireplaces and piles of chopped wood, and wherever they were, the gentlemen swiftly made a small campfire to boil a billy and toast bread, which they ate smothered in butter and honey, their preferred picnic food though Mrs Knight also included pressed tongue and chicken paste. The walk out of these valleys was so strenuous that once back at the Hurlstone they could do little more than relax by the fire in the drawing room and feast on the splendid array of delicious cream cakes, biscuits and sweet tarts laid out for afternoon tea. Apart from the cakes and pastry, the food served at Hurlstone was mostly ordinary; dinner was soup, a meat dish and pudding. The meat dish was a roast, hot pot or third-rate curry (the sort of dishes made from leftovers). One member of the party had even joked about how he was sure he had seen the very same potato from the Sunday roast in at least three meals since.

The older sister especially enjoyed her early morning walks to the edge of cliffs looking over valleys shrouded in mist, taking in deep breaths of bracing mountain air, and experienced what her guidebook promised: 'All sense of languor is lost; the step is buoyant and elastic, and life seems worth living' (although the buoyancy of the step was usually subdued after ascending steep paths and wooden ladders on the way out of a valley).

Sometimes they took a coach to travel further afield, one day to Wentworth Falls to see the view that Guérard had painted, another to Blackheath to see extensive valleys and the long, thin waterfall at Govett's Leap. Their coach driver was a talkative chap who introduced himself as 'Harry Peckman, Blue Mountains guide and poet, at your service', and was keen to show them the grand sights, and fill them in on local historical gossip, such as daring rescues of wayward tourists, and his favourite story of how the township came to be called Katoomba: 'In the 1870s an Aboriginal woman by the name of Bet—some say she was a princess—accompanied a few local Hartley residents on a picnic to what was then called "the Crushers". The picnickers asked her what was the Aboriginal name for the waterfall, and she informed them that the place was really known as "Katoomba", meaning "Tumble-down water"'.

He was such an enthusiast for what had been his home for the past thirty years, and took them to so many out-of-the-way places that some of the passengers wondered if they'd ever reach Blackheath. The day they planned to go to Mount Victoria they decided to take the train, quicker than a horse-drawn cab, allowing more time to explore their destination. They had the unusual experience of travelling in a goods train on their return journey.

One night Mrs Knight organised a lantern slideshow. Chairs assembled, lights extinguished, and there, projected onto a large, white sheet, were wondrous images of Blue Mountains scenery, taken by John Paine, a commercial photographer who had been photographing the mountain scenery since the 1870s. The audience decided there were similarities between landscape paintings and artistic photographs of landscape in the way each constructed perspective and conveyed a startling sense of depth and breadth entirely recognisable to those who had seen the scenery for themselves, with no sense of loss due to the photographs being in black and white. As the sisters discussed later that night, the black and white photography somehow enhanced the misty effects they so enjoyed here. In particular, the photographer had successfully represented the region's waterfalls, contrasting them with the surrounding cliff faces using a technique that brought the thin stream of foaming water to the forefront of the image. The next morning they told their friend's mother, who had retired early the night before, 'You could almost hear the sound of tumbling water'. Mrs Knight told them that a shop on Katoomba Street sold tourist copies of Mr Paine's work, and they decided to go there that afternoon.

The week had been a great success, even though there were no marriage proposals, except during a parlour game when a handsome young guest proposed to another guest who thanked him kindly, but said she must refuse his offer since she was about to celebrate her fortieth wedding anniversary. The night they arrived back at their aunt's house, they dissected the experience over an aperitif, a custom the aunt had adopted after her trip to the continent: the guests had all, remarkably, got on with one another; the accommodation was comfortable, reasonable food, delicious cakes, enjoyable evenings; the bedrooms were not adequately heated which meant the drawing room was a hive of activity at night with too many distractions for quiet reflection or reading. The best part was without doubt the excursions to see the scenery, especially the long, often arduous walks along mountain paths that wound around the escarpment, detouring to viewing platforms for different landscape perspectives, down rock faces via sturdy wooden ladders to enable close inspection of fern dells and waterfall pools. They felt refreshed, they told their aunt, in both body and spirit.

Later that week their party reunited for dinner. They had decided in advance that each person should perform an entertaining account of their week in the Blue Mountains, in poetry, drama or mime. Someone gently portrayed Mrs Knight in caricature. Two others joined forces to re-enact one of the especially arduous walks, but as the explorers Burke and Wills. One guest pretended he was Eugen von Guérard talking in a heavy Austrian accent about his painting, the *Weatherboard Creek Falls*, or the 'Vetterboard Falls' as he quipped. The younger sister stood up and recited a poem composed by their guide Harry Peckham. She performed in melodramatic fashion, delivering the first lines with intensity:

Katoomba, awake, the spring morning is breaking
Which breathes the glad tidings thy future is bright.

John Paine, [Blue Mountains Waterfall, Wentworth Falls], c. 1881.

She moved to crescendo with the passage:

> The pure winds, impatient with invigoration,
>> Implant the red rose with a smile on each face:
> The cloud-riding Storm King shouts 'Life! Preservation!'
>> And cleaves with a thunderbolt Death in his chase.

And then joyfully:

> Then come to the great sanatorium, Katoomba,
>> Ye searchers of scenery, peace, pleasure, and health;
> Take rest on her summit, where naught shall encumber,
>> The Blue Mountains Eden, fair garden of wealth.

After which she paused, and with the seriousness of someone delivering an important proclamation, carefully enunciated:

> Rich minerals abound in her veins, ripe for hewing;
>> Oh, hearts of Katoomba, awake and be doing![2]

The Blue Mountains were a major destination for visitors in the Australian colonies, and one of the first places for extensive commercial tourist development. They are a useful guide to business activity in a growing tourist market, and how commercial enterprise contributed to the directions of Australian tourism. Increasingly, tourism was not only for the upper classes in search of something novel and interesting, but also a leisure activity for anyone who wanted to and could afford to retreat from the everyday, and restore physical and mental energy.

In the second half of the nineteenth century the upper Blue Mountains developed from a few sparsely populated settlements into a group of six townships covering the area from Wentworth Falls to Mount Victoria. A major impetus for this development was the increasing number of visitors to the area, bolstered by the arrival of the railway in the late 1860s, and especially, the variety of accommodation built (or later, converted from existing structures) to house visitors. Some of this development was opportunistic and not always successful, but it was part of a pattern of development that emerged throughout Australia's mountain resorts during this period.

Places such as Mount Lofty and Mount Barker in South Australia, the Dandenongs, Daylesford and Mount Macedon in Victoria, Sutton Forest (and other townships in what later became known as the Southern Highlands) in New South Wales, and Mount Tamborine in Queensland, all started to show signs of a developing tourist infrastructure, particularly once the railways improved access. Comfortable lodgings especially designed for tourists were constructed. Active local business communities interested in tourist business developed. Influential local residents who wished to protect their immediate environs from large tourist developments, nonetheless helped lobby for public reserves and contributed to the construction of bush paths to local sights.

The scenic magnificence of mountain sights was an underlying reason for their popularity, and prompted interest in the tourist potential of other mountainous regions further afield. From the turn of the twentieth century extensive tourist facilities were being planned for parts of the Kosciuszko district, Mount Buffalo and the Grampians in Victoria, and Kuranda in North Queensland. Fashionableness was a factor, especially in those districts chosen by a colonial governor to establish a summer retreat, such as in the Adelaide Hills in South Australia, at Mount Macedon in Victoria, and Sutton Forest in New South Wales.[3] But where once mountain vistas, ferny dells and wispy waterfalls were the main reason for either a short excursion or an extended tour, mountain resorts were now building reputations as quiet yet sociable retreats from life's daily humdrum in a cool and restorative climate.

A study of the situation in the upper Blue Mountains shows how development in response to tourist accommodation needs and expectations was an important part of a local economy, and perpetuated, even transformed, a region's identity.

In 1866, the district around the roadside village of Weatherboard, the first settlement in the upper Blue Mountains on the road from Sydney, was described as 'a favourite one of resort for tourists in search of the picturesque'.[4] It had no grand hotels, not even modest boarding houses or private residences used for summer holidays. The village consisted of a few rough buildings and one inn providing basic refreshments, all that could be purchased from any wayside inn along the Sydney–Bathurst road. The land had not yet been surveyed for the establishment of a town, and it was to be a decade or so before the first public sales of land. 'Tourists in search of the picturesque' may have been a feature of the mountains in the 1860s, but businesses in search of the tourist did not seriously arrive until the 1870s. Early tourists had to share the wayside inns with a rougher range of road users, bullock teamsters and such. However, by the last decades of the nineteenth century more refined needs were being catered for.

From the 1870s to the early 1900s development in the Blue Mountains was providing a new range of services specifically for tourists: accommodation to suit different budgets and tastes, and businesses aimed at tourist activities, such as the bakery that provided picnic hampers and the coach company that toured nearby sights. Regional commercial interests developed their own perspective on tourist attractions, still exalting natural beauty, but adding amenities fashioned according to how they perceived the tourist market. This new commercial interest meant a pronounced concern in having tourists stay as long as possible, trying to attract newcomers, and hoping that first-time guests would return again and again. So, while making their amenities sound attractive, many entrepreneurs promoted the mountains not only for traditional attractions such as scenery and ferns, but also for the new idea of mountains as pure and healthy: tourists might stay (and return) for their physical well-being. In 1866 the term 'resort' (in the travel context) was used for the act of touring itself, but by the early twentieth century it had come to mean extensive tourist services and facilities at a particular place.[5]

An initial impetus for a local tourist infrastructure was the new railway to the upper Blue Mountains, first in 1867 to Weatherboard, and a little later, to Blackheath (providing easier access to Govett's Leap) and Mount Victoria. Although the railway's intended purpose was easier communication and transport between Sydney and towns servicing the rich grazing and agricultural lands west of the Blue Mountains, a side benefit was to shorten the journey between Sydney and the Blue Mountains from a couple of days to less than six hours: in theory people could visit the upper mountains for the day. A journalist in the late 1870s noted that with 'an hour and forty minutes rest before the down train to Sydney returns, there is just time for a flying visit' to see the 'Waterfall of the Weatherboard', especially if visitors hired a horse or horse and cart. Although it was possible to catch the morning train from Sydney (departing at 9 a.m.), and arrive at the Weatherboard (at 12.58 p.m.), with only an hour and a half before the afternoon train departed (at 2.34 p.m.), any delays on the way, as there often were, meant visitors would miss either the sights or the train back to Sydney. (The major cause of delays was ascending and descending single track zig zags where it was often necessary to wait in railway sidings until the track was clear of other trains. By the 1910s new tunnels relieved the congestion and so railway timetables were more reliable.)[6]

Much of the interest for the early few who undertook the journey was the train trip: to experience modern technology, marvel at steam power and, especially, the engineering triumph of mountain railroad construction, the series of viaducts zigzagging up the sides of the range creating a less steep gradient for trains, and so making the rail passage possible. But the train trip also meant that the sights of the upper Blue Mountains, instead of being mere diversions (awe-inspiring and unusual though they were), were toured and savoured for themselves rather than tasted briefly on the way to somewhere else. With more time, tourists along with the small but increasing number of local residents were able to explore the cliff tops for more views and for safe descents into the gullies. The railway also was more comfortable than even the most luxurious coach or carriage, and certainly provided a less stressful journey than had previously been the case. In 1861 Rachel Henning wrote that the road 'was *bad* when I was here before, but now there is no word that I should like to use that would least express its state'.[7]

Improved access attracted influential Sydney businessmen, politicians, judges and University of Sydney academics and their families who built holiday houses in the district—some of the types who were an important early influence in the development of Australian mountain resorts more generally. (A number also built train platforms near their estates in order to take advantage of the railway.) A holiday house in the mountains was a trend well established in the 1870s in the lower mountains, between Lapstone and Woodford, especially after notable Sydney residents Alfred Stephen, James Martin, Charles Badham and Henry Parkes had built country residences near one another at Linden and Faulconbridge. In the mid-1870s Henry Parkes had selected 600 acres of land near Springwood, on which he first built a small holiday cottage, and then in 1878, a much larger cottage facing the gully with superb views and according to his daughter Annie Parkes 'with a noble verandah and two very large front rooms'. He called this cottage Faulconbridge after his mother's maiden name. He had chosen the land for the 'wild solitude of mountain range and glen' and appreciated it as a refuge 'from the vapour-laden air of the coast district to the dry and exhilarating atmosphere of the mountains'.[8]

The term 'hill station' was not usually applied then to describe such collections of Australian mountain-nestled homes away from home. But there are some similarities with the British custom in India of escaping the heat of the plains to comfortable residences in hill areas, such as Simla. Certainly, by the turn of the century the health-giving properties of higher altitude air beckoned many members of Sydney society, and the equivalent in the other colonies, to spend their summers in nearby mountain resorts.

In the upper Blue Mountains the trend began in the 1870s at Mount Victoria when two friends of Henry Parkes, the newspaper proprietor John Fairfax and the

Holiday houses of well-known citizens *featured in travel writing. This picture of Sir Henry Parkes at home at Faulconbridge in the Blue Mountains was published in 1881 in the* Australasian Sketcher. *(F. A. Sleap,* A Visit to Sir Henry Parkes at Faulconbridge, *1881?)*

politician William Piddington, each built a large holiday residence suitable for house parties. In the 1880s the trend continued with the new Katoomba house of Chief Justice Frederick Darley (the house was called Lillianfels in honour of his daughter Lillian who had died of tuberculosis the year before it was completed), and a little later politician John See built a fine residence at Wentworth Falls with a grand view into the valley. At Mount Victoria Walter Scott, a bachelor, who came from England in 1885 to succeed Charles Badham as professor of classics at the University of Sydney, built a cottage, later sold to another University of Sydney professor, George Arnold Wood.[9]

WEALTHY COLONISTS WITH HOLIDAY HOUSES *helped to make mountain resorts fashionable. Some holiday houses were later sold to be turned into comfortable guesthouses. Pictured is 'Eurilla', Sir William Milne's country residence at Mount Lofty in the early 1890s. (Terence McGann, 'Eurilla', Mount Lofty, [the House 'Eurilla' Showing Garden and Front Approach], c. 1890.)*

Although many of these second homes were noted as modest compared to their metropolitan alternatives, some were substantial buildings, the finest yet in the upper mountains and they were a reminder that powerful people now lived in the region even if on an occasional basis. Their presence heralded what was to become an enduring function of the mountains: a location for a holiday house, a second home for those who sought a retreat from the day-to-day concerns of the city and its climate and were well-off enough to afford it. Often described as 'pretty' or 'lovely villas', most were weatherboard with iron roofs, although even this construction represented a not inconsiderable investment. Acre lots of land were available for about £80, and larger blocks, 10 acres or more, for between £300 and £400. In the 1880s with the cost of construction on average around £50 per room for a weatherboard house, it was not difficult to spend about £1000 in total, for which the landowner, assuming the land had already been cleared of trees, could expect a house that would meet upper middle-class expectations with at least twelve rooms on a 12-acre block of land. All this was before the cost of furnishing the house, planting a garden and building stables. Although there were houses with more than twelve rooms, such as the Manor House built at Mount Victoria by the Fairfaxes in the 1870s, local advertisements of the time indicate a fashion for such mountain retreats to have between seven and twelve rooms, including a separate dining room, parlour and kitchen, making these holiday houses usually more than twice the size of the four-roomed workers' cottages common in Sydney.[10]

Many part-time residents took an interest in local matters, but usually in providing or supporting facilities that might enhance their own enjoyment of the district, such as well-marked tracks to explore the surrounding bush or a school of arts to provide a focus for intellectual life and where, even if they did not need to borrow reading matter from the library, they could listen to visiting speakers lecture on botany, contemporary imperial politics and other topics. Frederick Darley was the first president of Katoomba's School of Arts, and in the 1880s Henry Parkes, who had acquired land at Wentworth Falls, was titular head of the local Reserve Trust, the organisation responsible for many of the bush tracks leading into the valley below the falls. It is unlikely that these residents had much interest in tourist development or increased opportunities for business—indeed many may have not wanted such changes—but their support for cultural institutions and most notably, for the introduction of a system of walking tracks that opened up the landscape, undoubtedly contributed to the district's reputation as a desirable tourist resort.

By the late 1880s speculators in the upper mountains had begun to subdivide blocks of land into up-to-an acre lots recommending sites suitable for 'business premises' (those located near the railway stations) or for residences. Also, owners of some of the newly constructed residences began to sell their properties, often complete with 'high class furniture', crockery, linen and even spring mattresses. Investors, lured by the prospect of quick profits upon resale, had been encouraged to purchase properties and then, as more residences were built, to recoup their initial outlay by renting their properties as holiday houses. For two guineas per week (up to three and a half times the amount paid in rent for a four-roomed worker's cottage in one of Sydney's more respectable working-class suburbs), one could spend the summer in a two-bedroom furnished cottage with a dining room, kitchen and perhaps a servant's room. There was little available for less than two guineas a week, with most cottages more expensive, especially if large.

Purchasers were encouraged to believe that land in the upper mountains was a good investment because the district was the preferred choice of eminent Sydneysiders, and thus a country branch of Sydney's wealthy suburbs. Newspaper articles and guidebooks describing the train trip often noted where 'influential colonists' and 'distinguished gentlemen' lived, and this information was used in promoting land sales. The speculator responsible for subdividing an estate into what became some of Leura's more exclusive streets, appealed to purchasers' snobbery with claims that the district was on its way to becoming 'aristocratic' with land acquired by people he proclaimed to be 'wealthy buyers, such as Bankers, Squatters, Merchants and Gentlemen of independent means'.[11]

The district's exclusiveness, however, did not mean its residents were only from the upper classes. Domestic residences in the upper mountains needed maintenance

COUNTRY HOUSES WERE BUILT FOR COLONIAL GOVERNORS *towards the end of the nineteenth century in most colonies, including Mount Lofty in South Australia, Sutton Forest in New South Wales and Mount Macedon in Victoria. Vice-regal residents could heighten the fashionable reputation of a resort. Pictured is the governor's country house, Mount Macedon, in the 1880s. (Engraver unknown,* The Governor's Country House *[Mount Macedon, Vic.], 1886?)*

workers, and if there were a big enough settlement, shops. Mount Victoria prior to the construction of the first country residences had a temporary settlement, a tent city for labourers and other workers on the zig-zag railway to Lithgow, and, although by the mid-1870s most had moved elsewhere a small number, including carpenters, gardeners and a house painter, as well as a baker, were still living in the area.[12]

Conveniently, then, in providing services for both the grand houses of wealthy Sydney families and the more modest holiday retreats of urban professionals, the mountain settlements saw the railway construction boom replaced with new opportunities for its working-class residents. James Knight, for example, having arrived in Australia from Scotland with his wife Rosanna in the late 1860s, worked in the upper mountains as a fettler and ganger on the railway, then opened a general store in Katoomba and, a little later, taking advantage of local building opportunities, he started a business constructing holiday houses on recently subdivided land. The number of shops throughout the mountains, including general stores and bakers and butchers, also increased in the 1880s, but this was probably an indication that more people now resided permanently in the area, sustained (or at least hoping to be sustained) by local work, such as odd jobs, gardening and construction, called for by the owners of holiday houses. There were several short-lived mining ventures around Katoomba from the 1870s, possibly providing some custom for the district's fledgling commercial enterprises, although mines located deep in the valleys between Katoomba and Blackheath did have their own settlement at Nellie's Glen in the Megalong Valley including a hotel, a butcher's shop and a bakery, and another near the Ruined Castle, although this one was not much more than a few huts. Once the settlements were abandoned it was possible that some miners and their families decided to try their luck in the mountain townships. Holiday house owners had begun creating opportunities in the building and related trades, which in turn had helped develop and maintain a small permanent population, which in its turn, combined with the seasonal demand from the occupants of holiday houses, had created opportunities for butchers, bakers, general storekeepers and even a hairdresser.[13]

The increased interest in the natural beauty spots of the mountains along with the convenience of trains encouraged more people to make the trip. There is no way of knowing how many people visited the mountains, but development in the variety and number of places of accommodation in the upper mountains from only two inns in the 1870s to nearly seventy hotels and boarding houses in 1900 suggests not only an increase in tourist numbers, but also significant concern for where one might stay. By the end of the nineteenth century, there was both interest in the sights and in the merits of the tourist amenities, in particular the hotels and boarding houses.

In the 1880s the idea of the benefits of the holiday house was extended with the new commercial interest in up-market hotel accommodation for tourists. Commercial accommodation in the form of small wayside inns had existed in the upper mountains for decades. The inns were so modest and so scattered that none of their proprietors were included in an 1867 list of New South Wales 'hotelkeepers' or 'innkeepers' published in the *Walter Samson Directory*. As a result of the new railway and the end of the need for overnight accommodation, by the 1870s there was little business for the inns, and most had closed, apart from a few at Mount Victoria, which probably survived longer because of the railway workers.[14]

By the early 1880s there were hostelries in the upper mountains mostly patronised by local workmen, although a few offered refreshments to tourists and even provided modest accommodation. Tourists were generally dissuaded from staying in these establishments, which were variously described as 'anything but inviting' and, in one case at least, 'execrable', and were advised instead to 'cultivate the friendship' of a person with a holiday house, with whom they might stay or possibly 'buy ... out for a month or two'.[15]

This state of affairs was soon to change. In 1882 a large hotel with sixty commodious rooms was opened at Katoomba, a settlement then barely more than a railway siding for loading coal from the district's mines and adjusting train loads for the descent to Sydney. Initially, the group behind its development had planned the hotel for Wentworth Falls, already prized for its attraction for tourists, but the

THE CARRINGTON, KATOOMBA, N.S.W.

bid for suitable real estate there failed due to local interests united against a major hotel development. Possibly Katoomba, closer to Sydney than Blackheath and Mount Victoria, and unlike them, with little residential development, lacked local interests to resist this proposal. Harry Rowell, a Sydney hotelier, bought the Katoomba site and built the Great Western Hotel, and upon his death, it was sold to Frederick Goyder, who changed its name to the Carrington Hotel.

By the mid-1880s, of the seven hotels then operating in the four townships of the upper mountains (Leura and Medlow Bath did not yet exist) only two, the Carrington at Katoomba and the Imperial at Mount Victoria, were recommended as providing the necessities of good service—a comfortable dining room, commodious guest rooms, and common rooms, such as a music room and a drawing room. Ten years later, however, about half of the district's hotels, now amounting to eleven, that advertised accommodation for tourists were highly recommended for their premises and services.

Modernity, spaciousness, extensive views of surrounding scenery and attentive service were some of the hallmarks of gracious hotels in the upper mountains. In the promotional material of the 1880s and 1890s, hotels made much of their innovations, in particular, the use of modern technology in facilities such as electric bells, electric lights and sanitary arrangements. In the 1880s the Carrington boasted of providing 'every sanitary appliance that modern science has indicated as effectual', which included a reliable water supply, hot and cold water and electric bells in every room, and a gas supply for lighting and heating. In the early 1890s, the Imperial Hotel at Mount Victoria announced that it had been 'thoroughly renovated'; the Belgravia Hotel at Medlow (before the Hydro Majestic was built in

GRAND HOTELS *like the Carrington at Katoomba in the Blue Mountains only became a feature of tourist accommodation late in the nineteenth century, although they did not replace more modest accommodation such as the mid-nineteenth century Watts Bridge Hotel at Fernshaw in Victoria, depicted here in the early 1880s. (Above: Nicholas Caire, The Hotel [M. Jefferson, Watts Bridge Hotel, Fernshaw], c. 1883. Below: Photographer unknown, [The Carrington], c. 1900.)*

1904 and the township became Medlow Bath) advertised its electric light as well as its 'hot, cold and shower baths', all supplied by 'the most powerful machinery'; and the Wentworth Hotel at Wentworth Falls, only recently constructed, stated that the 'hotel is modern' with up-to-date facilities and had been 'furnished throughout by Farmer & Co. of Sydney'.[16]

References to electricity were probably intended to impress potential guests, those who wanted to experience this new form of energy. Domestic electricity was not yet available in the Australian colonies, and there was certainly curiosity about its potential and its use in lighting a room, as the Belgravia Hotel promised in advertisements. In other words, a luxury hotel could provide facilities not yet ordinarily found in middle-class homes, like a bath with running hot water.[17]

The pride the bigger hotels took in their modern facilities would have addressed middle-class concerns about sanitation and cleanliness. By this period there was increasing awareness of the connection between infectious disease and easily contaminated water sources, not to mention open sewers. Also, new importance was given to high standards of cleanliness, fresh air, sunlight and ventilation, information particularly directed at women who managed domestic matters. Typical urban fears that sanitary arrangements in developing rural areas might be less satisfactory than those in metropolitan middle-class suburbs were probably not seriously entertained in the Blue Mountains given that the district's population was small and the region had long been valued for its majestic scenery and extensive views, images not usually associated with disease.[18]

In the late nineteenth century the size of a house, the extent of its grounds and its relationship to surrounding properties could indicate a response to these new concerns: a large house in its own grounds could more easily separate the living quarters of its owners from their waste. References to spaciousness in hotel advertisements would help attract customers aware of the relationship between overcrowding and disease.

Space was identified with luxury, and the large hotels made much of this in their advertisements. In the mid-1880s advertisements for the Carrington Hotel at Katoomba went into great detail about the generous expanses available to the up to eighty guests who could be accommodated in its sixty rooms at any one time. In addition to bedrooms (a choice between a bedroom only or a suite with a private sitting room) guests also had a choice of common areas in which to socialise, sometimes according to gender as in the ladies' drawing room or the gentlemen's smoking and reading room. The Carrington's main dining room which, according to one advertisement, measured sixty by forty feet, was almost seventeen times the size of the largest room in a worker's cottage. There were as well 'large lofty corridors and large verandah' (suitable, the advertisement suggested, for promenades in wet weather) and the two acres of gardens included areas carefully laid out with English fruit trees. Located on top of a hill the Carrington could boast of its 'magnificent and extensive views', implying spaciousness there, too. The impressive size of the Carrington was well illustrated in an advertisement depicting its driveway winding through landscaped gardens to the front door of a three-storey mansion.

Views and spaciousness were hallmarks of luxury accommodation. The Hotel Wentworth (opened at Wentworth Falls in the early 1890s on a scale that did not arouse local concern) also made much of its luxury and its views, one advertisement stating that 'this large new hotel is overlooking ... these famous falls, and commands an unrivalled view of what is admitted the finest scenery on the mountains'. Recreational facilities, such as croquet lawns and tennis courts, that were customary in the grand colonial residences, were also available at some of the bigger hotels.[19]

Large hotels aimed to present comfort and service on the scale of a grand house, but also to tantalise guests by offering modern conveniences. Hotels such as the Carrington, the Belgravia and the Wentworth offered more in facilities, space and decoration than most other hotels in country Australia, and were rivalled only by luxury hotels in Sydney and Melbourne. The period of the grand metropolitan Australian hotel, as J. M. Freeland notes in his study of hotels in Australia, was beginning at the same time as the mountains' grand hotels were being built; the Federal Hotel opened in Melbourne, and the Australia,

Metropole and Sydney hotels in Sydney. These were grand because of guest facilities such as smoking, writing and sitting rooms and because of ornate decoration, grand dimensions and their height, an impressive seven stories in the case of the Federal Hotel, made possible by new engineering and construction techniques and made accessible for guests by the addition of electric lifts.[20] Although mountains' hotels could get by without lifts, great attention was paid to their decoration, to spacious entrance halls and sweeping staircases and to extensive well-maintained hotel grounds.

The grand hotels of the upper mountains did not necessarily provide the type of accommodation that all tourists might want or could afford. In the early 1880s there had been little to recommend the upper mountains in the way of smaller hotels, but in the next ten years a number of smaller hotels were built or refurbished and they provided reasonable accommodation. Hotels without extensive grounds, views, modern facilities and a variety of common areas might have sounded less enticing for stays of a week or so, but they probably offered as much as was expected of a hotel on a tourist route, and mountains' hotels generally would have paid more attention to tourists than most other hotel accommodation then available in country New South Wales, looking to provide a reasonable dining room and perhaps even a drawing room.

Luxury was not necessarily sought by tourists. Although the appointments of large hotels might fascinate guests, satisfying one's curiosity was, for some, hardly worth the fuss and expense. After all, they were expected to be out and about, viewing sights, undertaking strenuous mountain walks, and in such circumstances hotel facilities really needed to offer little more than polite service, varied menus for meal times, a good bed in a comfortable, well-ventilated room, proprietors able to arrange transport to tour the district more extensively than was possible by foot, and staff to meet trains and take departing guests to local railway stations. Although some moderate-sized hotels did offer suites these were usually for families. Some also offered facilities such as a drawing room or a billiard room, but more extravagant extras were not necessarily sought by guests, even those who would have seen themselves as cultivated ladies and gentlemen. Some even regarded 'extras' as a distraction from the main purpose of the visit and, instead, recommended certain smaller establishments for their particular hospitality and (according to one writer) in one instance, 'apple-pie order'.[21]

By the late 1880s another type of tourist accommodation had developed, offering short-term board and residence. These were the boarding houses. Until the late 1890s there were not many, the 1894 *Wise's Directory* listing only seventeen boarding house proprietors in the upper mountains (although some of these probably provided longer term board and residence for the increasing number of workers in the district). There had been boarding houses at Mount Victoria in the late 1860s and early 1870s during the period of railway construction, providing meals to labourers and some modest accommodation, but these probably had little to do with tourists.

In the late 1890s, however, the number of boarding establishments increased at such a rate that by the turn of the century *Wise's Directory* listed more than fifty boarding house proprietors. A number of the new boarding houses specialised in accommodation for tourists, usually for a period of between a week and a month. Since colonial gazetteers, such as *Wise's* did not distinguish between board for permanent residents and temporary accommodation for tourists and invalids it is impossible to be precise, but it is likely that this trend, most significantly the large increase apparent at the turn of the century, had tourism as its basis. The evidence is twofold: the number of boarding houses in the upper mountains was the largest outside Sydney, more than listed for large population centres such as Newcastle or Tamworth; and there was a large (and increasing) number of advertisements at this time in both local newspapers and tourist directories for boarding establishments offering tourist accommodation. The greater number of boarding houses in the upper mountains was not part of a colony-wide trend, but a result of particular local conditions, most notably, tourists requiring accommodation. It certainly did not reflect a significant increase in population in the upper mountains as there were just over 3000 in the 1891 census and only 500 more ten years later.[22]

Proprietors seeking the custom of tourists in advertising their establishments rarely used the term 'boarding house' (although guidebooks and some newspaper writers were less concerned about such sensibilities). Instead, advertisements emphasised that they were privately operated establishments, perhaps selective about whom they would accommodate, promising the comforts of home. They catered for guests from the middle classes who were keen to travel, yet conscious of cost and wanting respectable lodgings. The notion of 'home' was important and could help attract those who did not want to stay in cheap hotels, which, especially those with public bars, were neither select enough nor able to cater properly to the needs of tourists. Yet the larger, more luxuriously appointed hotels were less friendly, more expensive and provided a number of facilities believed to be superfluous, and attracted people not necessarily congenial to a dedicated mountain rambler. As one writer put it, at the larger hotels fellow guests were likely to be 'English and American tourists, clothed in checks of fearful and wonderful construction' as well as a smart local set, perhaps a 'Melbourne millionaire, and ... a maiden fresh from Potts Point [and] ... a Government House exquisite [with] a portly chaperone'.[23]

'Home' also implied a familiar structure: set times for breakfast, lunch and dinner, with guests congregating for meals, and after dinner settling down in the parlour or drawing room for some light entertainment, perhaps to read, play cards,

GUESTHOUSES *were the preferred accommodation for many tourists. Pictured is a 1905 advertisement for a Blue Mountains guesthouse describing features such as 'spacious verandahs'. (Photographer unknown, 'Shirley', Katoomba, c. 1900.)*

"Shirley," Katoomba.

Mrs. CLARENCE LINDEN

Offers Superior Accommodation to Visitors, with Full Comforts of a Refined Home.

The House is beautifully situated off the main road, and has an extensive view.

SPACIOUS VERANDAHS,
open and enclosed.

TENNIS COURT AND SMOKING ROOM.

TERMS : - **TWO GUINEAS** per week.

listen to other guests sing or play the piano, join in chit-chat or parlour games, or watch lantern slideshows. Just as the idea of 'home' suggested social relationships between family members, boarding establishments, also, traded on a reputation for providing a suitable environment for congenial company, with the expectation that under the guidance of the proprietor, who might, for example, provide a picnic hamper, guests would start doing things together, perhaps organising an excursion to Jenolan Caves or a trek into one of the surrounding valleys. When lone guests arrived at their chosen boarding establishment, the general expectation was that upon departure they would have made new friends.

Even as early as the 1880s there was a wide range of boarding establishments. The largest was the Manor House at Mount Victoria, formerly the grand country residence of the Fairfax family, and presented as similar in style to the Carrington. Able to accommodate seventy guests in 'large ... lofty rooms' and private suites, it was set in seven acres of well-laid out grounds with English fruit trees, a croquet lawn and tennis courts. Others were smaller, offering accommodation to a dozen or so guests at a time, although some took in only half this number. Many of these boarding establishments were probably first intended as country residences and, when up for sale, advertisements offered a number of well-sized rooms including dining and drawing rooms, a separate kitchen and laundry, and probably one or two small rooms for servants. At this time most houses in the Blue Mountains were sited on good-sized blocks, large enough to include both a garden for guests at the front of the house, and enough land behind for clothes lines and possibly a chook yard. The architectural fashions of the time meant there were front verandahs, often furnished with cane chairs and tables. Some boarding establishments, such as Balmoral House at Katoomba (from the 1880s), had two storeys, enabling the entrance hall to terminate in an ornate staircase, perhaps not as grand as those of large hotels, but nevertheless providing an architectural statement. Most such establishments did not offer the modern sanitation facilities of the large hotels, but by promising the 'comforts' of home the implication was that such arrangements would be no less than guests would hope for in their own houses.[24]

The large number of tourist boarding houses had a particular effect on local demographics—specifically in female numbers—that made it different from statewide trends. By 1901, according to the official census, the proportion of women in the region's total population had increased by about 11 per cent since 1891. This demographic change meant women now outnumbered men there by 1.3 to 1, whereas in the state population men outnumbered women by 1.1 to 1 (and in Sydney, women outnumbered men only by 1.04 to 1). There is a parallel between this and the increase in the number of upper mountains' boarding houses. This trend was most pronounced in the two largest townships, Blackheath and Katoomba, where about 58 per cent of each town's population was female, a figure that was 10 per cent more than for the rest of New South Wales.[25]

A reason for this statistically significant gender imbalance was that running a boarding house was seen as a suitable female occupation, and more women than men were likely to work in them. By 1900 almost two-thirds of boarding house proprietors in the upper mountains listed in *Wise's Directory* were women, and there was a prevalence of contemporary advertisements for tourist establishments listing a woman as their proprietor (or, more usually, 'proprietress').[26]

A boarding establishment with a woman ensuring the smooth organisation of the daily household routine could be seen even more as a large, comfortable home. Even those owned by men usually had women, either their wives, female relatives or perhaps an employed housekeeper to deal with guests, organise meals and manage the housekeeping. The increasing demand for tourist boarding establishments in the upper mountains indicated new business opportunities. Women taking them up were possibly attracted by the ability to use their homes to earn an income, particularly after the death of a male breadwinner. Menie Parkes, in financial straits since the death of her husband years before, had thought of turning Faulconbridge into a boarding establishment to keep the property within the family and enable her to maintain a certain standard of living. Nothing came of this proposal (which was only one of several she wrote about) but her correspondence on how she was to support herself indicated this option was a respectable one whereas only in the most dire financial circumstances would she become a shopkeeper. By 1901 the *Woman's Sphere* recommended running a boarding house in holiday resorts to those women struggling to make ends meet: 'a comfortable living could be made by scores of women if they would turn their attention to this great want. For half the year they could rest from their labours and live well on the profits earned during the busy months.'[27]

Boarding establishments in the upper mountains were not always successful, nor were they easy options. Indeed, the list of proprietors managing upper mountains' boarding establishments indicates that many women went out of business after a year or two. Nor was it simple to maintain a well-run house, one that guests might want to return to or might recommend to friends; high standards of cleanliness were crucial and, according to advertisements and newspaper articles, good food and company were important considerations in choosing where to stay. A proprietor would almost always need some domestic help: in the larger establishments, usually paid servants; in the smaller establishments probably relatives, women for household and cooking duties and men for general maintenance, luggage duties and running errands. An enterprising woman might open her house to tourists, but unless she was prepared to maintain the residence in tip-top condition with chores done, guests' needs met, and menus varied enough to sustain interest, as well as to be a welcoming hostess, considerate of her guests, the woman might soon decide it was all too much trouble and close down her business, or guests, hearing that standards were not as they ought to be, might seek out another house.[28]

Hotels and boarding houses, along with an increasing interest in the mountains as a tourist destination, remodelled the public faces of the townships and also the business opportunities available. Hotels, although soon outnumbered by boarding establishments, were prominent because of their position and size (even the smaller ones were larger than other buildings).

Almost always they were new structures. Some were weatherboard, but the larger ones, such as the Carrington, the Wentworth Hotel and the Belgravia were brick. Other large hotels, such as the Mount Allen at Wentworth Falls, the Hydora Hotel at Blackheath and the Imperial Hotel at Mount Victoria, were also imposing: most were two storeys (some had a third floor of attic rooms), covered an extensive area and were surrounded by grounds that were sculptured and cultivated into sweeping driveways, green lawns, and newly planted trees and shrubs.

The size of these premises and the needs and desires of guests required a diverse and reasonably large workforce able to construct buildings, maintain them and their grounds, cook, clean, wait at tables and drive conveyances to and from the railway station and around the sights. There were opportunities for long-established locals who were able to adapt to changing local circumstances. In the 1860s Harry Peckman, then a young man, had been employed by an innkeeper at Hartley (in the valley below Mount Victoria, along the Sydney–Bathurst road) as a cart driver transporting goods between Bathurst and the terminus of the railway. In the late 1870s once the railway superseded the road he earned his living driving carriages for tourists keen to view upper mountains' sights, and by the late 1880s this had developed into a full-scale business, offering transport around the mountains and even to Jenolan Caves.[29]

Opportunities for paid employment developed not only for established locals but also for new residents attracted to the district by the prospect of work. It is possible to gain an idea of the increase in opportunities in the 1890s from the business sections of *Wise's Directories*. By 1894, soon after the completion of the Wentworth Hotel at Wentworth Falls, the Belgravia at Medlow Bath and the newly renovated Hydora Hotel at Blackheath, *Wise's* listed thirty-nine Blue Mountains residents working in various building-related trades, as carpenters, builders, painters, plumbers, a mason, a timber merchant and even an architect. This was more than a 100 per cent increase on the number listed two years previously. In 1892 there had only been two gardeners listed, but by 1894 when work began on landscaping hotel gardens there were twelve, a number that remained more or less the same well into the 1900s.

Employment opportunities created by serving the needs of tourists flowed on to other sectors of the mountains' economy. The number of shops in the upper mountains increased substantially between 1892 and 1894 (the number of businesses listed as 'stores' doubling, from five in 1892 to ten in 1894), and new types of shops emerged. In 1892, *Wise's* listed twenty-seven shops in all, including bootmakers, bakers, butchers, tobacconists, grocers, cordial manufacturers and one chemist. By 1894, there were forty-four shops, with notable additions such as fruiterers, a poultry dealer, a fishmonger and a confectioner, as well as shops dealing in specialised products, such as a stationer, watchmaker and a tailor. The shops specialising in fresh produce and particular services would have hoped for the trade of hotels and boarding establishments, even if only indirectly by gaining the custom of their employees. By 1910 *Wise's* listed sixty-nine shops and local manufacturers in the upper mountains.[30]

These new businesses well and truly established Katoomba as the district's commercial centre. Whereas in 1886, soon after the Carrington Hotel at Katoomba had been extended to accommodate more guests, the number of surrounding shops was about the same as at Mount Victoria, by 1894 Katoomba was the site for more than half the total number of shops in the upper mountains. Katoomba's significant development resulted directly from being the site for the district's first large hotel and the commercial focus it created. It is also likely that the relationship between a major hotel development and local commercial activity was to some extent mutually supportive, helping produce a group of community leaders whose livelihoods to some extent depended on a flourishing tourist industry. Katoomba's Progress Committee (formed in the late 1880s) included among its founding members the proprietor of the Carrington Hotel, a land developer, the owner of Katoomba's largest general store and the proprietor of a smaller hotel. When the township was proclaimed a municipality in 1889 many of its aldermen were also members of the Progress Association with commercial interests in the district generally and Katoomba specifically. Progress Associations aimed to ensure the provision of amenities for local residents, but they also discussed and implemented policies that might increase local tourist trade, such as lobbying the colonial government to improve access to tourist attractions and discussing ways and means of advertising the district more widely.[31]

From the late 1880s onwards local commercial interests, largely concentrating their businesses in Katoomba and Blackheath, represented a significant force in the development of the upper mountains as a tourist resort. Hotels and boarding houses offering accommodation to tourists also helped establish opportunities in building, decorating, gardening, and shopkeeping, so that by the end of the nineteenth century townships had been established in a district that only a few decades before had been little more than a road to Bathurst, with world-famous views along the way. The district also continued as a location for holiday houses, and although these occasional residents may have grumbled about the increased numbers of tourists coming to enjoy the sights, their own support for walking tracks and certain cultural institutions such as a school of arts made the district more attractive, and these features were promoted by guidebooks and newspaper tourist columns to encourage visitors.

The problem, however, was that businesses whose incomes depended upon tourists either directly or indirectly (because proprietors of boarding establishments and hotels needed cash flows to buy local services and goods) had to find ways that would ensure tourists continued to seek out their services. One obvious way was to persuade tourists to stay longer. The very word 'touring' implied the tourist staying only a few days before moving on, so the desirable notion of a tourist staying, say, a month, involved an incentive to change the meaning of the term 'resort' from an activity to a destination where tourists could rest and enjoy the surroundings.

In the Blue Mountains as in other mountain resorts this was largely achieved by marketing the environment as especially healthy with particular curative characteristics, most notably in its pure air. The mountains came to be seen as restorative for those seeking peace and quiet from the daily grind, as well as those recuperating from a range of illnesses. Whereas previously, physical exertion had been seen as part of an excursion to the mountains, now the opportunities for peace, quiet and physical well-being were also being promoted.

In the 1880s and 1890s the strong belief in the effects of climate on health reinforced the idea that certain types of climate, particularly the humid air of tropical regions, were unhealthy for those of European stock. Late nineteenth-century discussion focused on the beneficial effects of a dry inland climate at altitudes higher than sea level. For the most part this belief was shaped and promoted by concern to find a cure for pulmonary tuberculosis (and to a large extent reflected changes in European and English thinking on the topic), but it also came to inform treatment for other complaints such as asthma, lumbago, skin irritations and general debility, and it was this application, particularly to something as non-specific as general debility, that was useful in broadening the appeal of suitable tourist districts. Whereas earlier in the century the Australian colonies generally were promoted as a large sanitarium, a healthy environment to live in, (and thus an appropriate place for consumptive emigrants), by the end of the century particular regions were presented as valued for their pure air and cool climate during summer months, a retreat from the hot and tiring life of the city.[32]

From the belief that Australia's inland regions, particularly its mountains and tablelands, possessed desirable climates, there followed the promotion of Australian mountains for the curative properties of their climate. Some of the earliest mentions are in guidebooks published around 1880 and although brief—rarely more than a short statement about how '[invalids were] ... seeking health' in the 'bracing nature of the [mountains'] climate'—they indicate a reason for people to spend more time in the mountains. In the case of the Blue Mountains, the first significant tourist promotions to persuade people of this were advertisements for boarding establishments, circulated by the few then operating in the late 1880s. Most proprietors advertised their establishments as a 'quiet and comfortable home' for visitors desiring a 'change of air'. Although active tourists were included in the types of people who might stay at these establishments so, too, were 'invalids', a term loosely applied to anyone who felt a little jaded or was convalescing from illness, and hoped the climate, the change in air, might have curative effects.

It is difficult to determine whether many tubercular patients, in fact, deliberately sought out the mountains in the late nineteenth century. Indeed, contemporary evidence suggested that the health-giving properties of the Blue Mountains' climate were recommended for asthma, heart disease, 'general debility, nervous afflictions [and] liver complaints' rather than pulmonary tuberculosis. James Inglis quoted what he called 'one of the leading physicians of Sydney', who argued that the best climate for 'consumptive invalids' was at Bathurst and Orange, in the western district past the Blue Mountains, and Goulburn in south-western New South Wales. By the mid-1890s, although *Wise's Directory* listed four 'surgeons' ('physician' was the usual term applied to those caring for tubercular patients) living in the district, this probably reflected an interest in medical attention being readily available for a wider range of tourists as well as an opportunistic streak in those setting themselves up as medical men. In the late 1880s, a 'Surgeon Dentist' at Blackheath advertised that he would provide accommodation for his patients so that they could 'combine their dentistry with visits to the various places of interest on the Blue Mountains'. There was also the question of infection. By the late nineteenth century pulmonary tuberculosis was widely accepted as infectious and special convalescent homes were established in restorative climates. Even if infected visitors to the Blue Mountains were there to take 'the cure', it is unlikely that those not infected, including the proprietor and staff, would wish to share the same accommodation. Nor was it likely once the infectiousness of tuberculosis was established that the proprietors of boarding establishments advertising accommodation suitable for tourists and invalids intended the term 'invalid' to include consumptive patients. (From the early twentieth century several private hospitals—also called 'sanatoria' to indicate they were places of treatment and isolated from the wider community—were established and the district did, indeed, develop a reputation as a pleasant retreat for tubercular patients.) [33]

From the late nineteenth century, the restorative qualities of the upper mountains' climate were promoted generally, and helped create a new image of tourist pursuits in the Blue Mountains, one that still favoured touring the area in search of 'magnificent scenery', 'natural wonders' and the like, but also included a search for physical well-being. Although there were still strenuous activities for tourists, such as long walks up steep paths, perhaps coming across the unexpected (the path destroyed by a landslide, or a misplaced sign leading in the wrong direction), now there was also encouragement to rest, enjoying the peace and quiet of a pleasant resort during a long stay.

By the 1890s tourist writing—guidebooks and newspaper articles—sought to explain the benefits of a district's climate, such as that of the upper mountains, to personal well-being. William Dymock, in his guidebook to Sydney and New South Wales, attempted to provide scientific evidence for the effect of cold mountain air on humans:

> Many people shudder at the idea of mountain temperature forgetting the physiological fact that animal bodies, at low temperatures, rapidly *lose* heat by the sea coast, while they *generate* it under the influence of inland or mountain air; this partly explains the rapid beneficial effect or *change* upon the human system, and why people feel vigorous under dry inland cold while they are shrivelled up under the damp cold of a littoral position.[34]

Bodies would not shrivel during a sojourn in a beneficial climate such as that of the upper mountains, and because the district was at the correct altitude for a 'good atmosphere', lungs could fill to capacity with pure air, 'the mere inhalation of which [would] ... give new zest to existence' and by enlarging their 'vital capacity', indeed exercising 'little-used organs ... the tendency to ailment [would be banished]'. Appetites, also, could expand:

> [this] delightful temperature ... produces one very marked effect on visitors. After having spent a day or two at Katoomba their appetites became wonderfully keen and, as many a mountain hotelkeeper can testify to, it takes a wonderfully large quantity of food to satisfy boarders.[35]

The promotion of a combination of touring and restorative powers, largely initiated in the 1880s by the proprietors of boarding establishments in the upper mountains, was taken up in major campaigns to persuade people to visit country Australia. In 1895 Thomas Cook & Son prefaced their first guidebook to New South Wales by proclaiming its 'great attractions as a tourist resort and sanatorium [since] [w]ithin its area almost every climate may be found, from the tropical district surrounding the Northern rivers to the cool regions in the vicinity of the Australian Alps and Kosciusko'.[36] In the early 1890s, also, the New South Wales Railways incorporated the 'change of air' theme into their advertising campaigns for tourist destinations in New South Wales and this was prominent in their promotion of the Blue Mountains. These advertising brochures presented mountains' townships as an escape from Sydney's 'sweltering day[s] in January and February' and recommended that when a 'change is needed ... the metropolitan [dweller] looks with longing to the hill-tops where he knows the sweet cool breezes blow among the forests and dells and waterfalls'.[37]

PUTTING UP THE SIGNPOSTS AND LAYING DOWN THE TRACKS

In which civic-mindedness and the pattern of development of nineteenth-century nature tourism are explored

There is only one place in the world where the red tingle *Eucalyptus jacksonii* still exists. The trees can be found in an area of about 6000 hectares between Walpole and Denmark in Western Australia's fertile south-western forests, and have become a local attraction for people wishing to see for themselves great natural forests of the karri and the tingle that are so tall as to make other eucalypts look like shrubs. It is still possible for tourists to climb a few of the karri trees to see the view from their tops, those that had originally been adapted as fire-spotting towers in the 1950s, but they must negotiate metal rungs nailed into the trunk to reach the canopy.

In regards to the red tingles a particular environmental issue arose that could have compromised tourist access to the region. Red tingles are tall trees, and can grow to a height of 75 metres because their shallow roots spread as they grow older, allowing the trees to buttress for greater stability, and to gain nourishment from the rich surface humus. But the very circumstance that helps prevent them from falling down, and that contributes to their striking appearance, also leaves them vulnerable to damage. People walking around their considerable bases to admire them were inadvertently packing the surface humus into a hard mass. The tingles were slowly starving to death.

The state authority which manages the forests wanted to encourage tourists and preserve the tingles. In 1994 in an ambitious and imaginative move it resolved to re-invent the area, to attract more tourists yet also minimise their impact, educate them in forest ecology, and broaden their visual and sensual experience by taking them where very few had ever been. Some of the first tasks in this project were literary, to conceptualise what captured the imagination. There were the trees themselves, of course, the ancient landscape and a proposed boardwalk that would eventually wend its way around the base of the tingle trunks, delicately placed to avoid the roots.

But the daring part of the project turned out to be a walk that took people up through the forest canopy. A team of architects, structural engineers and an environmental artist came up with the winning design, a 600-metre wheel-chair friendly walk along a narrow, see-through steel span bridge that was especially designed to sway as tourists followed the gentle inclination to reach a height of 40 metres above the forest floor.

The environmental artist was crucial to the design, an artistic eye to seek out perspectives that would transform the experience. Instead of simply creating a means of getting people safely to the canopy, he wanted them to feel what it was like to sway on a branch and to look from high to the ground far below. The sensation is so effective that occasionally people (some after only a few metres of the gentle ascent) scuttle back to earth, willing to forsake the experience even though they know the walkway is structurally safe. For those who persevere there are sturdy platforms at various points where people can congregate, savour a brief respite from vertigo, survey the scene and perhaps look down upon a white-tailed black cockatoo or western rosella flying from branch to branch. It is a modern phenomenon, when environmental managers, artists, writers, structural engineers and architects work together as a team to preserve the environment, initiate greater understanding of its fragility and importance, and give controlled access to unusual sights and experiences.

The Tree Top Walk was opened to the public in 1996. Yet this pattern of development, this organisation of tourist views, can be traced well back into the nineteenth century, to artists and writers bringing a trained eye to capture the essence of what they saw. Their 'eye' judged the best view; tracks were literally beaten to the chosen spots that were later marked by signposts or on local maps or were simply known to local residents prepared to act as guides. Writers had a further role to play in tourist-oriented developments, describing the terrain and tourist routes in terms of perceived requirements, whether of adventure-seekers, sightseers, the less agile, or even the 'fair sex', thus helping to organise the tourist experience and the sights they had come to view. With such increased accessibility civic sensibility demanded the sights be protected from the enthusiasm of visitors and the exploitation of developers, and be preserved for the enjoyment of current and future generations. Signposts, tracks, paths, viewpoints, painting exhibitions, published writings, creation of reserves, local knowledge were all part of the web that encircled and marked out places of wonder.

With the creation of reserves, land around natural attractions was reserved from sale for public recreation, not only for the people's enjoyment, but also as a statement of the nineteenth-century belief in the importance of the contemplation of nature as a means to intellectual and spiritual inspiration. Nature was omnipotent, full of lessons for the advancement of human kind. It followed, of course, that natural wonders with the power to inspire should be preserved, their magic protected from the commercial interests of an industrial society. In addition, people argued that, in deference to the democratic principles of colonial society in the mid-to-late nineteenth century, these natural wonders should also be made accessible to all.

The notion of reserving land for common use is ancient, and was included in the various nineteenth-century Australian lands acts to regulate the alienation of crown land. The legislated reasons to reserve crown land from sale included its use as 'commons' as well as for other utilitarian purposes—to protect water supplies, ensure wood availability, provide land for churches, contain Aborigines. This, it was believed, would help serve the public interest. But there was, too, an emerging idea that 'public interest' should not only include public utility, but also enlightenment. In New South Wales, for example, the *Crown Lands Alienation Act 1861* stated that the 'public interest' included reserving land for a 'mechanics' institute, public library, museum or other institutions for public instruction, or amusement ... or for public health, recreation, convenience or enjoyment'.[1]

The system of reserves that emerged around the world in the 1860s onwards started a revolution in thinking about how the public interest might be served in protecting natural attractions. A long way from our modern understanding of national parks and their role in the conservation of the natural environment, nonetheless, the legal mechanism used to reserve land became a rallying point on many occasions in the second half of the nineteenth century. Interested parties argued for the preservation of a particular piece of land for its natural attractions, even if at that stage they only occasionally succeeded in having the land permanently reserved as a public asset.

In the nineteenth century this revolution in thinking was not always matched by a resolution of action. Large parcels of land initially proclaimed as temporary reserves in recognition of their scenic value and potential for public enjoyment, were often whittled away—usually alienated for sale—until they consisted of just a few acres around the attraction itself, when finally it would be declared inalienable and held in trust for the people. A problem was that although the legislation prevented the sale of declared reserves, it also allowed for reserves to be made temporary, and governments could revoke temporary reserve status in order to alienate the land for sale. The original intention of 'temporary reserves' was to protect land before it had been properly surveyed. Coral Dow has equated this nineteenth-century practice with present-day 'interim development orders'.[2] It was a chance to pause for reflection and evaluate the worth of landscape as a natural attraction. But the clauses were also used to shelve the issue.

In the early 1860s there was public discussion about protecting Ferntree Gully in the Dandenongs, and in 1862 the surveyor recommended that the Victorian government reserve the gully and surrounding land for its scenic qualities. But Ferntree Gully was only declared a reserve in 1882 after many of its ferns had been uprooted for sale to suburban gardeners, and this belated declaration did not protect it from further onslaught.[3]

So, despite the means to declare permanent reserves around natural attractions, most remained temporary (if longstanding), and were sometimes made smaller under revocation clauses, or revoked altogether. The large reserve of 44 square miles (about 114 square kilometres) extending from Lawson to Mount Victoria in the Blue Mountains suffered such a fate. The reserve was declared in 1867 to protect 'natural features, such as waterfalls, fine views etc.' until a surveyor had determined which parts should be kept. In 1870 and again in 1876, much of the

SUPPORT FOR THE CREATION OF SCENIC RESERVES *was often a consequence of artistic and literary works. Paintings such as this one helped promote early public discussion about preserving the gully, although Ferntree Gully in Victoria was not finally proclaimed a reserve until 1882. (E. von Guérard,* Ferntree Gully in the Dandenong Ranges, *1857.)*

original reserve was revoked to make land available for sale, with much smaller reserves being declared around waterfalls and other scenic wonders. Also in the Blue Mountains, the cliff edges between Leura and Katoomba were not initially reserved from sale and public outcry arose in 1880: articles in newspapers argued for public ownership and a petition went off to the Legislative Assembly—in spite of the protests, an individual received a land grant that even included part of the Katoomba Waterfall. It was a pattern repeated around much of Australia.[4]

Still, a revolution in thinking it was. Whether or not governments were prepared to set aside large tracts of land noted for natural attractions as permanent reserves, they were prepared to consider seriously this course of action as a matter of public interest. Certainly, early on, colonial governments experimented with the permanent reservation of smaller tracts of land around natural attractions.

On 2 January 1862, shortly after the New South Wales *Crown Lands Alienation Act* came into effect, the government directed a survey be undertaken of the land which contained the Fish River Caves 'which it is intended to exclude from sale'. There was a long delay in conducting the survey, but the directive demonstrates that more than four years before land surrounding the caves was actually reserved, and three years before the New South Wales Wombeyan Caves and two years before Yosemite in the United States became subject to public policy, the New South Wales government was already thinking of protecting natural attractions as public assets.

Such enlightened thinking was also apparent in other colonies. In Tasmania, from 1858 legislation specifically allowed for scenic reserves to be protected for 'public purposes, including recreation and enjoyment'. It was under this legislation that Mount Wellington was reserved for the people. In Victoria, the politician Sir Henry Wrixon spoke up for such reserves to be declared permanent, arguing that 'all public reserves, parks and gardens, and every piece of land of the kind should be securely tied up in the hands of the Government for the use of the people. They belong to everybody, and they ought to be kept for everybody'.[5]

As the century advanced, the case for reserving natural attractions for use by the people, for all time, became more formalised, with local advocacy groups sending deputations to the relevant authorities, mounting petitions to their local parliamentary member, all in defence of land valued because it was beautiful, sublime or contained natural marvels. In Victoria, debate about the appropriate use of land around the Gippsland Lakes, a tourist destination for some decades, resulted in the 1881 declaration that the 'Gippsland Lakes, beds and banks' had been reserved for public purposes. In South Australia in response to public opinion, the Field Naturalists' Section of the Royal Society and the Australian Natives' Association argued for Mount Lofty to be reserved 'as a national possession for all time'. They won a temporary respite in 1883 when legislation was passed prohibiting the subdivision and sale of the area, but continued the campaign until the area was declared a national park in 1892. In Victoria, a similar story of public outcry over timber-getting and mining at Mount Buffalo led to the formation of the Bright Alpine Club, which in 1898, a decade after its formation, succeeded in having the region temporarily reserved as a future site for a national park. In the 1890s, the Western Australian government accepted public interest arguments and declared a large permanent reserve around the Yallingup Caves (although subsequently reducing the size of the reserve, giving in to local farmers who did not want such a large amount of land permanently reserved). And in the same decade, the New South Wales government finally capitulated to public outcries over its decision to allow mining in Sydney Harbour in the Cremorne area and preserved for 'the people' in the words of the parliamentary opposition, 'a magnificent heritage—a water frontage … unequalled in Port Jackson'. But the political will to ensure that large reserves and (later) national parks were kept for the public for all time was long in coming.[6]

The declaration of a reserve did not guarantee its protection from destruction. In a society where wealth was based on wool, wood and minerals, these last two commodities especially were usually the reasons for defiance of regulations intended to protect scenic reserves, particularly in locations where there were no caretakers to enforce the rules. Wilsons Promontory, the southernmost point of mainland Australia, some 200 kilometres from Melbourne, accessible only by boat until the road was completed in the 1930s, provides a good example. In the early 1880s a group of Victorians decided to argue for the protection of the area 'to preserve', in the word of one proponent, 'its rugged grandeur'. The Field Naturalists' Club of Victoria took up their cause and over the next twenty years argued for the establishment of a national park held in perpetuity. A major public campaign was conducted including Town Hall meetings and deputations with representatives from several prominent organisations such as the Royal Society and the Public Library as well as 'leading public men' to senior government officials. In 1898 they

DIFFICULT ACCESS TO NATURAL ATTRACTIONS *did not prevent tourists from seeking them out. Pictured are tourists disembarking at Wilsons Promontory in Victoria, a destination accessible only by boat until the 1930s. (F. A. Sleap,* Sketches on the Coast—Landing Passengers at Wilson's Promontory, *1884?)*

finally succeeded in having much of the area temporarily reserved as a sanctuary for native flora and fauna in preparation for its declaration as a national park. Various commercial activities such as timber-getting and mining were forbidden, yet without appropriate policing of these regulations, such commercial activities continued, as did the deputations to local members and the petitions to parliament to do something to preserve the area properly and permanently from such ravages.[7]

Despite the temporary status of some scenic reserves, the fact that they had been reserved at all set powerful precedents for preserving natural attractions for public use. The question of temporary or permanent status was not often easily resolved, but the general expectation was that in the meantime governments should provide money to maintain the reserve as the trustees they appointed saw necessary, and parliaments often voted small sums of money to maintain and develop reserves for public use. Many scenic reserves, including those in the Blue Mountains, were managed by a board of trustees, generally local property owners, some with considerable political leverage as in the case of Wentworth Falls Reserve, which in the 1880s had as one of its trustees, the New South Wales politician Henry Parkes.[8]

These days the terms 'public recreation' and 'national parks' (particularly those with wilderness areas) are sometimes seen as mutually exclusive. The public interest in preserving natural attractions is seen as best served by strict regulations about permissible activity in national parks. This development has occurred not only because of new intrusive activities, but also because of greater understanding about ecological systems: interfering with water sources around limestone caves might affect stalagmite and stalactite formation; destroying coral on a reef could devastate the rest of that reef. This ecological understanding was rarely part of nineteenth-century environmental thinking. With hindsight it is easy to condemn past practices in spite of their historical context. Yet these practices before the development of particular lines of ecological thought were based upon thinking and an outlook that are still current. Natural attractions were valued because they were natural. By being 'opened up' to the public the short-term effect may have meant sites deteriorated. But a long-term consequence was educating the public to see the natural environment as a public asset. Another consequence was continuing reappraisal about the best way to preserve natural attractions for the future, yet also promote their use in the present. This early establishment of natural environments as public assets, and of a belief in balancing preservation practice and public expectation of access, was essential to the development of a conservation-conscious tourist industry. Perhaps we can be hopeful for the survival of the red tingles.

Tracks and paths were central to the organisation of tourist views (as they still are), the physical means of entry to see sights and experience wonder. Behind their development lie many stories of civic duty and sensibility in opening up these sights to the people. Their development also encapsulated an optimistic spirit, a celebration of natural attractions for being natural, where signposts, tracks and paths encouraged Australians to go and see for themselves unusual and delightful scenery, both above and below ground.

Tracks to natural attractions had long existed and in many places were probably the same used by local Aborigines in their journeys. In the 1830s, both Charles Darwin and Louisa Meredith walked the track the Macquaries and others had used in 1815 to view the Weatherboard Falls in the Blue Mountains. By the 1840s the track to the summit of Mount Wellington in Van Diemen's Land was well used (despite the sixteen-hour round trip) and public subscriptions had funded a well-made pathway for part of the way.[9] In the 1840s and 1850s rough tracks took tourists into the valley of the Fish River Caves in New South Wales. Many of these tracks and early pathways were suitable only for small groups of tourists, and if visitor numbers were to increase, and the extent of riches revealed, these sights had to be opened up with paths, lookout platforms, direction signs, and strategically placed benches for weary walkers.

In the second half of the nineteenth century local citizens as well as governments did much to open up natural attractions. Existing tracks were upgraded, railings (often made of saplings) were installed at various viewing spots, makeshift bridges were constructed over gullies, wooden seats installed along newly signposted tracks.

Take the case of the Blue Mountains, where some local property owners led by example. By the 1860s, even though the Blue Mountains had an international reputation for sublime mountain scenery that was unique to Australia (and there were marked tracks from the main road to points of interest), there were still no paths from the ridges into the deep valleys, which were believed to be 'inaccessible' by many of those looking down. From the 1870s in response to increased interest in the region's waterfalls and the gullies, a few paths were 'hewn out of the solid rock', although the more adventurous (in at least one documented case) took a tomahawk, rope and a flask of whisky and climbed down the rock face. Many of these paths were constructed and maintained by landowners on their extensive properties. Henry Parkes was one of the first to do so, designing pathways on his property that had stone steps, bridges and seats, and took in fine views. Many owners encouraged the public to use their sight-seeing paths, which by the end of the century in the Blue Mountains altogether totalled about 45 kilometres.[10]

Resorts in other colonies, such as at Mount Lofty in South Australia and Mount Macedon in Victoria, and later Tamborine Mountain in Queensland, followed similar patterns of development. Owners of the larger estates developed extensive pathways, through gardens they had planted with exotics, and beyond into the natural surroundings, perhaps leading through a fern gully, or on to a waterfall or a fine view. Not all pathways were open to the public—David Syme, proprietor of the *Age*, had fenced off the fern gully on his Mount Macedon property against 'fern-getters'—but those that were part of a local sight-seeing infrastructure could be held up as an example for other landowners. Some of these paths were later to pass into the public domain, and Jim Smith's Blue Mountains walking track heritage study makes the point that paths in the Blue Mountains public reserves were similar in design to these earlier paths on private estates.[11]

ORGANISING ACCESS TO VIEWS BECAME A CIVIC TASK *in the second half of the nineteenth century, with local residents often working together to establish and maintain a system of paths and lookouts for the benefit of tourists. Pictured is Sir Henry Parkes on his mountains property, where he designed a series of pathways to mountain lookouts for public use. (Photographer unknown,* Sir Henry Parkes at Faulconbridge, NSW, *1880s.)*

The amounts of public money directed to reserves were hardly ever large and relied on the willingness of locals to contribute their skills to the process of opening up sights. In the second half of the nineteenth century local volunteers everywhere, despite limited resources, created a number of public pathways to natural attractions. The waters of the South Esk Cataract rushing through a deep, narrow basaltic gorge

near Launceston in Van Diemen's Land had been earlier in the century the subject of several widely exhibited paintings by John Glover, Eugen von Guérard and others, and had become an excursion for people visiting Launceston. In the second half of the nineteenth century, Launceston residents established a local association and raised money to build pathways and bridges, stairs and seats to help people see and experience the cataract from almost every angle. Tree ferns and other trees and shrubs were planted to enhance its appeal even further. From the 1860s, local residents aware of the tourist potential of South Australia's Mount Gambier lakes introduced points of access to view them from different perspectives. Punting parties took to the waters, footpaths were cut out of the steep sides to the lakes' edges, and in 1875 a road around the lakes, funded out of public revenue, was opened to tourists. The Tasmanian Tourist Association was formed in 1893 to provide assistance, including small amounts of money, to town improvement associations for publicising local assets, building public amenities such as shelters and walking tracks, and generally improving the accessibility of Tasmania's tourist spots.[12]

Sometimes governments could be persuaded to provide substantial amounts for basic tourist infrastructure, such as that voted by parliament for Jenolan Caves in the 1880s and 1890s, in part to open up regions for public recreation, but also as public investment to stimulate local commerce. In the mid-1880s the New South Wales parliament voted £2500 for the construction of a 26-mile-long (about 42 kilometres) bridle track from Katoomba to Jenolan Caves. Half of the sum was spent on the first 6.5 kilometres from Katoomba into the Megalong Valley, constructing a steep zig-zag path down the rocky ravine (and the same as that taken by the party of three ladies, four gentlemen and Punch the packhorse, as recounted in the third chapter, 'Travel as Celebration').[13] Public money was also available,

PUBLIC SUBSCRIPTIONS *often raised money to build pathways and other amenities, as was the case with the pathway at Cataract Gorge in Tasmania, pictured here. (J. W. Beattie,* Track from Crow's Nest, Cataract Gorge, Launceston, *1890s.)*

although generally only a pittance, to maintain natural attractions for public use, and in many cases committee-run trusts and associations were formed to help with decisions about opening up natural attractions to the people.

Organising tourist views had become, in the phrase of historians Jim Davidson and Peter Spearritt, a 'civic task', where committees helped provide the expertise to make realistic decisions about such things as the expenditure of public money and give advice on how to make ideas work, bring dreams alive. A combination of meagre public funding and the willingness and commitment of local volunteers—holiday-home owners, owners of local businesses and others willing to join working bees—enabled the construction of paths, shelters and other amenities, and the erection of signage directing the way to specific sights with an explanation of what might be seen. Even if the signs no longer exist many of these nineteenth-century paths are still in use in areas that are now national parks, recognised as places of great natural environmental significance. Yet all of this might have turned out so differently but for this early expression of civic pride in the natural environment (as piecemeal as it sometimes was), this busyness and willingness to create the means to enable others to seek out and experience nature's offerings from the best vantage points.

Development of tourist paths in the second half of the nineteenth century also took advantage of what was already there. The bridle path from Katoomba to Jenolan Caves took in parts of the Mount Victoria to Jenolan road. In many areas industries such as logging and mining led the way for tourist developments. Roads, tracks and tramways opened up difficult terrain, and many continued to be used by tourists long after industry had moved on. In Victoria's gold rushes in the 1850s new tracks and trails were marked out from Melbourne to the goldfields. What became known as the Yarra Track passed through the forests in the region of today's Healesville and Marysville, allowing travellers access to tree-fern gullies and waterfalls including the Steavenson Falls and Fernshaw. Timber-splitter tracks in the Dandenongs were used by tourists in the 1860s and later, as access was extended, to view giant eucalypts and tree ferns. When the timber tramways were constructed, tourists used these too.[14]

Towards the end of the century in the Blue Mountains there were coal-mining enterprises in the Jamison and Megalong valleys below the cliffs of today's Leura and Katoomba, although most were short-lived (in one case, a mine closed after a year, and most lasted only a few years). The service tracks along the cliff tops and down into the valley provided access to a whole range of sights not previously available to tourists. The mines themselves were rarely mentioned in tourist literature, although at least one writer saw tourist potential: 'a visit to a coalmine would at first sight appear somewhat prosaic, but that at Katoomba is unlike any other of its class in Australia, by reason of its unique position and surroundings'. Ferns and majestic cliffs made the trip worthwhile.[15]

Although tracks up mountainsides, along the tops of cliffs, into valleys, beside waterfalls or underground into caves increased opportunities for tourism, they also exposed tourists to difficulties and sometimes even danger. If people wanted to reach the bottom of waterfalls they had to descend steep tracks that were often slippery with mud, and they had to walk up again. Nor did improvements, such as attaching long, wooden ladders, almost entirely made out of rough bush timber, sometimes springy saplings, over sheer rock face and widening tracks overcome the difficulties noted in the tourist writing of the 1880s. The tourist development of limestone caves in the 1880s and 1890s provides a vivid example.

Up until then, tourist experience of caves had often involved hours underground—at Jenolan Caves, an eight-hour tour was not unusual—though only one or two large chambers were explored. Much of the time was spent getting in and out of steep, narrow entrances, and exploring the smaller highly decorated chambers off the larger ones. In the accounts of these excursions little was made of physical exertion or the need for stamina. But once cave guides started to take

NEW VISTAS *could be attained using conveyances designed for industrial use.*
Pictured opposite is the Main Incline of the 1880s Coal and Shale Tramway
(now the Scenic Railway) into the Jamison Valley in the Blue Mountains.
The tramway at Geeveston in Tasmania, above, also enabled tourists to explore
the region's tall trees and tree-fern groves. (Opposite: John Paine, Shale Mining,
Scenic Railway, Blue Mountains, NSW, *c. 1890. Above: J. W. Beattie,* Tramway
at Geeveston, *1890s.)*

tourist parties further into caves, made possible through systematic surveys of the
tunnels, travel accounts began to make much of the cave tour itself, eagerly
describing difficulties that would be encountered.

Travel accounts describing Jenolan Cave tours warned: one 'false step would involve a broken leg' or would result in 'scattered fragments' of limestone. Advice was given to prevent bodily harm: for instance, wearing clothes well padded at the knees and elbows 'and an old pair of sand shoes as these grip the floor and save many a one from backsliding'. Once the tour began the first expression of concern was usually at the entrance to the cave, which was mostly narrow and sometimes vertical before reaching a landing. One commentator described how he and other members of his party were 'crawling, crouching, slipping, sliding, squeezing' in order to drag their 'bodies through the awful passage'. The entrance to another cave was described as 'no joke for even a thin man … [being] a narrow, rocky, tortuous entrance'. Some commentators made cave inspections sound like a trapeze act; entering one cave involved sliding down a 'steep funnel-shaped place for about 50 feet', then down an iron ladder for about thirty-five feet (10.5 metres) before being lowered by 'aid of a strong rope' to the 'finest waterhole'.

Once inside the cave it was necessary to climb over rocks on all fours, or to lie full length in order to engage in 'rolling over and over' while being directed by the guide, 'Now! get your back against the rock. Put your foot on this point'. Rarely was the mode of progress upright except when descending a 'well-like opening on a rope ladder some 40 feet long' or when negotiating long wire-ladders 'which vibrated most alarmingly'. One commentator used the terms 'serpent man', 'corkscrew' and the 'many-footed caterpillar' to describe the contortions necessary. Descriptions of 'climbing and squeezing, stumbling and jumping, now up, now down, now in, now out, under and over' peppered accounts of people's trips to the caves throughout this period.[16]

Improvements that actually made new access routes safer and easier to nego-tiate—stone stairways, iron bridges—were to come later. In the Blue Mountains, for instance, the construction of a sturdy path down the cliffs at Govett's Leap in 1899, an ambitious, but successful project since the cliff was sheer, inspired plans for others, some of which were completed while some were left to languish. The series of wooden steps and ladders descending to the valley below

Katoomba Falls was not replaced by a 'magnificent stone stairway', Furber's Stairs, until 1909.[17]

Long before stone stairways and iron bridges, tracks and paths were being beaten to new and daring depths and heights, to increase the opportunities for people to feast upon nature's delights. Often this persistence to mark out paths to the best vantage points exposed visitors to a heightened sense of adventure and the peril of, say, standing on a cliff's edge to admire a view.

The first materials used as protective railings were usually saplings tied together firmly and attached to large trees and were really only useful as a warning of nearby precipices, not as a barrier on which to lean and look below. There were iron railings at a couple of cliff-top lookouts, for example at Govett's Leap, but the expense of more solid materials and the number of lookouts necessitated saplings as a cheap and easily erected alternative.[18] Iron railings were usually commented upon in tourist literature because their existence implied security as did the existence of ladders—sometimes referred to as 'rustic stairs'—down sheer rock face. If writers briefly mentioned 'precipitous descents' it was to emphasise that ladders (flimsy-looking to our modern concern with public liability) had made them accessible.[19]

Tracks were also subject to natural deterioration, and although the trustees attempted proper maintenance of them, the task was large. In mountain areas, landslides were of particular concern, not only because of possible physical injury, but also because they could, overnight, obliterate a track. Lucy Broad described how in 1904 she and her lady companion were forced to spend a night on the track in the valley below Katoomba because of damage done by a landslip.[20]

Trustees of the Blue Mountains reserves had used the money granted by parliament to provide tracks to more vantage points, but improvements in the nineteenth century were rarely enough to remove many of the accustomed difficulties, although some, such as wooden log seats and the fountains constructed out of stone for drinking water would have alleviated specific discomforts. Other facilities, such as fireplaces and firewood, were provided not only so that tourists could enjoy, say, tea boiled in a billy in an area designated for such purposes, but also to protect the

VIEWING PLATFORMS WERE OPENED UP QUICKLY AND CHEAPLY *with railings made from saplings and other easy-to-hand material. Pictured is one for the Three Sisters in the Blue Mountains erected in the late 1890s. (Ernest Brougham Docker,* The Three Sisters, Katoomba, Blue Mountains, NSW, *1898.)*

surroundings from the burnt patches left after campfires and to prevent native flora from being used as firewood. In some reserves the trustees had signs installed at the beginning of the tracks, though usually they were more descriptions of what might be seen than descriptions of where to go.[21] Such installations probably meant most visitors (except those who went caving) no longer took a guide—certainly, newspaper articles had stopped advising the need for one—there was, however, concern at the reliability of the signs and particularly of their vulnerability, either to pranksters who might change their direction for a lark or to the strong winds that might dislodge them and the heavy rain and bright sunlight that might fade painted words.

Tracks closer to the towns were often presented as safe, even enticing to the less adventurous, with homely images—a place to have a cup of tea, perhaps—and the trustees were often praised for their thoughtful provisions for tourist comfort. Much was made of what were called 'rustic seats', mostly modest benches made of roughly hewn logs, and readers of the tourist material were assured that the 'tiny, natural fountains [of] pure mountain spring water' ('deliciously cold' some noted) found in carved-out rock basins, were protected by iron bars from the 'refuse' of 'rodents'. A special comfort was that walkers need not cup their hands to drink the water since 'glazed mugs' were attached to the rock by an attractive metal chain, and were small enough to pass through the bars (although it was not explained why small rodents could not also pass through).

Amid all this activity of opening up natural attractions for the public's appreciation there were also the travel writers, the producers of reams of published material about Australia's natural attractions, who helped to shape colonial perceptions about the natural environment, extolling its virtues, critiquing its worth as scenery. How they did this will form the basis of the following

chapters. For now, we will focus on a literary device used as a means to organise tourist sights. The literary device was the use of gender and represented a heightened consciousness of tourist activities appropriate for ladies and gentlemen.

This was a new development in tourist literature, a consequence of the conventions regarding feminine and masculine behaviour that came to dominate much writing in the late Victorian era. With cautions such as ladies should avoid certain caves, we can see the stark contrast with today's representations of tourist developments to introduce visitors to nature. Imagine reading a sign at the Valley of the Giants warning women against undertaking the Tree Top Walk, or alternatively, advising men that they are likely to suffer vertigo.

Travel accounts about Jenolan Caves clearly show the emergence of this literary device. In the period before the early 1880s the women who had toured the caves had done so without much published concern about their abilities. Their presence was noted, and although there is little evidence about how they (or, for that matter, the gentlemen) actually negotiated difficult cave passages, there was no expression that this was an inappropriate activity for women.[22] Neither before the late Victorian period did unpublished sources express the attitude that caving was unfeminine, not even by someone as sensitive to ladylike behaviour as Rachel Henning, who mentioned in a letter that people in Bathurst had been:

> going to see some wonderful caves ... said to be most magnificent, running for an immense way under the mountain, and some of them are so large that there is no roof to be seen ... Several parties have been formed to go and visit them, and the week before last Mrs Machattie, the doctor's wife here, got up a party of twenty-seven, chiefly young ladies, to go and see

ACCESS TO HARD-TO-REACH PLACES *such as scenic valley floors came with ladders and stairways. Pictured opposite is a wooden stairway and bridge replacing the earlier ladder (far right of top picture), and a seat, somewhat the worse for wear, with a view of Linda Falls, Leura, in the Blue Mountains. (Above: G. A. Druce,* Track to Linda Falls, *1900s. Below: G. A. Druce,* At Linda Falls, *1900s.)*

them. They all rode, as there is no road for any vehicle, and took three packhorses with provisions, and each carried a blanket for a bed. The journey took two days each way, and when they got there they camped in the outermost cave, where a tent was pitched for the ladies and the gentlemen slept round the fire. They were out exactly a week and enjoyed themselves exceedingly.[23]

Although there are implications about acceptable types of behaviour for lady tourists—the long horseback ride was justified because there were no carriage roads and certain proprieties were observed at the campsite—she did not refer to the cave inspections themselves as either a masculine or feminine activity.

From the 1880s, however, certain images of femininity, especially to do with frailty and other physical characteristics on a cave tour, were invoked in published descriptions written by men. Serious caving was now presumed to be a male pursuit. Authors of articles were keen to advise where a woman could or should not go: an article published in 1881 advised 'ladies' not to venture into the Elder Cave as 'it is very difficult nearly all through', whereas the Imperial Cave had 'the easiest of access' for inspection by 'ladies'. Another author advised 'lady tourists to forego' the Arch Cave because its 'traversing … may be considered the most tedious and fatiguing—the mode of progress being seldom upright'. Yet, both these caves had featured for at least thirty years on earlier tours undertaken by women and men. The idea of women descending narrow rope ladders also concerned some later male writers, who recommended only caves with passages enlarged, bridges and steps built and handrails installed, since these could be inspected 'with comparative ease', and concentrating on them would solve the possibility of a woman's physical frailty holding up cave parties (and inconveniencing the men) in the more difficult sections. Women who persevered in touring caves considered by at least one author 'difficult enough for men' were described as 'strong-minded', 'deterred by nothing' or having 'sufficient strength of nerve'—such phrases were not used about men who traversed the same areas. Women who were determined to visit caves considered difficult were advised by at least one guidebook to 'adopt the "bloomer" or semi-knickerbocker costume' to ensure ease of movement.[24] (Such practical advice also might have been a reference to women's emancipation since bloomers had become a feminist symbol of independence.[25]) Caves that 'no lady [could] ever hope to see' (not even if she wore bloomers) required such 'courage' that only a few men would ever succeed in touring them.[26] It was even suggested that cave touring could be severely detrimental to women's mental health. A copy of a late nine-teenth-century guidebook to Jenolan Caves (held in the Mitchell Library collection in Sydney) has a hand-written annotation (possibly emanating from a caves guide) giving international backing to this rumour:

> It is … stated that in 1840 a lady from Boston swooned from fatigue while making the underground tour [in the Mammoth Cave, Kentucky, USA] … The remainder of the party went on without missing her. On their return after an absence of only 2 hours the poor woman had become insane and was observed sitting on a stone chattering to herself. She never recovered her reason and died 2 years afterwards in the Massachusetts asylum for the insane, a raving maniac.[27]

Raising questions of women's physical and mental ability helped present cave tour-ing as a masculine activity, but it did not follow that all men were able to undertake tours. Anyone of a nervous temperament was advised not to enter more difficult caves, those which had narrow wire-rope ladders and passages just big enough for one person, and those of stouter build were advised to forego narrow passages.

In theory men's character might be able to sustain much that was dangerous, but in the face of extreme danger and difficulty it was understood that the physique of many might be inadequate, and it was this possibility that presented the more inhos-pitable caves as accessible to only a few. By the late 1880s some writers had raised to heroic heights the guides who conducted the tours. For example, one equated the exploring skills of Jeremiah Wilson, the keeper of the caves, with those of Christopher Columbus and Captain Cook. He and other guides were praised for their 'physical strength' and 'strong [enough] nerve to worm along narrow passages, without any certainty of being able to reach a turning place, and with the risk of being so wedged in as to make retreat impossible'.[28] In 1891 admiration was well illustrated in a series of photographs taken by Kerry and Co., the Sydney-based photographic studio, showing guides dangling from ropes, crawling up walls of sheer rock and standing on one another's shoulders as they went about their tasks.[29] Although such manoeuvres had been required on occasion during earlier cave tours, and were probably undertaken by both men and women, now they were presented as extraordinarily daring, requiring 'physical strength' and 'strong nerves', that is, masculine stamina.

At the same time as some caves were being presented as physically and mentally demanding, others with passages newly widened and handrails installed, were being portrayed as safe. Jenolan Caves could offer something for everyone. Yet, even the new images of caving relied on what were now preconceptions based on gender. A cave's difficulty could be measured by its physical and mental demands. Caves with the greatest demands were the preserve of men—of cave guides and 'daring enthusiasts'. Indeed, noting in tourist literature the presence of women in a cave, even one accepted as demanding, usually indicated that the cave was safe for most agile people, provided they followed instructions and took due care. From the late 1880s writers of most substantial guidebooks to the caves put this view: Samuel Cook argued that the 'journey [in one of the more difficult caves opened to the public] is not perilous to persons who possess a fair share of agility and nerve ... It is frequently performed by ladies, of whom the guide is specially careful'. J. J. Foster explained that, in caves opened to the public where there were no 'artificial paths, steps ... or railings', as long as visitors followed the guide's instructions there was little chance of a 'serious mishap .... [and] no-one, lady or gentleman, need be afraid'.[30]

Interestingly, this literary technique did not extend to women's published accounts of their cave tours. Throughout this period as notions of caving difficulties extended and the idea of caving as a masculine rather than also a feminine activity was being established, women were still touring the caves, even some sections considered arduous. In their accounts women did not mention fear, physical inadequacy, or the need for strong nerves. They did note difficulties involved, but they did this because cave touring was presumed to be difficult and adventurous, not because they saw it as an unsuitable activity. In an article, 'A Lady's Visit', the anonymous author provided much detail about one cave tour describing the rough and tortuous descent to one cavern and to another, stooping and crawling through a passage not one metre high and at its end, descending a wire-rope ladder. In another account Mrs M. I. Stevenson, then in her sixties and mother of Robert Louis Stevenson, explained that it 'was really hard work going through the cave'. The steps were steep, there was much stooping, crawling on hands and knees and tearing of petticoats caught on sharp rocks. The American journalist and social reformer Jessie Ackermann also remembered cave touring in the late nineteenth century as 'hard work': 'this wriggling along narrow passages and crawling snake-fashion through others, emerging with blistered hands, red face, and disordered locks'. In another account an anonymous woman writer described how their guide took them to a 'less beaten track' to see a cave only recently discovered, warning them of possible disaster to clothing in that they 'could scarcely expect to carry out a button'. At one point they were told to slide down the side of a large rock and then climb up another. She wrote: 'We undertake it as directed, sit down and let ourselves go; but oh! the shaking and laughing en route, and the … inartistic ascent. Our candles are out, but clutched vigorously … for foothold there is none.' Despite the 'hard work', cave touring was fun.[31]

For all the warnings to lady tourists, and the representation of prowess among a 'very few gentlemen', there were also times when the literary device was not explicitly used in travel and tourist literature. The late Victorian obsession with feminine and masculine conventions meant readers would likely have interpreted its absence as a statement in itself: access to the described tourist attraction was suitable for women. Travel accounts about the Blue Mountains, for instance, did not present access to natural attractions in terms of feminine ability.

Of developed Blue Mountains resorts very little was ever written about paths particularly suitable for women. In the early 1880s one writer who descended a new track from Katoomba into a valley and up again, exhausted, stated that 'a track by which ladies could descend into the valley could be made'; the existing track was thus rated difficult, and its use a masculine activity.[32] But, statements indicating feminine frailty were not usual in Blue Mountains tourist publications, not even a decade later when much was made generally of the easy access provided by newly developed tracks and specific reference to their suitability for women might have been expected.[33]

Some articles by the 1890s were indicating that a walk down the cliffs had become a family activity, although differences were noted in the ways each sex descended the ladders—men faced the ladder, whereas 'ladies found it necessary to face about [in the direction of the valley] so as better to secure their footing' without being caught on their long skirts. The presence of women was not remarked upon as either a sign of their courage or determination or as a statement of a tourist attraction's stage of development, that is, the idea that if ladies could do it then it must not be too risky. There are also hundreds of photographs of men and women climbing up 'rustic stairs' and walking along tracks with, on the valley side, a sheer drop down the cliff face, without protection from railings, not even slender saplings. Such an image today we might interpret as intending to indicate these women were defying convention, but at the turn of the twentieth century, it seems this was not the case. Contemporary texts indicate that this type of mountain walking (unlike cave touring) was sufficiently undemanding as not to be a gender-specific activity, and so the idea that even women could undertake these walks would not necessarily have had the same effect on a readership as writing 'even women' could tour certain caves. This type of mountain walking as an activity presumed an equality between the sexes that was even accepted by writers of tourist articles.

MANNERS IN THE COLONIAL PERIOD *governed tourist behaviour and permeated contemporary travel writing. This engraving published in the* Illustrated Australian News *tells an ironic story of a party of ladies and gentlemen ascending Mount Wellington in Tasmania: the gentlemen attend the needs of the ladies, and the ladies, not the men, reach the summit unscathed. (H. N. Robertson,* A Holiday Ramble in Tasmania—Ascending Mount Wellington, *1885?)*

A HOLIDAY RAMBLE IN TASMANIA—ASCENDING MOUNT WELLINGTON.

TOURIST DRESS *in the nineteenth century, although formal to modern eyes, allowed some relaxation of dress codes such as rolled up shirt sleeves for men, and sturdy hiking boots and corset-free dressing for women. Pictured is a party on a two-day hike from Jenolan Caves to Katoomba in 1886. (Photographer unknown,* Looking for the Blazed Trees, *1886.)*

On the whole women's accounts of their walks suggested they were strenuous but included such beautiful scenery as to be worth it. One of the few women, and that anonymously, to publish a newspaper account describes several walks into the valleys with a party of ladies and gentlemen. Although mostly describing the scenery and the comforts provided along the way (images typically presented in such articles), she also mentioned a climb down 'very steep ladders' and how, when others preferred a rest and a cup of tea, a few continued until she, also, 'must admit to myself that I am tired'.[34] A woman on her round-the-world trip to New Zealand, Australia and the Far East in the 1900s described how she and her 'lady companion' (an indication that women walked these tracks without a male escort) 'went down and down, always anxious to get to the next corner, heedless … that every step would have to be retraced in an upward trend beneath the blazing sun', but were prepared to continue because the scenery was so beautiful.[35]

Ironically, because of the fashion in women's clothes in the late nineteenth century walking up steep mountain tracks was probably less easy for women than touring difficult caves at Jenolan. At the caves the well-established practice was to wear old, loose-fitting clothes provided by the guides, that enabled women to breathe more easily, have greater movement and undertake more physical exertion than the tight-fitting corsets and clothes of contemporary fashion. Certainly, there was discussion about how women should dress for mountain walks. One commentator noted that women's fashion constricted breathing in activities such as mountain walking where 'strong lungs and hearts' were needed, that tight clothing around the torso was unsuitable for an activity, like walking, which required long, deep breaths especially when proceeding uphill, and that women in such clothing were often exhausted by the struggle just to breathe. Men, also, would suffer, she said, if they wore constrictive clothing, and recommended that the 'masculine tourist' should wear loose clothing made of strong material, for instance, a flannel shirt or a blouse belted at the waist and a sacque, a loose coat suitable for activities requiring freedom of movement. Women's dress, she advised, should also be practical, including a wider than normal skirt just reaching the tops of shoes to allow 'perfectly free movements', and made from a strong dark-coloured material, but without 'the usual muslin lining' (probably because it was too flimsy not to be easily torn on sharp rocks). She recommended a broad belt as usually sufficient to satisfy the feminine fashion for slim waists, but if 'the figure is not slender enough to make this becoming' then a corset could be worn if left untied.[36] Thus dressed, in clothing that later would seem both impractical and dangerous, ladies and gentlemen were ready for strenuous mountain walks.

WRITING IT
ALL UP

*In which a brief history of nineteenth-century
travel writing is presented*

REVIEW

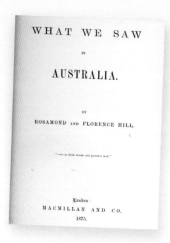

WHAT WE SAW IN AUSTRALIA.

By Rosamond and Florence Hill. London: MacMillan and Co. 1875.

THE RAILWAY GUIDE OF NEW SOUTH WALES (FOR THE USE OF
TOURISTS, EXCURSIONISTS, AND OTHERS).

Sydney: Thomas Richards Government Printer. 1879.

Yet another travel tale came across our desk, authored not by one but two English lady travellers.* As we pondered the possible delights from the feminine pens of these astute observers, a second book skidded across the same desk, this one a slim volume aimed at excursionists in search of the picturesque. On the one hand, the memory of past travels, on the other, the promise of future travels. Let us turn first to *What We Saw in Australia*.[1]

The literature of tours now-a-days, as every reviewer knows to his cost, is voluminous and exhaustive. The fiords of Norway, the steppes of Tartary, the ruined cities of South America, the prairies of the North, have, each and all, at one time or another, been grist to the mill of ambitious young undergraduates with money and geographical theories.[2]

Ambitious young undergraduates these ladies most certainly are not, nor are they filled with spinsterly small talk.[3] Miss Florence Davenport Hill is known to us as the author of an interesting treatise on pauper reform in England, *Children of the State: The Training of Juvenile Paupers* (London, 1868). Both sisters are energetic in English social reform, and here they turn their well-trained eyes towards our own colonies. The result is an admirable compendium of interesting information on our manners, charitable institutions, colonial gaols, reformatories, mission stations, and mode of government *inter alia*.

We learn about the benevolent work of the Governesses Institute and Melbourne Home for Servants, which provides board at nominal charges and helps to find suitable employment for governesses, sempstresses and domestic servants in straitened circumstances. This institution is managed by a committee of ladies who make the majority of decisions, rarely seeking assistance from the gentlemen's committee.

On our art and literary institutions there are intelligent and interesting observations. We learn that Australian scenery is best represented in Melbourne's Public

---

* This section of the chapter is a fictionalised review drawn upon reading many late nineteenth-century reviews of travel books and tourist guidebooks. The reviewed books are real. For further details see note 1.

Library, Museum and Art Gallery by the artists Nicholas Chevalier and Louis Buvelot; that the art critic Mr Ruskin chooses paintings in Europe for purchase by the Gallery, and that the Public Library has more than 600 visitors a day.

The sisters provide one of the more sensible accounts of our Houses of Parliament that we have yet had the pleasure of reading. Along with personal observations of the curious spectacle parliament is, there are also facts and figures about franchise and parliamentary membership. The manners and customs of our colonial ladies are also scrutinised. There is an account of the emerging colonial sericulture export industry, for which companies, often managed entirely by ladies, produce healthy silkworm eggs for export to Europe.

The travels of the Misses Hills also took them to picturesque places, and although their experiences were neither wide nor novel they do provide their readers with satisfying accounts. Our favourite is the description of Govett's Leap in the Blue Mountains, which is a remarkable valley, 'one of the lions of New South Wales'.[4]

Now let us turn to the *New South Wales Railway Guide*. For a guidebook there is nothing to desire but that the book should successfully contain the kind of information which it professes to supply in a pleasant, well-arranged and readable shape.[5]

The aim of this guidebook, we are told, is to provide an illustrated itinerary for the traveller in search of the picturesque that is within easy reach of the railway line. The volume is well arranged: sections on the history and development of railways in New South Wales, suggested itineraries and descriptions of scenery, remarks on the flora of the Blue Mountains and the geology of the Fish River Caves and a number of lithographs giving some idea of the sights. There is also a map showing the Great Western Railway crossing the Blue Mountains from the Nepean River to Bowenfels, and a geological survey map of the Fish River Caves. We would have preferred the inclusion of an excursionist's pocket map showing railway routes and destinations, but the guidebook although not small enough for a pocket is at least of a size and weight that could be carried under one's arm or in a knapsack.

Our railways now extend in a radius of more than 100 miles in all directions from Sydney: to Goulburn in the south-west, to Bathurst in the west, to the Hawkesbury in the north-west and to Tamworth in the north, and this guidebook tells us there are 24 picturesque places along the way to stop at and savour. We decided to rail-test the volume with an excursion to the Blue Mountains. We are happy to inform our readers that it passed our tests, and is an excellent addition to the growing number of excursionist guidebooks.

As instructed we dropped a line to the keepers of the accommodation houses to arrange bed and entertainment, and arrived at the Sydney terminus a full 15 minutes before departure time to ensure our baggage was suitably stowed and to inform the guard that we wished to be set down at Weatherboard (having decided to take advantage of the opportunity to see the far-famed nearby falls).

The morning train had been recommended for its views both of the scenery and the zig-zags from Emu Plains to the mountain summit. The scenery we admired, the zig-zags we experienced—the train shunting laboriously backwards and forwards for miles to a plateau and then a clear run over the remaining 20 or so miles to Wentworth Falls, which our guidebook tells us is the new name for Weatherboard. The volume also identifies interesting buildings along the way, and the stately mountains' residences of some of our distinguished citizens such as Sir Henry Parkes, Sir Alfred Stephen and Sir James Martin.

The inn keeper, Mr Charles Abraham Wilson, apparently had not received our note, but was able to accommodate us and organise a local guide for a walk to the Weatherboard Gorge and, the next day, as the book recommended, to a pretty waterfall called Water Nymph's Dell, this last request delighting Mr Wilson who explained few visitors had ever heard of it. We collected fern fronds with the specific intention of seeing if we could identify them using Miss Harriet Scott's excellent illustrations of 36 different types of mountain ferns in the guidebook's appendix. Not being of botanical inclination, and being uncertain whether what we had collected were actually ferns, we gave up on the experiment and will leave this task to our more expert readers.

After our stay at Wentworth Falls we continued on the 'up train' from Sydney, this time requesting the guard to set us down at Blackheath, a larger village insofar as it has the odd substantial building or two. Leaving our luggage at our accommodation we walked about one and a half miles through pleasant scenery to Govett's Leap, where we conducted another experiment, comparing the descriptions in the two books of what the guidebook says is 'one of the greatest natural wonders of the world'. We can only say that the Misses Hill's description not only does justice to the scene but is superior to the descriptions by Messrs Burton and Du Faur that the guidebook quotes at tedious length. For the pleasure of our readers we append the ladies' description:—

We followed for a considerable distance the high road to Bathurst cut through the bush. The mass of gum-trees on either side looked beautiful in their fresh summer foliage. The young shoots are crimson, and when seen against the blue sky, the sunshine gleaming through them, the tree seems covered with gorgeous blossom. Leaving the road we turned into the scrub, and drove over a sandy soil among small gum-trees and mallee scrub. When at length we quitted the carriage and had followed our guide for a short distance, we suddenly came upon what appeared to be an enormous rift in the ground, which yawned beneath our feet. Far below was an undulating mass of foliage—the tops of a forest of gum-trees, which covered the whole bed of the valley. Vast was the height from which we looked down, so that the trees had the appearance of perfect stillness, forming in the glorious sunshine a lovely crimson-tinted carpet, the shadows cast upon them by the clouds giving continual variety to the colouring. At the upper end of the valley towards the west, the cliffs on either side were somewhat depressed. Here a streamlet fell over the rocks, a sheer descent of 1200 feet, but so gentle its fall appeared, as we watched it obliquely across the valley, that the water looked like marabout-feathers softly floating downwards. Towards the bottom it vanished from our sight among large stones, and if in that dry season the stream made further progress its course was hidden by the forest at its feet. Turning towards the south, the brown, grey, and yellow rocks, rose perpendicularly, the sunshine softening them into a delicious harmony of colour; and so great was the width of the valley, that a waterfall on the opposite cliff looked from where we stood like a silver thread against its side. Beyond, the valley bore away in a southerly direction until it was closed in by ranges of overlapping hills of lovely blue—indigo or cobalt; as the blaze of the sun or the shadow of the clouds fell upon them. But for the faint murmur caused either by the falling of the water or the wind among trees the place was silent, and it was almost devoid of animal life. A bird or two overhead, and the noiseless

THE BLUE MOUNTAINS ZIG-ZAG RAILWAY *was a mid-nineteenth century innovation to convey trains over steep inclines. In 1892 the Lapstone zig-zag was superseded by rail tunnels, which considerably reduced travel times. The Lithgow Valley zig-zag, pictured, remained in use until 1910. (Robert Bruce,* The Zig Zag, Great Western Railway, from the Lithgow Valley, at the Foot of the Blue Mountains, NSW, *1869?)*

lizards who ran over our dresses as we attempted to sketch the scene, represented the whole animal life within sight or hearing.

A long with pictorial art, travel writing has been one of the most significant ways of creating a European notion of Australia, particularly in the late eighteenth and nineteenth centuries. Explorers, residents, travellers, tourists, botanists and artists have often used the genre for observations of social and cultural aspects of Australia and its natural history as well as the political and economic dimensions of an antipodean society. Although much of this writing was initially intended for audiences outside Australia, where publishers might expect to sell a larger number of copies, it was from early on an important basis for colonial self-definition.

Implicit in much early travel writing was 'wonder', especially associated with observing what to European explorers and travellers were unusual phenomena, and this prepared the ground for an increasing Australian interest, even pride, in local surroundings. Travel writing described those natural wonders as attractions where travellers might savour their surroundings, appreciate landscape, and learn about science, nature and the manners and customs of the local residents. In this sense travel writing was guide, teacher and image-maker.

Travel accounts published in Australia increasingly urged residents to undertake tours so that they might see for themselves natural and social phenomena, the geological curiosities of underground caves, the magnificence of tree ferns, the bountiful colours of delicate wildflowers, prominent public institutions in major towns and cities, poor areas, rich areas, Aboriginal communities, town life, country life. In these accounts Australia was a place where nature, the picturesque and the sublime might be studied as might the workings of a modern society, its democratic principles, the outcomes of public welfare, its cultural interests and commercial enterprises—a splendid and interesting destination.

The most useful type of writing for prospective tourists was a one-volume handbook that usually included statements from well-known travellers and from geologists, botanists or others explaining the significance of particular sights and practical information on transport (for instance, would a horse and carriage be available) and points of access (were the tracks well marked), and types of accommodation available. Many also had a map marking routes and features along the way.

In Australia some of the earliest relevant publications for tourists were the colonial directories and almanacs. While these early directories, published from the 1820s, included much information not relevant to tourists (such as the names of senior civil servants and importers of fine wines), they did provide useful details about businesses and such. A person setting out in the 1830s from Windsor to Sydney could consult *The New South Wales Calendar and General Post Office Directory 1832* for the time and point of departure of a coach, the cost of the fare and the name of the coach proprietor, as well as choose a place of accommodation from a list of 'family hotels' and use the reproduction of Major Mitchell's drawn-to-scale map to wander the streets of Sydney Town. A tourist planning a journey up the coast could consult the list of vessels employed in local trade and their usual destinations. If the tourist intended to travel within the colony, then the section on 'Itinerary of Roads throughout New South Wales' would assist in establishing what could be expected along the way and what interesting or unusual sights should be looked for: 'a very good mountain inn' at the Weatherboard Hut was noted on the Great Western Road at what is now Wentworth Falls, where, 'a short distance to the southward … the wild scenery of the inaccessible valley … is well worth the traveller's attention'; and, east of the Great North Road towards Brisbane Water (near today's Gosford) was observed to be 'a very interesting portion of the country'.[6] Directories from other parts of the colonies provided similar type of information. Most of these directories came out annually or every two years and regularly updated their information. These directories were not published as tourist guides, but their presence indicates that early on there were attempts to compile, organise and publish helpful details of colonial life. The subsequent tourist guide-books, then, were part of an already existing colonial practice of cataloguing information for those looking for it.[7]

The beginnings of the 'tourist guidebook' (published in English) as we know it today appeared in the British Isles from about the 1820s.[8] Travel reference guides had previously been published in a series of several heavy volumes that were not very practical to take out and about, but this new style of travel book combined into one volume travel advice, authoritative notes on significant sights (and sites) and on a destination's history (often also its botany and geology, and other features con-sidered noteworthy), all presented so that travellers had easy access to what they needed to know. In addition, the guidebooks gave details on transport and accom-modation, and for foreign travel, relevant phrases in the national language. Before the 1820s travellers seeking to organise a continental itinerary had to consult sev-eral books. But, thereafter, many publications consolidated relevant information into a single volume containing information about particular itineraries and, with little of the personal narrative central to older forms of travel writing, aimed to pre-sent touring as practicable.

A further development was the introduction (by the English publisher, John Murray, in 1836) of a tourist's handbook, an even lighter publication, not to be left with the baggage, but to be used for on-the-spot reference while visiting particular attractions. The new format, similar to small hand-held bibles with small print and a little later, lightweight paper (particularly useful as guidebooks began to include more and more information), took much of the guesswork out of where to go, how to get there and what to see. Travellers' accounts continued to be published, catering for readers regardless of their travel intentions, but there were now com-prehensive books specifically aimed at those wishing to undertake a tour.[9]

These handbooks were primarily prepared for travel to European destinations. By the late nineteenth century British publishers still did not produce handbooks to the Australian colonies. John Vaughan, the historian of English guidebooks, has concluded that for those travelling beyond Europe, emigrant's handbooks that began being published in the 1830s were most likely the source of travel information for tourists. Certainly, British travellers of the time in their travel accounts did not mention the use or availability of tourist handbooks on Australia.

English publishers, however, did continue to publish travel adventures about the colonies. Such volumes rarely gave specific advice about organising a tour, at least not the practical guidance that might help a tourist choose travel routes, accommodation or type of transport. These books, including explorers' journals about specific expeditions and the more general travel accounts of a lady or gentleman on tour, were intended to excite, intrigue and inform readers about the world beyond their own surroundings. Travel writers were often so concerned about distinguishing themselves as independent travellers that they gave little practical advice or encouragement for people to undertake similar tours (although their writing did help identify potentially interesting tourist attractions). This type of travel writing generally consisted of the author's own impressions (supposedly gathered while travelling), relying on story-telling ability to convey information and usually including descriptions of possible difficulties and dangers.[10]

Potential difficulties and dangers had been an underlying theme in travel accounts of Australia: explorers running out of food or water, threatened by bushfire or loosing their footing while scaling ridges; gentlemen travellers getting lost in the bush or suffering other hardships associated with outdoor life; and lady travellers, because of their sex and class status, having to cope with a number of occurrences that were not usually part of their daily existence. Some travel adventures did include practical advice, perhaps providing information about coach or steamboat fares, say, or recommending accommodation. The message, though, was that such tours had difficulties, although perseverance could be rewarded by unusual and interesting sights that were worthy of being recorded in a travel book.

From the 1830s, many English publishers began to include emigration handbooks in their publication lists (for example, *Mann's Emigrant's Guide to Australia*,

c. 1845 and *Murray's Guide to the Gold-diggings*, 1852). Most of these included useful travel information such as the particulars of the voyage, its cost, conditions at sea, what items passengers should take on board, and, upon arrival in the colonies, typical costs of goods and services. Authors of such books were aware of general readership interest in learning more about the colonies. In the 1860s the Rev. James Baird prefaced his guide to the colonies:

> This work has been written for persons about to emigrate to Australasia, and will furnish, it is believed, all needful information respecting the colonies ... Man, however, does not live by bread alone. Hence, climate, scenery, social characteristics and culture ... have received a full share of attention. Thus it is hoped that the work will also prove acceptable to general readers ...

Descriptions of natural features and scenery, the manners and customs of the inhabitants, the appearance of the towns, notes on colonial history as well as the economic and social prospects of the residents were all relevant to travellers wanting to be well informed about their destination.[11]

The first handbooks specifically for tourists were published in Sydney and Melbourne in the 1850s and 1860s. One of the earliest was *The Stranger's Guide to Sydney, in a Series of Walks; with a map of the City, and Directory of the Various Streets and Public Buildings* (1858). It was prepared and published by James Waugh as a 'a cheap and portable *Guide* for the use of Strangers visiting Sydney', especially for those visiting for only a short time.[12] Waugh, the youngest son of a Scottish publisher who immigrated with his family to New South Wales in 1840, was employed in William Piddington's book-selling business until the late 1850s when he established his own book and stationery business. He wrote to his mother of his intention to publish a colonial almanac and how, by selling it cheaply and circulating it widely, he hoped to advertise his business. About the same time as the *Australian Almanac* he also published the guide. There is no indication of his motives in publishing the guidebook, but he may have decided to use some of the information gathered for the almanac and reorganised specifically for tourists as a speculative venture. A few years later he published a country directory of New South Wales based on the postal districts of the colony with brief descriptions of where they were located, what industries might be found there and a note about worthwhile scenery, although this would have been of little use to visitors in search of tourist destinations.[13]

In the *Stranger's Guide* Waugh provided a map marked with various buildings and other places of interest noted along with an alphabetical listing of Sydney streets, public buildings and other destinations of interest with descriptions and instructions about how to find them. He also included information about local transport—where to pick up a hackney carriage, omnibus departure times, the cost of steam ferry fares—as well as suggested walks around the centre of Sydney itself. By the early 1860s revised editions included a brief history of the colony, a list of 'pleasure excursions' that might be undertaken in a day or less and, for those travelling further, a list of major booking offices for mail and stage coaches, wagons and vans. The book did not see local excursions as extending beyond Botany Bay, Manly Beach and Watsons Bay, and provided little beyond what most Sydney residents would have already known. The *Stranger's Guide* was not the type of travel writing concerned with an author's individual impressions and adventurous spirit, but a local response to the needs of visitors to Sydney, which, with its information directory format, presented Sydney as interesting and practical to tour.

In Victoria, *Guide for Excursionists from Melbourne*, a volume of collected articles describing short excursions from Melbourne, was published in 1868. The pieces with travel hints embedded within the general description, read like newspaper articles, and that's how they may have originated, given the large number of travel articles published in newspapers. From the late 1870s there were detailed guidebooks for colonists including those using the local railways who might wish to learn more about what they passed, those 'in search of the picturesque', and those seeking 'relief … from the worry and turmoil of business'.[14]

Some guidebooks, notably those published by the colonial railways, were general and included information about the whole colony, but others were detailed accounts of specific tourist areas, such as Jenolan Caves and the Blue Mountains. They were organised to provide information from a range of sources about a region's townships and settlements, scenic possibilities, and other attractions, as well as transport and accommodation. They drew on techniques long part of travel adventure writing—perhaps describing a scene as sublime or picturesque, or a general discussion of an area's scientific relevance.[15] Many of these guidebooks quoted at length scenic descriptions first published in early travel books. Guidebook after guidebook quoted Charles Darwin on Govett's Leap in the Blue Mountains, Louisa Meredith on Tasmanian scenery, and Anthony Trollope on the Hawkesbury River. To these were added the perspectives derived from commercial interests in a particular region, the comforts and entertainments of a particular resort or the physical benefits of a mountain climate.

Publishers included those already experienced in printing and circulating publications of interest to a local readership. Gibbs, Shallard & Co., publishers of the *Illustrated Sydney News*, the *Australian Journal* and *Sydney Punch*, produced guidebooks on Sydney, the Blue Mountains and New South Wales. William Dymock, one of the first native-born Australians to establish a major book-selling firm, during a period of expanding this business in the 1890s, published a guidebook and a series of publications with views of Sydney.[16]

Writers of newspaper articles that were of practical interest to the traveller also published travel books intended as guides. In 1880 and 1881, around the time of publication in England of his travel account about Australia, James Inglis (writing as Maori) also published a number of articles in newspapers about holiday trips to different parts of New South Wales. A little later, Samuel Cook, assistant editor and manager of the *Sydney Morning Herald* for most of the second half of the nineteenth century, published a series of articles about Jenolan Caves in the *Herald*. In 1889 'due to popular demand' the series was republished as a 190-page book, containing a detailed account of each cave known to the authorities as well as information on which caves to tour in safety and other details that might contribute to a well-planned tour.[17] Many of these handbooks were regularly

GUIDEBOOKS AND LOCAL DIRECTORIES *were important tools for travellers in the new colonies. Pictured is Mount Victoria in the Blue Mountains, from James Maclehose,* The Picture of Sydney and Strangers' Guide in New South Wales for 1839. *This edition was 'embellished with 43 engravings' of public buildings, picturesque land and water views, although illustrations were not commonplace in guidebooks until later in the century. (Engraver unknown,* Mount Victoria in its Original State, *c. 1838.)*

updated—at least in their travel-related details. Each new edition usually noted that the books had been reprinted because of demand. They provided a more permanent source of travel information than the accounts published in colonial newspapers, although the sources of both, in some cases, were the same.

Along with the local development of tourist guidebooks an important source of information continued to be local and metropolitan newspapers and the weeklies, such as the *Sydney Mail* (first published in 1860), the *Australian Town and Country Journal* (first published in 1870), the *Leader* and *Australasian* in Victoria, the *Chronicle* and the *Observer* in South Australia, the *Western* Mail in Western Australia, the *Queenslander* and the *Tasmanian Mail*. As historians of nineteenth-century Australian journalism have shown, Australian newspapers were the major outlet for local writing talent, since the population was not big enough to guarantee the commercial viability of a local book publishing industry. Australian authors had books published in England, but they were usually chosen and 'improved' according to the perceived tastes of an English or empire market, rather than one specifically Australian. Australian newspapers (along with what local book publishing there was) could publish material for a specifically Australian market. Initially, country newspapers, which have been judged by the Australian literary historian Ken Stewart as attaining 'a "literary-ness" and quality unimaginable today', provided items about nearby places of interest that alerted local readers of opportunities for acquiring knowledge about their surroundings. Some of the first accounts of the Fish River Caves were published in a Bathurst newspaper, and encouraged people to see for themselves nature's curious and wondrous handiwork.[18]

From 1860 such accounts were regular features in 'the weeklies', the newspapers-cum-journals published usually as a companion to a daily newspaper. They had been developed largely for the literate metropolitan and country population. They catered for a variety of interests including literature, science, rural issues, music and religion as well as the newspaper staples of political and general news.[19] In addition, regular columns described particular districts in the colonies from the point of view of a tourist, and many called upon readers to observe these places for themselves.[20] For example, in 1860 the second issue of the *Sydney Mail* published the first article in a series called 'Rambles in the Suburbs by a Stroller'—by the end of the year it had given lengthy accounts of people, places, views, interesting buildings and other observations about three Sydney suburbs, Woolloomooloo (including Darlinghurst), Paddington and Waverley.[21] There were other regular features on tours further afield—an account of a trip to see mountain views near the Kiandra goldfields included advice about local travel conditions and accommodation—and shorter pieces (although by the mid-1860s the tendency was to long articles)

Engraver unknown, Railway Guide Map Showing Pathways at Leura Falls, *c. 1890*.

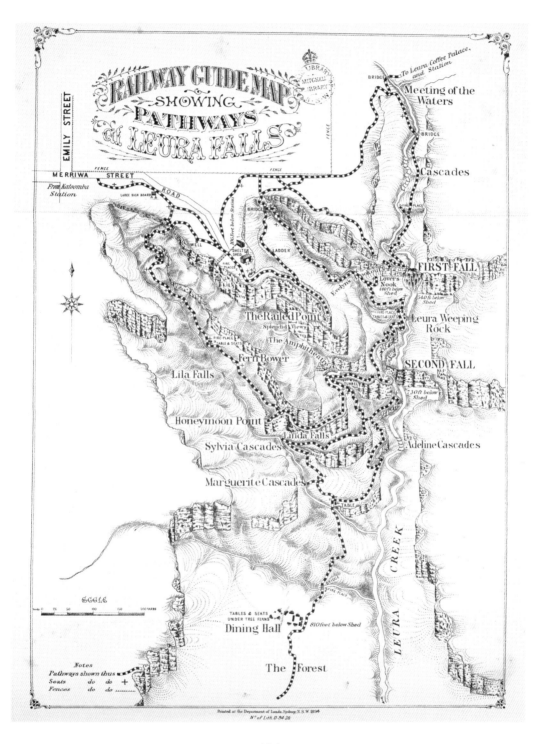

describing tours the writers had recently undertaken, perhaps to the Hawkesbury or the Illawarra, and urging readers to do likewise. From 1870, with the new *Australian Town and Country Journal*, there were even more travel accounts about colonial districts and townships. In the first six months of production the *Journal* included more than thirty-five travel articles about destinations in New South Wales, from large towns like Newcastle to settlements as small as Trunkey (a mining settlement between Bathurst and Goulburn), and including places as distant from Sydney as Bourke or as close as Parramatta.[22]

The dailies continued to publish articles on colonial travels, such as the 1865–66 series, 'Impressions of Victoria', published in the *Argus* as a series of more than twenty articles. But the production techniques of the weeklies meant that, unlike their daily counterparts (which used high-speed printing and paper of lesser quality), they could include illustrations (and by the late 1880s, photographs); thus, readers could see depictions of what was described—interesting rock formations, gentle waterfalls, celebrated views and inviting mountain paths, as well as local personalities.[23]

The type of travel writing that urged residents to visit different parts of the colonies often proclaimed how beautiful the country was. Sometimes, writers lamented that local scenery—at least the equal of what was sought by tourists in Europe—was rarely visited. For example, a writer describing 'a flying visit' up the Hawkesbury, commented on its 'truly magnificent' scenery, the surroundings:

> being all that was required to make the scene at least equal to that which daily attracts from all parts of Europe—aye, and Australia too—such numbers of excursionists … [I]ts charming scenery that would in the old country attract visitors from all climes, but which, alas! is almost unknown to the people at Sydney, although at their very doors.[24]

Another writer was even more emphatic: 'In scenery as in a thousand other things, Australia has something peculiarly original, something of which the counterpart is not to be found, in any other portion of the globe.'[25]

It was not only scenery that interested these writers. Many also described—often in great detail—ordinary encounters along the way. Those writing about tours of the Hawkesbury often included vignettes of colonial life, perhaps reporting a conversation with a local settler about farming, or commenting on social, economic, religious or educational circumstances of the district. In addition to its Blowhole (an ocean cavern notable for the seawater that spurted high out of the surrounding rock), Kiama was also known for its butter and cheese, and at least one writer urged tourists to organise a visit to one of its dairy products manufacturers. Populous districts, such as Wollongong, might prompt writers to remark upon local trade and industries and, often, they described the architectural features of prominent buildings. Older colonial districts, such as Parramatta, Richmond or Windsor, were valued for their historical associations with the first years of British colonisation, and could be the subject of informative articles, as writers attempted to re-create the past by explaining the significance of particular structures or sites, called by some the 'antiquities' of the colony.[26]

In the 1850s and 1860s before new transport services were properly in place, writers of travel articles often commented that the main hindrance to increased numbers of people touring was inadequate transport. A writer predicted that once the western railway was established, visitors to the Fish River Caves would no longer be 'so few and far between … [keen as they would be to see] the greatest natural wonder of Australia'. Another, commenting on how few of Sydney's citizens are 'acquainted with [the Hawkesbury River's] beauties', explained that since 'the colony is not yet populous enough to support steamers by pleasure traffic alone … those who wish to travel find that the only established routes are those which there is commerce enough to keep open'.[27]

Nevertheless, writers of newspaper travel accounts often urged their readers to see the attraction for themselves despite the difficulties. One writer, upon returning from a trip up the Hawkesbury, proclaimed 'a feeling of intense satisfaction with the trip—confidently recommending its imitation to all our friends; and the lovers of the sublime and beautiful in nature'. Others implied that the effect of what they saw while on tour was often so profound (echoes of the concept of the 'sublime') as to defy description and warrant a personal encounter. One wrote:

I have given you the above description ... my memory serving alone as my guide, but I should advise all who have the opportunity, to visit the spot, and they will ascertain that it is impossible to express by words one tenth part of the beauties of these wonderful works of nature.[28]

Calls for readers to undertake similar tours were usually sustained by details on how to organise travel arrangements. Most writers provided details of transport, for example, for travel by water, the names of particular steamers (sometimes even the owners' names) and where they operated. Advice was also given about alternative travel routes. Prospective tourists from Sydney who wished to tour the Hawkesbury but wanted to avoid the ocean were advised either to take the train to Windsor and then board the river steamer, or to travel to Pittwater from Manly and pick up a steamer there. Accommodation information was also given, usually a brief description of what could be expected as well as the name of the local hotel or boarding house proprietor with the warning that it was best to secure beds before departure (if possible, by sending a telegraph message). Where there was a choice of accommodation, as in the upper Blue Mountains from the late 1870s, writers might make recommendations, although this varied considerably, from those critical of all offerings to those seeing some virtue in every one of them depending on the particular requirements and resources of the tourist.[29]

By the end of the nineteenth century natural wonders as a destination in themselves helped create local tourist interest, and concerned primarily with attracting Australian residents they were part of a broader image-making process providing information about colonial life, its social, economic and political characteristics, and its built and natural environments. In addition to visitors' representations of Australia and the stereotypes created by late nineteenth-century artists and *Bulletin* writers—the bush worker and mateship, swagmen and freedom, gumtrees and the Australian countryside—there were other perspectives on colonial urban and rural life. Picturesque beauty spots, sublime scenery, geological curiosities, native ferns (but also colonial social and political institutions)—all increasing colonial self-confidence.

In a substantial reference guidebook to Jenolan Caves, *The Jenolan Caves* (1890), J. J. Foster enthusiastically made this point. The words might be flowery, the sentiment nationalistic, but the point (in a book designed primarily for the local market) was the promotion of colonial wonders as world class:

> The author … having visited most of the important caves throughout the world, viz., the Ajanta, Ellora, and Elephanta Caves in India, the Great Moulamein Caves in Burmah [*sic*], others in Java and Japan, and the principal ones in Europe, can with confidence say none of them can compare with the Jenolan Caves for their marvellous variety of formations, dazzling brilliancy of lustre, and exquisite colouring.[30]

In this literature Australia was not just a land of sheep, wheat, bushmen and pioneers. It was also a place of sublime landscape, natural beauty and stimulating travel.

In the twenty-first century, most Australians are familiar with descriptions of Australia's leading natural attractions: the 'red centre', the 'tropical north', the 'high country'. All these phrases help shape our view and expectations, and can obliterate other perspectives. In his study of the Blue Mountains, the cultural historian Martin Thomas borrows W. J. T. Mitchell's phrase, the 'dreamwork of imperialism', to describe the process of the cultural acquisition of land, whereby certain stories such as the crossing of the Blue Mountains in 1813 by Blaxland, Lawson and Wentworth are given such importance as to erase equally pertinent stories such as the physical and spiritual occupation of the area by the Gundungurra.[31]

Natural attractions physically exist—they are real places that can be visited by real people. But they are also, in a way, figments of the imagination. Their physical existence provokes an imaginary artifice, a canvas, upon which people pour words

HOLIDAY RAMBLES.—MOUNT MACEDON.

1.—THE FALLS.]   2.—THE FORD.   3.—THE ROAD UP.   4.—THE DEVIL'S HOLE.   5.—MOUNTAIN MEG'S HUT.   6.—SUMMIT OF MOUNT DIOGENES.—SEE PAGE 26.

and images shaped by particular intellectual traditions (such as the picturesque and the sublime). The British historian Simon Schama explains that our perceptions are shaped by 'culture, convention and cognition', and this 'shaping perception' makes the difference between 'raw matter and landscape'.[32] A simple example of this cultural specificity is the attempt to explain in certain languages the meaning of an 'arcadian or sylvan scene' or of the 'grandeur of wilderness'—descriptions that saturated nineteenth-century writing about Australian scenery. In some languages, difficulties arise when translating notions of rural idylls or grand wilderness without also distinguishing them from a belief that rural areas are backwaters. The 'raw matter' exists, but it is its shaping by people that determines whether we see it as grand or uninspiring.

ILLUSTRATED WEEKLIES *were, from the 1860s, a major outlet for travel writing and views of colonial scenery. For example, in the 1870s the 'Holiday Rambles' series was published in the* Illustrated Australian News for Home Readers. *(Samuel Calvert,* Holiday Rambles—Mount Macedon, *1874?)*

HOW MOUNTAINS
BECAME SUBLIME

*In which the attractions of
Australia's mountains are explained*

For much of the first half of the nineteenth century there was an urgency about establishing the sublime characteristics of Australian mountains similar to the rush to establish the existence of exploitable natural resources. Establishing the existence of such characteristics might not provide material wealth, but would present Australia as a place with resources for the cultivation of spiritual strength, nobility of character and creative energies. Australian landscapes challenged and extended European expectations of mountain scenery, and through the lens of the sublime, which itself was evolving until its demise at the end of the century, Europeans began to come to terms with Antipodean mountains.

The Blue Mountains, the vast hill ranges west of Sydney, were the first Australian mountains to capture the colonial imagination. Generally, early accounts presented the ranges as inhospitable with difficult precipices, endless ridges, little water and certainly no land suitable for agriculture. Even though the region was noted to be 'covered with trees', it was also described as 'barren', more than suggesting it was unproductive, useless to the colonisers, uninviting even to travellers. As early as 1789, the ultimate Enlightenment man Watkin Tench wrote an account of William Dawes' failed attempt to cross the Nepean and 'penetrate the Carmarthen Mountains'. His observation was that,

> as far as the eye can reach from very high hills, [the range] bears the most dreary, barren appearance that can well be imagined, nothing to be seen but ridge beyond ridge of mountains covered with trees and in many places with rocks, without a single visible interval of plain or cultivable land.[1]

Tench presented the land as unproductive (no plains or 'cultivable land'), but his view also reflected contemporary attitudes inspired by scientific developments. Before the seventeenth century, in England at least, there had been little artistic, literary or scientific interest in mountains. Then developments in astronomy, particularly Galileo's description of lunar mountains, initiated interest, not only in the cosmos as infinite (a challenge to dominant theological and ideological views that presented space as finite), but also in the mountains of earth. From the mid-seventeenth century, especially after the publication of Thomas Burnet's *A Sacred Theory of the Earth*, mountains came to be a major object of scientific enquiry into the age of the earth and the universe.[2] Thus, by the late eighteenth century, Tench's description of mountainscapes in New South Wales as 'dreary' and 'barren', and his term 'ridge beyond ridge' (suggesting an endlessness akin to infinity) did not so much express distaste for the landscape confronting Dawes as engage with the terminology that was beginning to express interest in mountains as a source for understanding the natural world. He could as easily have written that the mountains had no cultivable land and end it at that, but in choosing to embellish his description with phrases like 'as far as the eye can see', he had borrowed from the literary conventions used to describe mountains and helped to create a growing intrigue about this local variety.

Early European explorers of the Blue Mountains had hoped that just a few ridges separated the Sydney plains from what lay beyond: only climb the cliffs and over the precipices they would view hoped-for farming land. Instead, there was Tench's 'ridge beyond ridge'. But the concept of ridges, once established, meant the development of a routine for explorers to seek and describe views from the top of precipices that foreshadowed the attraction to future travellers. The mountains became known as a place to view fantastically shaped rocks and cliffs dropping away dangerously into valleys (or glens, as they were called in the fashion of the time). The observations of the explorers of this novel and challenging landscape were the beginning of an enduring image of these mountains as sublime.

A major experience of the sublime came from dangerous encounters with nature that tested the limits of explorers' physical capabilities, and early exploration of the Blue Mountains provided many such challenges. Francis Barrallier, who as aide-de-camp to Governor King undertook various official exploratory expeditions, described in his Blue Mountains' journal a precarious climb, in which his feet and hands had become bloodied. Yet the climb also provided a noteworthy view. He wrote: 'I glanced at the plain from that great height with a feeling of admiration mingled with awe'. Knee-deep in the finest of sands with sharp stones falling around them they came across 'immense overhanging rocks, which seemed to be attached to nothing, [and which] offered an appalling scene'. While attempting to hold onto one of these 'enormous masses' of rock they experienced a landslide accompanied by 'a thundering noise'.[3]

The language used to describe the perilous hazards of mountain explorations as well as the sights helped create early European expectations and images of Australian mountains, and for a short time at least, Australian mountains were reputed to test the courage and determination of even the bravest colonisers. In a world attracted by the sublime, suggestions that mountains were unconquerable raised the glory stakes for those who prepared to tackle unimaginable challenges and succeed in the face of the impossible. And, despite doubts about the usefulness of official explorations to these rocky regions (probably also partly due to financial constraints), Europeans continued to undertake expeditions into the Blue Mountains—one can speculate that the very image of the mountains as unconquerable inspired some to take on the challenge.

Responding to Gregory Blaxland's enquiry about the feasibility of a passage over the mountains George Caley, appointed by Joseph Banks to collect botanical specimens in New South Wales, replied that it was 'impossible'. According to Blaxland, Caley went on to explain that 'the Blue Mountains must inevitably remain an insurmountable barrier to the extention [sic] of the settlement'. But Blaxland had an economic imperative—he wanted more pasture for his sheep.

Having discussed his planned route with Governor Macquarie, Blaxland invited William Lawson and William Charles Wentworth to join his party. They set off in 1813 and their route along with adequate planning was to prove successful. Each kept a journal noting their observations and the difficulties they encountered. In these accounts, danger was not the main motif because, unlike previous expeditions, Blaxland's party was not to seek evidence of the sublime; it had decided not to climb precipices, but instead to cut a crude track wherever it seemed easiest, which their horses loaded with supplies could follow, in all likelihood utilising various Aboriginal tracks that criss-crossed the region.[4] Of course, difficulties still abounded: clothes torn by the thorny brush, little feed for the horses, few animals to hunt to supplement provisions. Although they did come across some 'fine streams of water', at other times the supply was inadequate, and they developed 'bowel complaints'. Indeed, after only a week—on their first rest day—Blaxland noted that his men decided it would be safer not to continue and persisted only after some persuasion.[5]

It was only occasionally that Blaxland and his party came across an environment recognisable in descriptions by earlier Europeans. There were remarks on the irregularities of the terrain: the 'impassable clift [*sic*] of rocks' that seemed to prevent westward progress was likened to a 'stone wall rising immediately perpendicular out of the side of the mountains'. Crossing a narrow ridge, Blaxland observed the 'very deep rocky precipice on each side'. Wentworth admired the physical strength and mental determination of earlier explorers who had attempted to cross the mountains by climbing one precipice after another. He wrote, 'Nothing coul[d] have afforded a stronger proof of the indefatigable perseverance of man than His surmounting these almost Insurmountable barriers'.

The 'insurmountable barriers' physically challenged humans, the mystery of their existence mentally challenged them. The emergence of the new science, geology, was integral to the interest in mountains, looking to give them a scientific basis as a source of sublime power barely comprehensible to humans. On the directions of the British government, early explorers were expected to return with specimen bags filled with samples of soil and rocks. They would be sent to England to be analysed, often under the guidance of Sir Joseph Banks. As Bernard Smith has suggested, this frenzy for collecting meant that the Pacific became better known to the English and to Europeans than did less distant regions, such as Ireland. Since it was soon realised that the Blue Mountains would not easily become economically productive for Europeans, the continued collection of soil, rocks and fossils from the mountains represented an interest in collecting and classifying samples purely for scientific purposes, whatever practical application they might have later.

By the time of Blaxland's expedition, some European scientific circles considered fossils useful in classifying geological strata. This interest in geological stratification had given rise to the new theory that the earth was composed of layers, which could be used to measure its age. Blaxland endorsed this theory from his own observations of the cliffs of the Blue Mountains, so tall and old they must, he suggested, contain 'stratas of earth', the study of which would reveal the immense geological age of the land. His expedition tried to collect rock and mineral specimens at different heights from these particular cliffs for further analysis, but found the descents too risky.

All three were intrigued by the physical environment. What they couldn't collect for further scientific analysis, they observed and described, speculating about the creation of these great precipices. Wentworth wrote that the 'immense unconnected perpendicular masses' must originally have formed one entire mass that was to be separated by some 'mighty convulsion in Nature'. Their observations on ruggedness, great dimension and the extraordinary power of nature, could not help but present the landscape as sublime.[6]

From 1815, a navigable if difficult route over the Blue Mountains had at last, against all colonial expectations, been established. Geological findings were beginning to attest to the great age of the mountain range. And with the new Romantic movement, which included the concept of the sublime, rejecting classical formalism in favour of the imaginative and a deliberate preoccupation with subjective reactions to art and nature, accounts of the mountains increasingly focused on the landscape's effect on European sensibilities.

An extensive and laudatory pronouncement on the mountains as sublime was written by Governor Macquarie, and an account based on his observations was first published in the *Sydney Gazette* in 1815, soon after his tour. Macquarie valued British discovery and exploration as signs of imperial greatness and it was for this reason—to publicise imperial discoveries—that in the steps of explorers he toured the colony so extensively, mostly with his wife, various gentlemen, and a huge entourage who ensured the group's untroubled progress. It was largely because of the governor's journeying that roads were built so soon after initial explorations had been conducted; apart from any future use, without them 'imperial progress' would have been greatly impeded, certainly more uncomfortable, and the public relations angle less potent (particularly if the governor and his wife had become lost in the bush or injured in a fall).

The first road across the mountains was not much better than a rough track. Intended for Macquarie's journeying it was built quickly and cheaply as an earthen road for carts. Tree stumps and roots were covered over and firmed down with earth, but rock platforms were left exposed where they occurred naturally. New South Wales, of course, was still a penal colony and in parts the road was extremely steep in order to deter escaped convicts and other law-breakers.[7] Its completion, though, signalled a new era of touring in comparative safety and comfort and helped develop new notions of mountainous scenery. No longer drawing so much upon the earlier reputation of the Blue Mountains as unconquerable and dangerous, it was easier now to contemplate the effect of the mountains' magnificent views and rocky outcrops on human sensibilities.

There were still dangers and difficulties, but they were more predictable and mainly the result of the difficult and tiring journey. In private correspondence Macquarie commented on the fatigue caused by travelling for hours on end over rocky and steep terrain. He was especially concerned about the effect of such strenuous activity on Elizabeth Macquarie, his wife. The road certainly meant that travellers did not have to cut through dense bushes or scramble up slippery precipices, but general unevenness and occasional steepness were to cause concern for some decades, even after new passes at Mount Victoria (on the western side) and at Lapstone (on the eastern side) were constructed in the 1830s. Heavily laden carts and passenger coaches made slow progress on the perilously steep sections of the road. Conditions for the horses could also cause anxiety: feed was not always available and horses were likely to tire before they reached grass for grazing. Travel by night was dangerous with quagmires, deep ruts and the threat of stumbling out to a precipice, but delays and the distances between established, if primitive, travellers' accommodation meant night travel was often unavoidable. Up until the 1840s some published travel accounts warned of bushrangers, although they did not cite actual personal experiences. The emphasis of travel accounts had now shifted from physical and mental strength as a prerequisite for the journey, what Wentworth noted as the 'indefatigable perseverance' of the early explorers 'surmounting these almost insurmountable barriers'. Now more attention was given to describing views than to the physical and mental challenge of reaching them.[8]

GOVERNOR MACQUARIE'S 1815 EXPEDITION *across the Blue Mountains to the Bathurst Plains included the artist John Lewin, who painted at least twenty watercolours of the expedition's progress. Above:* Spring Wood, *the first night's camp. Opposite above:* Pitt's Amphitheatre, *near the present-day Katoomba. Opposite below:* [Cox's Pass. View of Camp Beside Cox's River], *on the western side of the mountains. (John Lewin, 1815.)*

Governor Macquarie's expedition was the first large group of Europeans to use the road. His party included Mrs Macquarie, eight gentlemen and dozens of others who looked after them as well as tending the livestock, labouring with the carts, and managing other physical aspects of the journey. On 26 April 1815 the Macquaries set off from Parramatta to begin their journey. Lachlan Macquarie, an experienced traveller, was looking forward to this three-week excursion. The road to the Bathurst Plains was part of his grander plan to extend the boundaries of settlement and offer small lots of land to agriculturalists, hoping to realise the Lockian ideal of agriculture as a civilising force. Like others in his party he was also intrigued by the scenery in the Blue Mountains, descriptions of its grandeur and ruggedness having long peppered colonial conversation, and he planned to spend time during the expedition taking detours to worthy sights. The trip also afforded a break from the demands of Sydney life and the political machinations that went hand-in-hand with being a colonial governor. Macquarie gave strict instructions that he was on no account to be disturbed except with news of their young son, who remained in Sydney, too young for the rigours of the expedition. Macquarie wanted to devote his full attention to the task at hand, to assess the land in terms of his grand vision.

In his daily journal descriptions of scenery were as important to his assessment as the more practical observations of the land and the local Aboriginal people. A Scottish highlander whose career had encompassed travel to many parts of the world including North America, India, Europe and Persia, this personal experience had shaped his appreciation for scenery and gave authority to his exclamations. When Macquarie wrote of 'very fine picturesque grand scenery', people assumed he knew what he was talking about. But he also realised the value of consultation and had requested the company of at least 'two or three intelligent persons' with whom he could discuss the 'true value of the discovery'. Macquarie's account of the journey probably represents a consensus of views about each new sight and experience, derived from conversations with his travel companions, with his wife during rides in their coach, with the Surveyor-General John Oxley and his deputies, with the painter and naturalist John Lewin and others over dinner and cards. Captain Henry Antill, the author of the only other surviving journal of this expedition, noted the camaraderie among the travellers, a willingness to discuss and share views about what they had seen and experienced. Such discussion may well have emboldened Antill on the second day of the expedition to declare the scenery at King's Tableland as 'one of the grandest views that can be imagined'. After the first day of travelling, the party arrived at their campsite to the three cheers of the servants, who had travelled ahead to make ready for the governor's arrival. A table was set, ready for dinner under some lofty trees. The party dined, they played cards, drank tea and retired early in preparation for the next day's travelling and sight-seeing, a pattern that was repeated over the rest of the journey.[9]

An account based on Macquarie's journal was published in both New South Wales and England soon after the conclusion of the tour 'for the information of the Public (whose curiosity was all alive on the subject)'.[10] Its vice-regal connection and the fact that it was reprinted in several journals made it the first well-publicised account of the Blue Mountains, indeed of any Australian mountains. The account, predictably, suggested that Macquarie was primarily interested in the potential productivity of the land west of the Blue Mountains. But it also revealed enthusiasm for the mountainous landscape, and expanded the observations made by early explorers. Macquarie wrote:

> [King's Tableland in the upper mountains] is extremely beautiful and has very fine picturesque grand scenery, consisting of deep finely wooded glens, stupendous rocks and cliffs, with high distant hills and mountains. ... On the S.W. side ... the mountain terminates in abrupt precipices of immense depth; at the bottom of which is seen a glen as romantically beautiful as can be imagined, bounded on the further side by mountains of great magnitude ... [Further on] a view is obtained particularly beautiful and grand. Mountains rising beyond mountains, with stupendous masses of rock in the foreground, here strike the eye with admiration and astonishment ... [W]e passed a very extensive deep romantic glen, full of very picturesque and wild scenery.[11]

In the eighteenth and early nineteenth century, the prevailing concept of the sublime assumed that humans were capable of rising above everyday concerns and achieving true greatness. To a romantic of the time, it would not have been fanciful to see in Macquarie's interest a hope that New South Wales would one day emerge from the desolate landscape of convictism to something nobler, that the love of liberty and worthy sensibilities would be born in people with such scenery to contemplate. He had expressed similar sentiments a few years earlier in 1811 on a tour of Van Diemen's Land, when he wrote favourably of the colony's scenery, the combination of 'fertile plains', rivers, lofty mountains' and 'high rocky cliffs' as 'highly gratifying and truly sublime, and equal in point of beauty to anything I have ever seen in any country'.[12] Nor was Macquarie's hope particularly idiosyncratic; the symbolic importance of mountains was an element of national 'self-fashioning' in Creole independence movements in early nineteenth-century Latin America, as well as the newly emerging nations of Europe, and these new discussions may well have influenced John Ruskin. The English art historian explored and expanded upon similar ideas in *Modern Painters*, an influential mid-nineteenth-century publication on landscape painting, arguing that mountains could greatly affect the development of the human intellect, particularly in artistic, poetic and literary endeavours. He stated that nothing of any intellectual or artistic importance could be inspired by flat land.[13]

The sentiment that majestic mountain scenery in Australia could ennoble and inspire those who viewed it appeared in many travel accounts in the decades following the publication of Macquarie's journal. James Martin, later chief justice of the NSW Supreme Court, proclaimed in his essay on the 'The Sublime in Nature' (1838) that mountain scenery, including that of New South Wales, was 'eminently calculated to inspire us with the most dignified ideas'. On the 1840 expedition to the Australian Alps organised by James Macarthur, the Polish explorer and scientist Paul de Strzelecki named a mountain after Tadeusz Kosciuszko, the Polish patriot—a figure 'dear and sacred to all Poles'—in order to extol the virtues of liberty and honour 'amongst a free people, who appreciate freedom' (although the spelling of Mount Kosciusko was changed to include the 'z' only in the 1990s). David Burn, the playwright and author who accompanied Sir John and Lady Franklin on the vice-regal tour from Hobart to Macquarie Harbour in south-western

Van Diemen's Land, wrote of Frenchman's Cap: 'It is a bold, isolated, precipitously scarped crag, surmounted by a peak resembling the cap of liberty. The cap of liberty!'. While the scenery of the Blue Mountains was proclaimed by one writer as certain to give 'vigour to the digestive powers, and cheerfulness to the spirits', others wrote that the Blue Mountains offered 'views of stupendous grandeur ... that will awaken the dullest imagination'.[14]

For the two decades after Macquarie's expedition, many visitors continued to describe the Blue Mountains in terms of the sublime without explaining that their physical characteristics were quite different from those of mountains in Europe, England, Wales and Scotland. In Macquarie's time English travel accounts of the Welsh mountains, the Scottish Highlands and the Lake district (the mountainous tourist region of England) had continued to make much of rocky chasms, mists, storms, precipices, piles of rocks, endless ridges and cliffs as examples of mountain wildness, encapsulated by William Wordsworth's description of the Lake District: 'the mountains … are endlessly diversified, sweeping easily or boldly in simple majesty, abrupt and precipitous, or soft and elegant … towering above each other, or lifting themselves in ridges like the waves of a tumultuous sea'.[15] These were scenic features readily familiar to observers of the Blue Mountains. By the 1830s, however, expectation that the tops of mountains should form craggy peaks, preferably, snow-capped, had become pronounced in England. By then there was a strong visual dimension to English travel description, developed by the growing number of English guidebooks illustrated with lithographs and sketches by artists who had toured various regions. Also, the Swiss Alps, with their most satisfactory display of snow-capped peaks, was increasingly becoming a destination for English tourists.[16]

Until the 1830s—four decades after the first European descriptions of the Blue Mountains—the physical features of the Blue Mountains had coincided with

EUROPEAN MOUNTAIN SCENERY *was also appreciated for grand precipices, endless ridges and rocky chasms, and only later for snow-covered peaks. This engraving is from William Gilpin's 1792 guidebook to the English Lake District. (Engraver unknown,* Dovedale, *c. 1790.)*

British descriptive conventions. But from the 1830s in both Europe and the British Isles the accepted convention of a mountain landscape required that peaks rose tall from their surrounds, and, at certain times of the year, were snow-capped.

The scenery of the Blue Mountains for the new wave of travellers in the 1830s challenged this preconception. Charles Darwin, who toured the mountains during his brief time in Sydney in 1836, was particularly intrigued. The 26-year-old Darwin was reaching the end of a five-year survey voyage around the world on the *Beagle*. The purpose of the British naval expedition, led by Captain Robert FitzRoy, was to complete a survey of South America, then to circumnavigate the world stopping off in specific places including Sydney, Hobart and King George Sound to take chronometric measurements in order to calculate longitude. Darwin had joined the *Beagle* serendipitously. FitzRoy saw the scientific potential of such a voyage, and persuaded the Admiralty to include as part of the expedition two civilians, an artist and a scientist, prepared to endure a long voyage for the chance to see and observe the natural history and society of distant countries. FitzRoy engaged the experienced Augustus Earle as artist, and through Cambridge connections and recommendations, discovered Darwin, 'a young man of promising ability, extremely fond of geology, and indeed all branches of natural history'. About eight months into the voyage Earle left the *Beagle*, too ill to continue—he was replaced by an eager Conrad Martens—but Darwin remained in the care of the *Beagle* for the entire voyage.

In 1839 his journal and remarks about the tour were published as the last of three volumes of the account of the *Beagle*'s 1832–36 voyage, and to such acclaim that within a matter of months the volume was reprinted as a separate edition with a new title, reprinted again, then revised and published in 1845, and continued to be reissued for many years after. In the 1840s Darwin also published various works on specific facets of natural history observed during the *Beagle* voyage—coral reefs, volcanic islands, geology—and edited a number of books based on his journals and specimen collections including *Birds*, illustrated with prints produced by John and Elizabeth Gould. These publications launched his scientific career and he was already well known by 1859 when *On the Origin of Species by Means of Natural Selection* catapulted him into posterity. But on 16 January 1836, four days after his arrival in New South Wales, as he started off on his journey across the Blue Mountains to Bathurst with a guide and two horses, he was just another young gentleman tourist with letters of introduction to influential colonists, in search of novel and interesting sights, curious to learn about the success of English colonies on the other side of the world with a professional interest in regional geology and natural history. The excursion to Bathurst, he wrote to his sister, 'was partly for Geology, but chiefly to get an idea of the state of the colony, & see the country. Large towns, all over the world are nearly similar, & it is only by such excursions that the characteristic features can be perceived.'[17]

He was surprised at how the Blue Mountains upset his notion of mountain landscape necessarily having peaks: 'From so grand a title as Blue Mountains, and from their absolute altitude, I expected to have seen a bold chain of mountains crossing the country; but instead of this, a sloping plain presents merely an inconsiderable front to the low land of the coast.'[18] Once in their midst (near what is now called Wentworth Falls), he was even more perplexed by what he saw, describing the sight in some detail so as to present as accurate a picture as possible:

> one stands on the brink of a vast precipice, and below is the grand bay or gulf (for I know not what other name to give it), thickly covered with forest. The point of view is situated as if at the head of a bay, the line of cliff diverging on each side, and showing headland behind headland, as on a bold sea-coast. These cliffs are composed of horizontal strata of whitish sandstone; and so absolutely vertical are they, that in many places, a person standing on the edge, and throwing down a stone, can see it strike the trees in the abyss below … If we imagine a winding harbour, with its deep water surrounded by bold cliff-like shores, laid dry, and a forest sprung up on its sandy bottom, we should then have the appearance and structure here exhibited. This kind of view was to me quite novel, and extremely magnificent.[19]

The notion that what he saw was comparable to coastal scenery was not new. In the 1820s Barron Field had likened the appearance of this region to a 'sea of harsh trees'. In the early 1830s George Bennett described the view from the ranges as 'a sea of country in the distance'.[20] New was Darwin's surprise that the Blue Mountains could be regarded as mountain scenery, and his view was at odds with the attitudes of previous travellers who, in describing the range's cliff-like appearance had used the vocabulary of mountain characteristics—'deep glens', 'stupendous rocks', 'abrupt precipices', 'mountains beyond mountains'. Thirty or forty years before Darwin's journey there was not yet a prevailing European image of mountains as having peaks, and almost all early colonial images of the Blue Mountains described the landscape without reference to the Scottish Highlands, the Swiss Alps or any other European mountain scenery. By the mid-1830s, however, descriptions of the Blue Mountains generally made a point of asserting their difference from typical European mountain scenery.

The importance of Darwin's descriptions of the Blue Mountains grew as his fame increased from the mid-nineteenth century onwards. European mountains they were not, but their own magnificence was indisputable, and his words were quoted repeatedly in travel accounts and tourist material. Since many other travellers also wrote descriptions of Blue Mountains scenery into their accounts, from the 1840s onwards visitors were better prepared for the differences between this mountainous landscape and what was typical in the northern hemisphere.[21]

I n the first few decades of the nineteenth century the Blue Mountains were the hilly showpiece of the Australian colonies. Elsewhere, notably in Van Diemen's Land, there was a growing appreciation of other mountainscapes. In the early 1810s, as already mentioned, Macquarie had expressed his views of Tasmanian mountains in no uncertain terms, but, initially, others were more subdued in their praise. By the early 1820s specific regions in Van Diemen's Land were beginning to be noted for their mountainous character, although more attention was paid to the grand scenery of the central lakes. The colonial surveyor George William Evans, who had officially corroborated the first crossing of the Blue Mountains, explained that 'in various parts of the island there are … high hills; but with the exception of the Table Mountain [Mount Wellington], Tasman's Peak and Ben Lomond, scarcely any of which deserve the name of mountains'. During the 1820s Ben Lomond began to develop a following of dedicated mountain lovers, and along with Mount Wellington, became a mountain notable for its extraordinary scenery, a place that could well excite a person's imagination. Edward Curr's account of Van Diemen's Land written for emigrants was largely a lament for what he believed could be 'one of the most delightful countries upon the earth' but for the 'moral evil' of convictism; some of this delight arose out of seeing 'the most strikingly beautiful scene of which the island has to boast … The butts [promontories] of Ben Lomond rear their lofty summits, crowned in eternal snows, and terminate their range majestically in one abrupt descent.' In 1823 assistant surveyor Thomas Scott, with his painting *Ben Lomond from Fletchers Hut*, provided one of the first visual representations of Tasmania's mountains. Despite such representations, there had been few colonial explorations of Tasmania's mountains especially when compared to the number of expeditions to the Blue Mountains.[22]

This was to change from the late 1820s after the appointment of George Frankland as surveyor-general of Van Diemen's Land. Frankland believed in exploration as an important source of knowledge, necessary to his official duties. His surveyors were required 'to observe and record every remarkable fact connected with the Natural history of the island'. They were to keep journals of their observations, to record the topographical nature of the land, provide the precise surveying dimensions for official use, and describe unusual and interesting items and sights. As part of their duties they were to climb mountains, and their journals recorded trigonometrical dimensions and other observations of the surrounding territory alongside accounts of how viewing certain mountains affected their sensibilities. When a number of expeditions went to central Van Diemen's Land, with the purpose of mapping the river systems, an unintended outcome was the systematic exploration of several mountain tops, which had excited interest because of their sheer size. Views from the summits, the expedition leaders believed, might help further exploration. But their descriptions established the mountains as exceptional in themselves, notable for scenic and romantic possibilities. In his 1832 expedition from Bothwell to Frenchman's Cap, assistant surveyor W. S. Sharland described the mountains near the upper reaches of the Gordon River as 'stupendous hills … ascending to a very considerable height, whose craggy summits appeared to vie with each other in their fantastic structure'. Having descended from one vantage point he was able to look up and see it 'as it really was—a stupendous mountain, with a most appalling aspect to the west'.[23]

Up until the 1830s, descriptions of Ben Lomond had generally been from afar and praised its majestic appearance and lofty summits. From the 1830s, mountain surveys had provided the first European close-ups of Ben Lomond. When assistant surveyor John Helder Wedge ascended Ben Lomond in January 1833, the first ascent for the purpose of colonial surveying, he described in his journal the immense columns of rocks at its summit as 'truly awful, grand. The whole of the surface of the mountain presents the most barren and desolate appearance, not a single tree is to be seen of any description, not a scrub [ie shrub] unless a thick prickly bush may be termed such.' The artist John Glover accompanied Wedge's expedition and made a series of sketches on top of Ben Lomond depicting its summit as desolate crags.[24] The majesty of this mountain was a consequence of its utter desolation and a potent reminder of what nature could do. A *Hobart Town Courier* reporter described how Glover's paintings might help draw attention to 'many of the romantic and characteristic views' in Van Diemen's Land. In 1835 Glover held an exhibition of sixty-eight paintings, more than half Tasmanian scenes and landscapes. Seven of these depicted various aspects of Ben Lomond, either looking up at the mountain rising majestically out of the surrounding foothills, or on the summit, looking across at rocks 'called the Stacks … of great height and evidently split asunder by great violence'.

Other mountains in Van Diemen's Land received similar acclaim, a consequence of both artistic expression and official survey. Several paintings of Mount Wellington by Glover were exhibited at the same time as those of Ben Lomond. A review of the exhibition in the London *Times* remarked that:

> the country itself is beautiful and picturesque … in some districts magnificent and sublime; and in the neighbourhood of Hobart Town, from the union of cultivated plains, stupendous mountain scenery and broad expanse of waters, delightful and noble. It bears … a resemblance of the views on the lakes of Cumberland, with the exception that the hills are more lofty, possess more of a primeval aspect … [25]

In the same year, on an expedition to the head of the Derwent River, George Frankland reported coming across 'a very remarkable mountain [Mount

Olympus]... It appeared of immense height, and perpendicular on all sides ... Its isolated and commanding position at once excited in us the desire of ascending its Summit.' They did make the ascent and Frankland noted the 'stupendous groups of columns hanging over our heads in an imposing manner'.[26]

From the 1840s with the parameters of travel extended, more was published about Tasmania's mountains, and accomplished and amateur artists produced a number of paintings. Mount Wellington's relationship to Hobart made it especially appealing, with picturesque scenes of Hobart Town nestled at the foot of a 'lofty mountain ... forming a grand feature in the landscape'. In his *Views of Australia* (1824) Joseph Lycett included several paintings of Mount Wellington looming above Hobart, which forecast the sentiments expressed by an enthusiast some years later: 'the stupendous Mount Wellington frowns the beholder into insignificance'.[27] In 1846 a *Sydney Morning Herald* review of John Skinner Prout's *Tasmania Illustrated* praised his painting of Mount Wellington (entitled *The Female Factory, from Proctor's Quarry*), explaining: 'we like [this] better perhaps than any of its companions because it gives us a very fine piece of highland scenery'. In a diorama of Australian views exhibited extensively in England from 1850 to 1855 Prout included a painting of the same subject, commenting that the 'bold and rugged sides [of Mount Wellington] present a magnificent appearance'.[28]

The proximity of Mount Wellington to Hobart meant it was possible to ascend the summit and return to Hobart in a day, although some parties camped overnight and rose early next morning to see the sunrise before returning. The twelve-hour excursion, allowing three hours to explore the summit, was recommended for 'any moderately active pedestrian'. In 1837, soon after Sir John Franklin arrived to take up the vice-regal appointment, Lady Franklin and her party made the journey to Mount Wellington to admire the views. They set out at 4.30 a.m., arrived for

THE IMMENSE ROCK COLUMNS *of Ben Lomond in Tasmania were admired by nineteenth-century lovers of mountain scenery. (Frederick Grosse,* Ben Lomond, Tasmania, *1867?)*

MOUNTAINTOPS. *The rocky peak of Mount Wellington in Tasmania in the 1880s, above, and the heights of Mount Macedon in Victoria, opposite. (Above: J. W. Beattie,* Rocks on Mount Wellington, *1880s. Opposite: Samuel Calvert,* The Heights of Mount Macedon, *1878?)*

breakfast on top of the summit, after which the ladies rested on couches under 'crude shelters' especially constructed for them. The rest of the day was spent looking at views, plants and rocks, before setting up camp for the overnight stay planned so they could rise early next morning to see the sunrise. One of the party wrote a lengthy account of the excursion published in the local press, in which 'the

courage and activity of the ladies' was praised for their daring to walk along such perilous mountain tracks. The writing made Mount Wellington itself the focus of descriptions, especially its sheer size and the coming together of rocks, its mountainous character revealed in this statement: 'The old fable of the Titans' attempt to scale Heaven by heaping mountain upon mountain, and rock upon rock, recurs to the imagination on contemplating this fantastic grouping'. The emphasis on the coming together of rocks in fantastic shapes as a sublime characteristic endured. About fifteen years later author and painter Louisa Meredith also wrote of Mount Wellington's sublime features. She praised 'its summit of basaltic columns' for its 'ever-varying, but never decreasing grandeur'.

The language of the sublime that had been used initially in Australia as a response to the difficulties encountered in attempts to cross the Blue Mountains was now becoming commonplace in descriptions of other parts of the Australian colonies.[29] The rocky cliffs, gorges and ravines of Australian mountain ranges made up a local version of the sublime. In Van Diemen's Land sublime mountainous scenery was extended to include the castellated and pillar-shaped rocks on mountain summits, although much of this scenery also had gloomy glens and ravines. When Tasmanian summits were snow-covered, some comparison might be made with the Alps in Europe, as Louisa Meredith thought on first seeing Ben Lomond, and Paul de Strzelecki on seeing Frenchman's Cap. But this was not the predominant image of Australia's mountains in the nineteenth century. In South Australia, the Adelaide Hills were admired for the 'naked granitic precipices [which gave them] a character of romantic wildness', and the 'romantic effect of the glen, and the steep declivities of the hills', images that persisted for the rest of the century. Describing the view from Mount Lofty as 'truly Australian', George French Angas mentioned the rocky gullies intersecting 'abrupt hills', a few gumtrees and coloured by 'verdant grass'.[30] The Grampians in Victoria, a section of which was praised by Thomas Mitchell on his 1836 expedition to the Darling River as 'a truly sublime scene', were still recommended by the end of the nineteenth century for their 'deep gorges and precipitous cliffs afford[ing] a succession of views, grand, spectral, romantic and Dantesque'.[31]

The Snowy Mountains, straddling Victoria and New South Wales, bore a closer physical resemblance to European alpine regions, and this was often remarked upon.[32] Strzelecki described them in his 1840 expedition report:

> On entering [this region] ... every feature of that division seems to bear the stamp of foreign grandeur ... The Australian Alps, with its [*sic*] stupendous

peaks and domes; and in front the beautiful valley which the Murray so boun-
tifully waters; unite to form attractions for the explorer of no ordinary kind.[33]

Strzelecki was not saying that these mountains were more scenic than any others in
Australia, nor that such European portrayals of the sublime were superior to distinctively Australian types. He made this clear in *Physical Description of New South Wales
and Van Diemen's Land*, published on his return to England a few years after his
Australian expeditions. In this book Strzelecki praised other Australian landscapes for
their sublime character. He described the Blue Mountains' 'yawning chasms, deep
winding gorges, and frightful precipices' that lay between the ranges as 'narrow, gloomy,
and profound', and spent some time documenting the features that made up this scene.
For him Australia had scenery that profoundly challenged contemporary notions of
mountainscapes, but that could still be categorised as sublime. It also had scenery, especially in the Snowy Mountains, that corresponded to European expectations.[34]

By the late nineteenth century the alpine character of Mount Kosciuszko was
beginning to be reinterpreted and the point was made that this mountain did not
have the peak common in the northern hemisphere. A writer for the *Picturesque
Atlas of Australasia* explained:

> There is no sharpness or abruptness in the form of Mount Kosciusko. An
> Australian driver would take his coach and four to its topmost peak and
> drive about the huge stone cairn. … Kosciusko is a hummock of a great
> table-land, not a cone of peak springing from a plain.[35]

There was also acknowledgement that the term 'alps' might be excessive: 'around
Mount Kosciusko' wrote F. H. Mackay in a chapter on the 'Australian Alps' published in *Cassell's Picturesque Atlas of Australasia* (1887), the range 'assumes the
pretentious title of "the Alps"'.[36]

The earlier image of them as exemplary mountains, sublime in character, majestic
in appearance, persisted until the end of the century. In 1902, the Art Gallery of
New South Wales commissioned William Charles Piguenit to paint Mount
Kosciuszko, selecting him for his mastery of wilderness landscapes. Piguenit chose
the best perspective from which to paint the mountain in order to emphasise its

W. C. Piguenit, Kosciusko, *1903.*

height and steepness. The result was a painting of a grand mountain top amid swirling mists, barren, rocky, conceivably a wild entrance to the heavens. Piguenit's *Kosciusko* was one of the last major Australian wilderness paintings.[37]

These two perceptions of Mount Kosciuszko were not so much contradictory as expressive of how people shape nature (and nature shapes people). Both captured characteristics of the mountain, but from different vantage points. Piguenit had chosen a vantage point with views of the north-east side of Kosciuszko, enabling him to observe and paint great masses of steeply inclined rock and deep ravines, which lent themselves readily to depictions of grandeur. Most visitors to the mountain took the track from Jindabyne, with less impressive views of Australia's tallest mountain, corresponding more closely to the description in the *Picturesque Atlas of Australasia*, a 'hummock of a great table-land'.

The difference was not only one of perspective: it also represented a philosophical transition. Whereas, since the second half of the eighteenth century the language of the sublime had provided the means for people to express their appreciation of bold mountain scenery, by the end of the nineteenth century this was no longer the case. It is difficult to pinpoint precisely when the term fell out of use in Australia, the transition occurring during the last two decades of the nineteenth century. In the 1880s, as we have seen, travellers were still describing certain types of scenery such as mountains in terms of the sublime, but the same emphasis was no longer given to the transformative possibilities of the sublime, the state of being that arose from contemplating sublime scenery in which the onlooker was lifted out of ordinariness towards a state of inspiration. By the end of the nineteenth century, terms that had once challenged humans to achieve metaphysical greatness, were now used as travel clichés to point out notable landscape features, the contemplation of which was gently pleasant, even uplifting, but did not unsettle the senses.

HOW LIMESTONE CAVES
BECAME WONDERFUL

*In which the attractions of caves
are explained and their
development as public asset is discussed*

In 1841 George Webb decided he wanted to do something he'd never done before.* He had arrived in the colony of Western Australia two years earlier, settled in Perth and obtained a position in the colony's Commissary Department.[1] A sociable gentleman with an acute sense of the dramatic possibilities of irony, he announced his intention one evening to a gathering of the local reading club: 'I think I will go into the bush, walk perhaps twenty or thirty miles a day, not shave, wash, or comb my hair, sleep in my clothes, without changing my linen. In fact, I will get as dirty and tired as I possibly can; come home, take a fine swig of beer, jump into a large tub of water, flounder about in it for half an hour or so, get shaved, washed, combed, and *clean linened*, as Fanny Kemble would say, and then sit myself down in my morning gown and slippers, and if I'm not as happy as a prince, never give me credit for knowing what real comfort is.'[2]

One of the reading club members took him up. 'Just read an interesting account of some caves about two days journey from Perth. Mr Roe, our Surveyor-General, you know, organised a party—included the Governor, would you believe. Apparently Mr Grey had spotted some remarkable caves during one of his explorations a few years back, and Roe wanted to investigate them further. Thought they might contain fossilised bones and the like, which they didn't. But the caverns themselves … ! Hang about, there's the *Inquirer*, I'll read you some of what he saw. Ahhhh, here it is …

> The roof and caverned sides of this beautiful cave were still wet with the petrifying process, and the gloomy stillness was disturbed only by the constant dropping of water … Some of the numerous little side caverns from this chamber were extremely beautiful and interesting, their structure resembling in some instances a large oven, the floors thickly covered with smooth stalagmite, and the roofs finely fretted with innumerable pointed stalactites, having large prismatic drops, pendulous from their extremities.[3]

---

* This section of the chapter is a partially fictionalised account of George Webb's excursion to the Maidin Cave (later Yanchep) in Western Australia. See note 1 for further explanation.

'The Governor and Mr Roe seemed to have had a hard time of it ... lots of scrambling through narrow passages. That should get you dirty enough, Webb. There's a challenge for you! They've marked the entrance with a large diamond painted on a tree, so you should have no trouble finding it. Not only something you've never done before, but also something you've never seen before, eh? It's a good 35 miles away:—you should be well and truly stretched by the time you return. I promise to have the beer waiting for you!' George Webb and the others all chortled, and the conversation moved on in other directions.

The next morning, George made enquiries. Why not see the Maidin Caves for himself? He found two friends keen to join him, and they quickly made their preparations. They engaged Warrup, the Aboriginal guide who had accompanied John Roe and the governor. They acquired a pony, which they loaded up with necessities such as sugar, bread and brandy, animal traps and Harvey's Sauce for freshly caught game, bivouacs and mosquito nets for campsites, and caving equipment including candles, a large ball of twine, hammers and pick-axes. They enjoyed their comfortably paced outward journey, the excitement of adventure, the serenity of clear, still nights and the pleasure of good food and company, all of which helped to overcome the daily torment of heat, flies and mosquitoes. On their fourth day, after a sound night's sleep, they emerged from their mosquito nets and set out to find the tree on which Roe had painted his large diamond.

At the cave entrance they tied the loose end of the twine to a rock firmly embedded in the earth, adjusted their pick-axes and pannikins on their belts, lit their candles, and holding the ball of twine entered the rocky cleft. The unwound twine was to guide them out if their candles failed as had happened to Roe and the governor (who retraced their steps by following their line of twine). Webb and his friends moved slowly down a passage, single file and, as Webb was to write later, because 'the roof by degrees got gradually lower and lower ... were compelled to proceed on hands and knees, and indeed, in one place the passage was so circumscribed that the tin pannikins ... were crushed in forcing our way; but the roof again got more lofty'. At last, they could stand upright.

Augustus Earle, Mosman's Cave, Wellington Valley, New South Wales, *c. 1826.*

To reach this lofty chamber they had spent three days walking 36 miles, three nights camping in the bush, several hours scrambling to find the cave entrance, and what seemed an eternity squeezing through a muddy passage. But here was a wondrous sight the like of which not one had ever seen before. 'We found ourselves in a chamber', Webb wrote, 'from whose roof hung an almost innumerable number of stalactites, some of them hanging down several feet from the most lofty part, while all round pillars of the same structure reached the floor in a most beautiful and on our parts, most admired disorder'. Rising from the chamber floor were stalagmites as smooth as glass, some combining with stalactites to form impressive columns. Webb and his friends lit more candles, and the limestone crystals sparkled in a way that could only be described as dazzling. It was, really, a wonderful sight, wonderful to think that here beneath the earth there were such richly decorated chambers, caverns large enough for people to walk around, and all within relatively easy reach from Perth. Webb and his friends broke off several stalactites to be used later to illustrate what they had seen. Like Mr Roe and the governor they found no fossilised bones, but as they squeezed themselves out of the ground, they reflected on the causes of such a wondrous formation.[4]

George Webb undertook this excursion to the Maidin Caves in mid-November 1841, about a fortnight after John Roe's account of his excursion was published. Webb also had his account published locally. Both drew attention to what would interest an educated public: the possible discovery in caves of fossils or other organic remains to help the advancement of science, and the appraisal of limestone formations as beautiful objects in impressive settings. Cave touring itself was not new, but there was a relatively new appreciation of caves as wonderful.

The fashion for cave touring was well established among the upper classes in England in the eighteenth century. Poole's Hole and Peak Cavern in England's Midlands, like other caves visited by travellers, were enormous caverns, underground chambers connected by narrow passages. Their entrances were large enough to contain dwellings for the people who made a living from the tourist trade, beggars, guides and sellers of souvenirs made from local materials. By the late eighteenth century lady and gentlemen travellers visited the caves to view natural and human curiosities, including the 'hags' and 'witches' who lived at the entrances of the caves, their sinister appearance as much an attraction as the size of the cavern. The romanticisation of the grotto emphasised the shape of its entrance, the size of its cavern and the gloominess of the setting, and visitors expressed interest in these features using the newly emerging language of the sublime.[5] But visitors were not much concerned with the limestone formations, possibly because their experience was largely confined to the outer caverns that were usually more exposed to the vagaries of weather conditions, rather than the protected chambers deep within the rock. Limestone formations in exposed conditions dry out and develop a craggy, weathered appearance, becoming grotesque features hanging from cavern ceilings and walls, which would have added to the general gloominess associated with caves. Nor was there much discussion among visitors about the potential of caves for scientific enquiry, either as a repository for ancient bones or as a living demonstration of the agonisingly slow processes of nature. At a time when a common belief was that God had created the world in six days in 4004 BC, the curiosity of many travellers was to see what sort of world God had created rather than how. But as travel continued to inspire curiosity, and discoveries continued to challenge perceived wisdom, the attractions of caves soon expanded in previously unimagined ways. Central to this change was the human capacity for wonder, and astonishment in the search for the meaning of unexplained phenomena.

Compared with other European countries, the English were somewhat late in taking up caves as a scientific study. In the seventeenth century cave exploration in the Karst region of Slovenia, directed to finding underground sources of water (an activity carried on well into the nineteenth century), instigated techniques in cave exploration still in use today, marking out and measuring passages and noting some of the more pronounced features in order to understand where and how each cavern is connected to the next. The modern geological explanation for the existence of limestone formations was proposed in 1812 by the French naturalist Georges Cuvier, who stated that lime deposits were a consequence of carbonic acid in solution which dissolved limestone rock, and upon evaporation left glittering crystals. The theory was not published in English until 1820 and had to compete in English scientific circles for several decades with a number of incorrect theories. In 1823 William Buckland, the first Reader in Mineralogy in England (appointed in the mid-1810s at Oxford), produced a book on bones found in caves, which was one of the first widely circulated books in English to examine the scientific significance of caves, inspiring much subsequent underground excavation and cave exploration among the British. British geologists began to visit caves to collect fossils, and to study rock strata. Their discoveries focused tourist interest on these subterranean regions. Connected to this geological interest was the particular manifestation of the idea of the sublime inspired by caves because their existence was due to phenomena independent of human intervention (although at this early stage there had not yet developed an appreciation for the particular beauty of stalagmites and other limestone features).[6] In Australia in the first half of the nineteenth century, travellers setting out to view caves were part of a broader trend of cave touring.

Augustus Earle's watercolour *Mosman's Cave, Wellington Valley, New South Wales* (at what later became known as the Wellington Caves), painted on his travels in New South Wales in 1826, depicts men within recesses black as night except where illuminated by hand-held torches. It is one of the earliest colonial pictorial images of caves in Australia, and is in stark contrast to other landscapes of the time. Only darkness and rock, the sublime underground.

The Wellington Caves were of early scientific interest, particularly for their fossil bones. In 1831, on the basis of local reports of sizeable bone deposits, Sir

Thomas Mitchell undertook an expedition to collect specimens to send to Europe for further study. The deposits were of such scientific curiosity that the caves became well known in the European world of science. Mitchell produced two artistic illustrations, one showing the entrance of one of the caves, the other, their limestone formations and the enormity of one of the caverns. He also produced a carefully drawn map, a cross-section of the caves, on which he marked the location of major limestone deposits. His written account was scientific not romantic, describing passage lengths and the geological nature of the caverns, but the drawings introduced aesthetic elements to the scene, the sublime characteristics of large, dark caverns and massive formations hanging from the rock.

Soon after and probably as a consequence of Mitchell's visit, the Wellington Caves began to be described as both sublime and beautiful. Hamilton Hume on an expedition led by Charles Sturt wrote of a 'very large and beautiful cave'. James Backhouse visited the caves during his Australian travels in the 1830s and published an account in the early 1840s. He was clearly impressed by the size of the main cavern, over 100 feet long (about 30 metres) he estimated, with immense walls. He also likened the limestone formations to icicles and described their mass in one place as 'stupendous and remarkably beautiful'. By the early 1840s, visitors to the Museum in Sydney could view milky white stalactites and stalagmites from the Wellington Caves. Now there was a new dimension to cave touring in Australia and elsewhere in the world, the stalactites, stalagmites, helictites, columns and shawls.[7]

'Beautiful' or words indicating beauty were not initially used for this newly found limestone landscape, but they became terms employed by commentators to describe its formations and decorative features. It is possible that the idea of the beauty of stalactites and the like developed in Australia, even pre-dating the subsequently famous Mammoth Cave in Kentucky, in the United States. Initially, Mammoth Cave had been noted as the source of substantial amounts of the saltpetre used by the Americans during the 1812 war against Britain. In 1816, an

Thomas L. Mitchell, Large Cavern at Wellington Valley, New South Wales, *c. 1836*.

article about a mummified native American found in the Mammoth Cave helped advertise it as an interesting tourist destination, and by the 1830s Mammoth Cave was being praised for its sheer size, the 'monarch of caves … in grandeur, in wild, solemn, severe, unadorned majesty, it stands alone'. Not until the 1850s was much made of its limestone features.[8]

In the 1830s and 1840s New South Wales developed a reputation as the place to see limestone caves. In addition to the caves in the Wellington Valley, visitors were also forming parties to see what were later named Abercrombie Caves (near Bathurst) and Wombeyan Caves (near Goulburn). Abercrombie Caves were a convenient distance for a day excursion, and Conrad Martens visited there in 1843 and sketched caverns and stalagmite chambers. Soon after his return to Sydney he sold some of these sketches and also two paintings of the caves to W. C. Wentworth, indicating a broader interest in cave phenomena among colonists. In 1849 at the Promotion of the Fine Arts in Australia Second Exhibition in Sydney, he exhibited four paintings of the caves, presenting the artistic possibilities of caves as landscape. Wombeyan Caves were more difficult to get to than the caves at Wellington, but a pleasant excursion for those staying at nearby homesteads or farms. In 1841 Conrad Martens stayed in the region at Hannibal MacArthur's homestead on the Wollondilly River, visited the nearby caves and produced several watercolours. In his paintings of cave interiors the emphasis was on the sublime underground in dark, rocky caverns. However, some of these paintings also depicted limestone formations as milky white—in contrast to the surrounding gloom—highlighting the contrast between the beautiful and the sublime.[9]

By the late 1840s people were setting out on camping expeditions to visit caves located a good day's ride from Bathurst, and later known as Jenolan Caves. Travel accounts expressed sentiments that combined both the sublime and the beautiful to remark on the 'most grand and beautiful ornaments ever seen' and how it was 'impossible to give any thing like a description of the wonders and beauties of nature which there presented themselves'. From the 1850s as more people published accounts of their visits to limestone caves, they also explained more

Conrad Martens, Interior of the Burrangalong (Abercrombie) Cavern, *c. 1843–49.*

fully why they believed the character of the caves was more sublime and beautiful than previously believed. In his study of South Australia's geology the Rev. J. E. Tenison-Woods, an enthusiast for Australian scenery and geology, explained the mid-nineteenth-century fascination with caves in terms of sublime caverns adorned with beautiful features:

> Of all the natural curiosities a country can possess, none tend so much to render it famous as the existence of large caves. There is such an air of mystery in the idea of long subterranean passages and gloomy galleries shut out from light and life—so little is known of their origin, and they are generally accompanied with such beautiful embellishments of Nature—

that one is never tired of seeing them, or of hearing the description of those that cannot be visited.[10]

Tenison-Woods also noted that no one had yet described the 'rich and varied beauties ... the extraordinary natural curiosities that are to be met' in South Australia's caves, and so he did it himself. He drew upon his experience of the Mosquito Plains caves near Naracoorte in south-eastern South Australia, taking seven pages in his serious scientific study to describe the 'subterranean beauties' of just one cave (part of this description was to be quoted in other writers' accounts of visits to these caves). He wrote of the:

> pillars so finely formed, and covered with such delicate trellis-work ... that the eye is bewildered with the extent and variety of the adornment. It is like a palace of ice, with frozen cascades and fountains all around ... There is above and below—so that the roof glistens, and the ground crackles as you walk—a multitude of small stalactites, which fill the whole scene with frostings that sparkle like gems in the torchlight.[11]

Tenison-Woods was also an early enthusiast for the limestone wonders of the Great Barrier Reef. In the nineteenth century comparatively few people were to see it, so its story really belongs to the twentieth century, but by the second half of the nineteenth century scientific theory recognised that limestone rock, out of which caves and stalagmites are formed, was once coral reef. In 1842 Charles Darwin published his theory of coral reef formation, developed from his observations of different types of reefs, and his puzzlement over the formation of barrier reefs in particular. Subsidence, he argued, caused living coral to submerge to a depth where it died, thus forming 'dead coral-rock'—which later came to be recognised as limestone. Travel writers noted this connection between limestone caves and colourful coral reefs. Of Jenolan Caves, one nineteenth-century commentator wrote that it was 'hard to believe that this narrow band of hard grey rock was once the huge but fragile coral bank glistening in the bright waters with a thousand hues.'[12]

Science provided the means to explain the physical appearance of limestone caverns. Wonder was no longer only an emotional response to the fantastical arrangements of nature, but was also becoming a rational response to the possibilities of nature; knowing how stalagmites were formed made them no less wonderful to look at. This development was partly a consequence of the publication in English of C. G. C. Bischof, *Elements of Chemical and Physical Geology* (1854), an authoritative text on mineralogy which included information about stalagmites and stalactites.[13]

From the late 1850s some information, mostly brief, about the geology of limestone caves was published in travel accounts. They varied in detail, some merely speculating on the forces that created large open-ended caverns with 'piled-up and scattered rocks', or pondering the formation of limestone features with a bare rhetorical flourish: 'by what agency were these caverns first formed? Ay, what agency and how has nature succeeded in thus adorning them?'. Others were more scientific, correctly explaining that limestone formations were the result of carbonic acid dissolving the surrounding carbonate rock depositing calcium carbonate 'by a kind of dripping process' that formed stalactites and other formations. But no account concentrated on geological explanation.[14]

Sound geological explanations for the limestone formations at Jenolan Caves began to be published from the late 1870s, as a result of the thorough geological and topographical survey of the caves conducted by the New South Wales government. Dimensions of some of the caverns measured by local guides had occasionally been alluded to in articles about the caves, but this was a systematic survey by professional geologists who categorised and preserved information for future use, and it was conducted at a time when only a few other such surveys had been undertaken elsewhere in the world, for instance in Ireland, Jamaica and Indiana (USA) in the 1860s.

Interest in the Jenolan Caves survey probably persuaded governments to support other such investigations, notably in New South Wales where systematic surveys of a number of other limestone caves were conducted from the mid-1880s.[15] It is also possible that this scientifically conducted geological survey prompted international interest in Jenolan Caves. The New South Wales Legislative Assembly recorded a parliamentary comment that the caves 'have been known and become famous to the

GEOLOGICAL SURVEYS OF LIMESTONE CAVES *began elsewhere in the 1860s, and in Australia from the late 1870s. This sketch shows the 1878 survey camp at Mosquito Plains in South Australia, near the Naracoorte Caves. (Stephen King, [A Survey Camp on Mosquito Plains, Near Naracoorte], 1878.)*

scientific world', and at least two articles about the caves appeared in foreign scientific journals.[16]

From 1878 there was a bank of publicly available information to inform future travel accounts of limestone caves. Charles Wilkinson, the NSW geological surveyor in charge (who had been a member of the 1878 survey team), wrote an account of Jenolan Caves that was published and quoted at length in the last two decades of the nineteenth century in almost every major guidebook about the area. Wilkinson sought to interpret for a general audience what he called the 'silent rock teachings' of the caves and he made it an exciting yet accurate story about the enormous amount of time taken to produce the caves. He drew attention to the fossils in limestone rocks, observing that this 'now compact grey marble was once a mass of living corals' beneath an ocean: when the climate changed the coral reef died, over time forming limestone; then a 'convulsion of the earth's crust' weathered and eroded it over time, producing subterranean cavities large enough to hold a party of tourists, as well as the stalactites, stalagmites and other forms of calcium carbonate deposits that they had come to observe. Inside the caves, he said, 'the vastness and silence … fix the attention of the observer on the mute but beautiful forms that Time has slowly amassed under it'. Astonishment was a natural reaction to the time it took to form a stalactite: by the late 1880s guides were pointing out how little a stalactite had grown in the decade since it had been first measured, and authors speculated how many thousands of years before it would be a floor-to-ceiling column. A visit to the caves had now become a lesson in geology, an example of the wonder of nature, and a statement about the almost unimaginable age of the earth.[17]

By the end of the nineteenth century no other Australian cave system had had as much government money spent on it nor as many guidebooks published about it as Jenolan Caves. Jenolan Caves had become Australia's premier cave tourist resort. Whereas once the Wellington Caves had more tourists than any other cave system in Australia, from the 1880s the New South Wales government spent more on Jenolan than on any other cave system in the colony. Jenolan was closer to Sydney. It had not always been easy to reach, but by the 1870s the railway reached Mount Victoria and Tarana (between Lithgow and Bathurst), and the journey to the caves took considerably less time. The caves also drew visitors from the nearby Blue Mountains, fast developing as a fashionable tourist retreat. The cave system itself was extensive, the largest of any New South Wales cave system, and had generous deposits of sparkling limestone, more than enough to impress curious visitors. It was these factors that persuaded the government to spend money to develop Jenolan Caves.

By the mid-1890s many of Jenolan's caves were open to the public with structures in place to protect the fragile limestone and provide visitors with easier access. The story of their development shows the importance of public interest in the decision of the colonial government of New South Wales to pursue the tourist potential of Jenolan and other limestone caves. By the turn of the century, other colonial governments were also taking similar initiatives, persuaded that to invest reasonably large amounts of money in the protection of limestone caves might enable them to be opened up to the public in a way that more or less ensured their continued existence. The alternative was to do nothing, leaving them unprotected, thus open to cave enthusiasts to carry off stalactites and other formations to show friends and associates back home. Soon, logic dictated, there would be nothing left to see. As geological knowledge increased about the formation of these limestone beauties, especially the huge slabs of time needed, so did the realisation that destruction meant no one would see them again. The geological lessons from these natural wonders, their inspiration to the human imagination, would effectively be lost forever. Saving them as a public asset, and developing them for the enjoyment and edification of the people, was the aim of the civic-minded public officials who set about protecting and developing Australian cave systems. And in this, Jenolan Caves eventually led the way.

Until 1884, when they were officially proclaimed as the Jenolan Caves, this region 170 kilometres west of Sydney was known variously as McKeown's Caves, the Fish River Caves and the Binda Caves, but, it seems, never as the Jenolan Caves. Since the late 1840s the occasional party of lady and gentlemen travellers had toured the caves, and colonial newspapers published the travellers' accounts, and this was the main source of information about the caves until the last decades of the nineteenth century. Indeed, the caves were so little publicised mid-century that well-known chroniclers of Blue Mountains travel before 1850 (such as the American explorer Charles Wilkes and the Polish explorer Paul de Strzelecki) did not extend their journeys to take them in. This may have simply been because interest in limestone caves was only just developing. But even for those already interested it was not a journey to be lightly undertaken. In the 1860s there were still no amenities at the caves, no food or accommodation except that which had been organised for the parties before they set off. At the very least, a tour to the caves required about two weeks for a party travelling to and from Sydney, allowing for the four or five days travel by coach from Sydney to Bathurst, two days from Bathurst to the Caves (via Oberon), three days at the caves, and then the return journey.[18]

By the 1860s and 1870s a satisfactory tour to the caves still involved careful planning to ensure appropriate transport, comfort at the campsite and the services of a guide who knew which caves to visit. With camping equipment and supplies arranged, a party of as many as twenty or so young lady and gentlemen travellers would ride about fifty kilometres from Bathurst to one of the farms closest to the caves, with the caves still a full day's slow ride away. Until the mid-1860s they negotiated the services of one of the local farmers to act as guide, his daughters as cooks and sons as camp hands, and such tours provided a useful income supplement for farmers who opened their homes to tourists. From the mid-1860s travellers were required to organise their plans through a local farmer, Jeremiah Wilson, who lived at Oberon and had been appointed caretaker of the caves by the government in 1867.

Distance and the difficult terrain usually meant an overnight stay before an early start next day for the ride to the caves. The last part of the journey to the caves was seen as unsuitable for the 'timid or faint-hearted traveller'.[19] The descent into the valley was so steep that riders had to dismount and advance cautiously through dense trees and scrubs, negotiating loose bracken and, in wet weather, slippery mud. At the bottom of the rough track a notably narrow valley led into two grand, airy caverns—the Devil's Coachhouse and the Grand Arch—

both open at each end, allowing entry to sunlight and continuous draughts. In one or the other, a campsite would be established including an area for the lady travellers and makeshift screens of cloth and fallen tree branches to create 'sleeping apartments'. The journey was attractive because of the mountainous scenery and the sense of adventure, and there was opportunity to climb precipitous rocky outcrops near the campsite, shoot native birds, observe wallabies, and dance on the floor especially erected in the Grand Arch in the late 1860s. But the main reason for visiting the caves was underground, to see the 'beauties of these wonderful works of nature'.[20]

There had been some attempts to make the caves safer for tourists and preserve them from vandalism in the mid-1860s, although the major work was not begun until the late 1870s. In 1866, five years after the passage of the Crown Lands Acts, the governor of New South Wales declared that the caves and surrounding land would be reserved from sale and, thus, remain crown land, an early public recognition by an Australian government that the natural environment had value as a tourist destination.

The prime mover in these official measures was John Lucas who had first visited Jenolan Caves in the early 1860s. Elected to the New South Wales Legislative Assembly in 1860, Lucas four years later became the member for Hartley, an electorate on the western slopes of the Blue Mountains near the caves. He showed genuine concern about providing general public access to the natural environment, had land set aside for parks in country towns throughout New South Wales, and appreciated that there were local interests in protecting the Caves. Under the 1861 land acts, public land could be bought for private use; thus without action, the caves could have become private property. The families on farms located within a day's

THE JENOLAN CAVES *in New South Wales were of interest to scientists in the late nineteenth century when the French illustrator Albert Tissandier completed a series of seven drawings,* Les Grottes de Jenolan, *four of which were published in French scientific journals. (Engraver unknown,* Grottes de Jenolan—Montagnes Bleues [Australie], Vue du Devil's Coach-house, *c. 1880.)*

ride of the caves who catered to the small tourist trade would be under threat of an outsider buying up the land and ending local individual enterprise. John Lucas believed that government-protected local industries presented advantages to farmers and the labouring classes.[21]

Lucas was a conservationist, not one in the modern sense of the word (after all he had returned to Sydney from one of his expeditions to the caves laden with limestone loot, over 100 'specimens of the Caves, some being four feet long').[22] He recognised that the caves contained 'beautiful works of nature' and extended his belief in government protection of industry to protection of areas that could be enjoyed by an enlightened public and perhaps advance scientific knowledge. His parliamentary colleagues might have been persuaded by this argument, especially given well-publicised concerns in the United States about the ownership of major natural attractions. The privately owned Niagara Falls had been a tourist attraction from the eighteenth century, but by the 1860s most American commentators considered it spoiled by uncontrolled commercial development, and used its example to warn against the private development of other natural attractions; in 1864 Yosemite Valley was reserved for 'public use, resort and recreation' partly as insurance against commercial ravages.[23]

Between 1866, the year the caves area became a public reserve, and 1879, when the road from Oberon was due to open, not much changed. The annual budget of £50 had been authorised by the Legislative Assembly in 1866 and was not increased until 1879. Part of this annual budget was a stipend to Jeremiah Wilson as keeper of the caves. Wilson was expected to protect the caves from tourists eager to collect specimens of limestone formations, to conduct cave inspections, to undertake minor improvements in day-to-day camp life for the comfort of visitors, to provide and maintain equipment for touring the caves, such as iron ladders and ropes, and to report to the Department of Lands, the government body responsible for the area, including when limestone was souvenired.[24]

Wilson's information was basic, not much more than a few details about visitors to the caves, but it did alert the authorities that numbers were enough to warrant concern about preserving the caves. In 1872 the Department of Lands issued a notice that 'persons are in the habit of mutilating and destroying the stalactites' and those caught 'will be prosecuted according to law'. In 1878 it organised the survey of the region that helped influence government policy. Philip F. Adams, the surveyor-general who led the surveying expedition, was horrified that 'so valuable a public property' was guarded by a part-time non-resident caretaker. (This was not to blame Jeremiah Wilson. After all, there was no caretaker accommodation at the caves, and Wilson had to make the difficult 20-kilometre trek from his property to conduct his inspections. Nor had Wilson been appointed a full-time keeper: the reasons for this are unclear, although members of parliament who voted for the position and these conditions probably wanted to save money.) To provide security Adams strongly recommended iron gratings and doors at immediately accessible openings. To ensure safety inside, he proposed steps and handrails to replace the wire-ladders erected by Wilson and recommended they be installed in all caves later opened to the public. With further access routes planned, such as the road from Oberon and a bridle track from Katoomba (built in 1884 by the government) he believed that the numbers of visitors would increase significantly and with insufficient protection the destruction of the caves would continue at an alarming rate.[25]

The aim was not to prevent people visiting the caves, but to establish a means by which fragile subterranean formations could be viewed without damage, even with greatly increased numbers of visitors. This new interest in the caves as public asset fitted in with the broader government policy of the time of providing edifying entertainment for the public's enjoyment. To this end several major public institutions were established, such as the national park south of Sydney (John Lucas, the same politician who supported the caves as a public reserve, was a park trustee), a public art gallery, a public library and, interestingly, a geological and mining museum, established in 1875 by the Department of Mines and under the direction of Charles Wilkinson, the NSW geological surveyor, who a few years later was part of the 1878 expedition to survey the caves. Throughout the 1880s and early 1890s the government spent thousands of pounds on the caves (compared with less than £500 for the whole period between 1867 and 1878).[26] Access roads were constructed or upgraded, passages within caves were redesigned, ladders were attached to sheer rocks, steps carved, bridges erected over chasms. These changes were designed to protect the caves, as well as visitors, by creating a clearly marked path past particular geological treasures, so that visitors would know where and where not to tread. In the 1880s the first electric lights were installed expressly to protect a recently discovered cave from the smoke damage apparent in other caves that had been caused by the candles held by visitors.[27]

These 'improvements' at Jenolan Caves became the standard for cave development with the NSW Department of Mines overseeing the protection, development and survey of the colony's main limestone caves at Abercrombie Caves near Bathurst, Wellington Caves, Wombeyan Caves near Goulburn and Yarrangobilly Caves in the Snowy Mountains. By the early 1890s accommodation houses had been built at remote caves such as Wombeyan and Yarrangobilly.[28]

By 1897 the New South Wales government had spent more than £23 000 on developing limestone caves—much of this during years of economic depression—yet in the previous year only 5569 people had visited seven cave systems, more than half choosing Jenolan or Wellington caves. Jenolan had the largest share—a total of 1816 visitors. The hope was that spending money to open up the caves for tourism would bring commerce to country regions as well as enabling colonists to be edified by natural wonderlands. But altruism was also involved since the government had decided visitors should not be charged for cave tours. Visitors did have to buy their own magnesium ribbon or candles to see the caves, but even with almost 100 per cent mark-up on these goods, in 1896 the profits were less than £100.

Members of parliament in other colonies urged development of limestone caves. Again, the point was not to make money out of the caves themselves: they were to be reserved and developed for public use and recreation. (But by advertising subterranean wonders, a chance to explore underground, there was the possibility of attracting visitors from other colonies, or the colony itself, and boosting local economies, although this was not explicit in debates about the public expenditure on caves). Steps were taken to preserve the caves at Naracoorte in South Australia by proclaiming them a reserve in 1885, appointing a caretaker and thereafter making 'improvements' to open up the caves for public recreation. In Western Australia at the turn of the twentieth century local residents of the Yallingup district in the south-western corner lobbied the government to protect their limestone caves. Visited since

A PARTY OF TOURISTS *at Naracoorte Cave in South Australia in 1890.* *(Photographer unknown,* Naracoorte Cave, *c. 1890.)*

at least the 1880s, by the 1890s there were already signs of 'vandalism' in the caves at Yallingup with names carved into rocks and limestone looted.

Following the example set with Jenolan Caves, the Western Australian government instigated a geological survey, proclaimed the caves a reserve in 1892 for the protection and development of the caves as a tourist attraction. But when moves were made to make the reserve inalienable under the new Western Australian *Parks and Reserves Act* (1895), local farmers objected to having so much land tied up for what they saw as a playground for city-dwellers. The government, wanting the caves protected, responded to this local lobby by rescinding the proclamation of the original reserve and instead making a number of small, inalienable reserves around cave entrances. A similar story surrounded the protection and development of the caves at Yanchep, those which Roe and Webb had explored more than sixty years before.[29]

The developments at Jenolan in the last two decades of the nineteenth century also became a model for other colonial limestone enterprises. One cave at Naracoorte was developed following preservation principles established at Jenolan: protect significant natural features with chicken wire barriers and fence paths with sturdy iron railings. Frank Wilson, once a cave guide at Jenolan, advised on developments at Yallingup and various limestone caves in Victoria, before becoming manager of Buchan Caves in Victoria in 1907 (visited for their subterranean features at least since the 1880s).[30]

Throughout the 1880s and 1890s along with detailed geological descriptions, publications about limestone caves still saw them as representing the concepts of the sublime and the beautiful. In terms of the sublime, caves were 'wild-looking', filled with 'ghostly shadows from the lights of our candles', where 'darkness and silence reign'. Cave features could provoke extreme emotions: 'involuntary shudders' when contemplating 'abysmal depths'; wonder, bafflement and puzzlement when considering the formation of certain features. In terms of the beautiful, writers vied to present lavish descriptions of these limestone formations, marvelling at their colour, shape, their smoothness, how they glittered. One writer said of a cave at Jenolan that it surpassed 'any other cave in the known world for exquisite beauty, extent and variety of lovely deposits'.[31] Their commercial development helped to open this experience to travellers, but the strong government involvement in financing them was a form of colonial altruism, a public investment in providing opportunities for the edification of the people through inspiration in response to the wonders of nature.

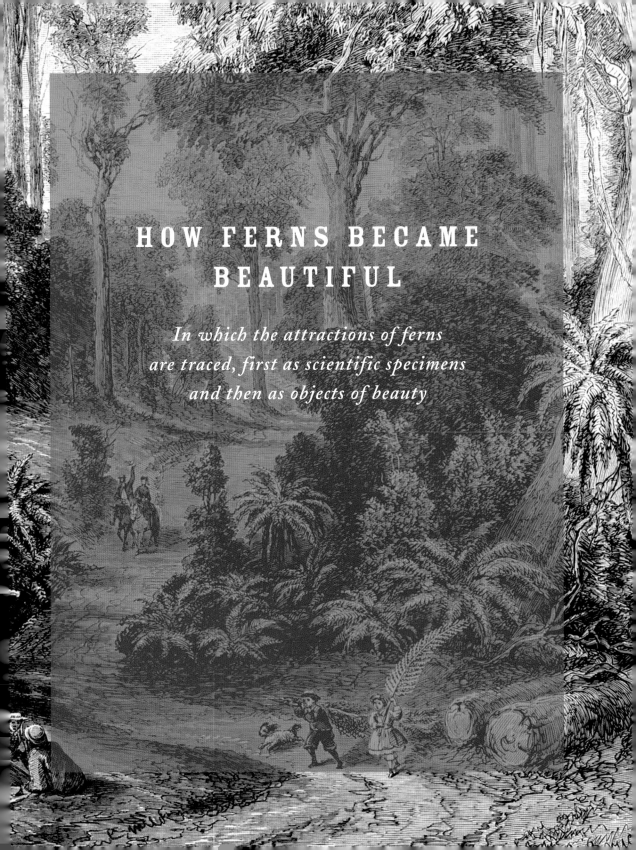

HOW FERNS BECAME BEAUTIFUL

*In which the attractions of ferns
are traced, first as scientific specimens
and then as objects of beauty*

B y 1900 the feathery fronds of the fern were well established as a symbol of middle-class taste. Ferns were a feature of suburban gardens and a decorative motif for silverware, and graced bridal bouquets, dining room tables and drawing rooms. They were also a reason for sight-seeing trips. Thomas Cook's *Railway Official Guide Book to Tasmania* (1895) recommended Tasmania's magnificent fern gullies. At Mount Wellington, tourists were directed to view 'a deep gloomy fern tree gully', and at the Hartz Mountains, 'natural ferneries'. Where gullies had no ferns, as in the case of Cataract Gorge in Tasmania, locals planted some to make a natural attraction even more appealing to turn-of-the-century taste.[1]

But unlike aesthetic appreciation for mountain landscapes, views or caves, ferns did not begin to receive popular consideration until several decades into the nineteenth century in Australia (and Britain, North America and other countries). There was, however, scientific interest in ferns from the late eighteenth century, as new ideas and frameworks of knowledge highlighted the importance of Australia's distinctive natural environment for expanding the horizons of scientific knowledge. This scientific interest was largely expressed in Latin, then the international botanical language, without the sentimental response that was increasingly a feature of travel descriptions about natural scenery. Nonetheless, this scientific interest aroused a more general appreciation of ferns, not just for their scientific value, but also as objects of intrinsic beauty and evidence of the wonders of nature.

This scientific interest arose largely as a result of botanical studies becoming a serious and professional pursuit by men of science. By then there was some knowledge of ferns based on varieties found in Europe, and Linnaeus had included them in his botanical schema. The observation of ferns in other parts of the world presented an intriguing problem about how these new specimens might be classified.[2] Ferns, along with mosses, lichens and fungi—what were then called cryptogams—did not have stamens or pistils, and so could not be easily classified using the Linnean method based on sexual characteristics. Improvements in the compound microscope in the first half of the nineteenth century helped with the correct identification of ferns, but before then, a number now separated into distinct species were thought to be the same, and vice versa.[3] Thus ferns were a scientific mystery, objects of curiosity sought out on travels, and this fostered the collection of a huge variety of samples.

Travellers keen on botany searched for novel specimens on their excursions, especially if their travels took them through moist, rocky terrain. La Billardière, naturalist on the expedition to the Pacific in search of La Perouse, observed many new Australian botanical species, including sixteen ferns from Van Diemen's Land. In 1806 he published the second volume of his large folio work on the botany of New Holland and Van Diemen's Land, which included botanical drawings of these ferns.[4] About a decade after La Billardière's tour, but before the publication of his work, Robert Brown, naturalist on Matthew Flinders' coastal surveys, collected at least 106 fern species, almost half of these from Van Diemen's Land, where his planned excursion of several weeks extended into many months due to unexpected delays on the return to Port Jackson. Initially frustrated by this delay (and unimpressed by the botany around the River Derwent), Brown turned it to his advantage making ten botanical excursions to Mount Wellington, where he collected most of his Tasmanian fern specimens. Although aware of previous French excursions to the same region, and the possibility that he was making no new botanical discoveries, he was, nonetheless, positioned as a British authority on Australian ferns.[5] He included details of the varieties in *Prodromus Florae Novae Hollandiae et Insulae Van Diemen* (1810), the first (and only published) volume of his major work on Australian botany.

Robert Brown was one of the first European travellers to present Australian fern varieties not simply as different from those in Britain: their extent was so great as to arouse further scientific enquiry. Ferns thrived in parts of Australia and to understand why would help advance botanical theory. He made these points in an article published as an appendix to Flinders' *Voyage to Terra Australis* (1814). Written in English and attached to a travel book with a more general readership than usual for scientific writings, the article advanced the theory that geography had a substantial bearing on botany, and on where species originated. (We now take this for granted, but this 'commonsense' was only being worked out in the first decades of the nineteenth century.) He established that ferns in their natural state flourished within strict geographical limits—the lower latitudes—but, there, could tolerate cold climates, even snow, as did the tree ferns of Van Diemen's Land. He also, in spite of classification problems, set Australian ferns in a world context. The Australian colonies had, he judged, about 100 varieties, or 10 per cent of fern species then thought to exist throughout the world. Of the Australian varieties, only a quarter were also native to other countries. Brown described some peculiar to Australia as 'remarkable' in their differences to other species. He was intrigued that only one of the species found in Australia existed in the same latitude in the northern hemisphere, and even more that there were no tree ferns in the northern hemisphere beyond the tropics, even though they existed in Australia's southern latitudes. But most interesting of all was the number of Australian ferns. He took Norfolk Island as an example showing how, despite its small area, it had as many fern species as were then thought to exist in the whole of Britain.[6]

By referring to a large number of ferns, both La Billardière and Brown helped raise interest in solving the puzzle of classification, which by the second half of the nineteenth century had been achieved. With a reliable methodology for identifying ferns, those interested in botany now might delight in identifying species when on excursions, or even make new finds. As well as seeing ferns in their natural habitat, travellers could also buy them (along with other native plants) from local nurserymen. In 1836 Daniel Bunce advertised ferns in his Hobart nursery catalogue, probably acquired on his regular tours of Van Diemen's Land to collect indigenous plants.[7]

In the Australian colonies, it was initially tree ferns that aroused most appreciation, a magnificent and unusual sight to behold, and from about the 1820s often noted by botanically inclined travellers wherever they came across them. At this stage the ferns were only mentioned in passing, and mostly for their height rather than their beauty. This development represented the change from tree ferns being sought after as botanical specimens, to their recognition as both botanically intriguing and notable features within interesting and spectacular scenery. Seeing just a few tree ferns during his trip through the Blue Mountains the botanist Alan Cunningham expressed delight at their 'grandeur and magnificent appearance', and their 'stupendous size'.[8] In the Illawarra, tree ferns and other vegetation, notably extensive tracts of cabbage palms, as well as sea views were praised as worthwhile scenery. Macquarie's description of his descent from the escarpment near Mount Keira to the Illawarra (in the region of today's Wollongong and Port Kembla) included satisfaction with the 'grand magnificent bird's eye view of the ocean … and the low country' before the descent through a forest of tree ferns, cabbage palms and the 'largest and finest forest trees I have ever seen in the colony'.[9] Macquarie's account was publicised—although nothing he published about his tours beat the publicity generated by his Blue Mountains' journal—around the same time that the Illawarra became a noteworthy travel destination in the 1820s.

The escarpment near Mount Keira afforded magnificent prospects of the Illawarra—sea, land and sky—before the descent to the coastal plains through a forest of tropical vegetation. Even Barron Field, not usually a lover of Australian forests, raved about the luxuriant dispersal of vines, cabbage palms and tall tree ferns among the cedar trees. The term 'rainforest' was not yet used by travellers. Instead they wrote of 'luxuriant' and 'tropical' growth. The cabbage palms gave a sense of Australianness to the scene; the tree ferns and vines, a hint of the tropical (a persistent connection, even though many Australian tree ferns grow in temperate climates). Augustus Earle presented this vegetation as the setting for his painting, *A Bivouac of Travellers in Australia in a Cabbage Tree Forest, Day Break*, exhibited at the Royal Academy in

Conrad Martens, Tree Fern, *c. 1835–36.*

London in 1838.[10] John Skinner Prout's painting *Tree Fern* was displayed at the 1849 Sydney show organised by the Society for the Promotion of the Fine Arts in Australia. Prout included *Descent of Mount Keera* [*sic*], *Illawarra* in his travelling diorama exhibition in England in the 1850s, describing the region as 'fertile, beautiful and romantic' with scenery 'diversified by [cabbage] palm trees, ferns, and nettles'.[11]

A tree fern valley on the lower slopes of Mount Wellington in Van Diemen's Land became a travellers' stop in the 1830s. From then developed the notion that a grove of tree ferns was a notable sight in itself, and even if not peculiarly Australian, certainly a remarkable feature of Australian scenery. These tree ferns became the subject of paintings and descriptive accounts, statements made about their attractive features and, for the first time, judgements about why they were beautiful. John Glover included a painting of these tree ferns in his 1835 London exhibition as an example of antipodean scenery.[12] Many travellers, including Charles Darwin and botanist Alan Cunningham, went to Mount Wellington both for its views and on account of its growing botanical reputation.[13] One favourable way to the summit was through this valley of tree ferns, many twenty feet high, some with broad trunks. The fronds created an interlaced ceiling above, concealing the forest canopy, the effect said to epitomise the elegance and splendour of tree ferns. James Backhouse, a Quaker missionary interested in botany, who visited the Australian colonies in 1832, was expansive:

> above was the noble crest of fronds … exceeding 11 feet in length … and of the tenderest green, rendered more delicate by the contrast with the dark verdure of the surrounding foliage … [There were also] small membranaceous [*sic*] ferns of great delicacy and beauty. On a rocky bank adjoining, there were other ferns, with creeping roots, that threw up their bright green fronds … decorating the ledges on which they grew. In the deepest recesses of this shade I could enjoy the novel scene—ferns above, below, around—without fear of molestation; no dangerous beasts of prey inhabiting this interesting island.[14]

Darwin in 1839 remarked: 'In some of the dampest ravines, tree-ferns flourished in an extraordinary manner … The foliage of these trees, forming so many most elegant parasols, created a gloomy shade, like that of the first hour of night.' It was the decorative effect of the fronds and other ferny elements that made the scene, the key element of which was colour—but a delicate and beautiful colour enhanced by shade. Soon after arriving in Van Diemen's Land, J. S. Prout, on one of his sketching tours to Mount Wellington, captured this setting with its restful, shady recesses, canopies of feathery fronds, and the delicate green of the tree ferns. One of his watercolours was included in *Tasmania Illustrated*, a series of lithographs published in 1844, and some were probably included in the Hobart Town Art Exhibitions in 1845 and 1846.[15]

Backhouse also included in his travel account a sketch of a similar setting, noble crests of fronds, and luxuriant growth, reaching towards the sky. It inspired a fellow Quaker Frederick Mackie many years later to find that exact spot: 'I was highly delighted with the splendour of the tree ferns … Their ample spread, their light and feathery appearance with the bright hue of the green cannot fail to attract even a careless observer'.[16] Mackie's account was published posthumously, but, earlier, as an unpublished journal of a Quaker mission it was probably read by other Quakers.

By the time Louisa Meredith published her Tasmanian travel account in the early 1850s, there was already concern about the destructive tourist element, and she lamented that the Mount Wellington tree fern valley, now a favourite resort of picnic and sketching parties, was littered with champagne bottles and 'sandwich papers'. Tree fern gullies were magnificent sights, but not when filled with litter, and Meredith recommended, instead, the splendid tree ferns in the Port Sorell area, about which she too used words from the developing conventions of tree fern description: an 'enchanted valley … exquisitely beautiful', green with ferns of all descriptions, tall tree ferns forming a thick canopy overhead.[17] For her, Mount Wellington was still a sight to behold, but as a rugged mountainous backdrop to Hobart, and for the extensive views of surrounding districts from its summit. Despite the litter, Mount Wellington's tree fern valley remained a favourite place to

TREE FERN GULLIES *were a favourite excursion destination. J. S. Prout captured the much admired effect of sunlight on the green fronds in this painting. (John Skinner Prout, [Fern Tree Gully, Possibly Mount Wellington], 1844–48.)*

visit throughout the nineteenth century, largely because of the continued interest in ferns, its proximity to Hobart (Tasmania's major port) and the magnificent views from Mount Wellington's summit. Travellers could combine in the one trip up Mount Wellington the requisite experiences of a successful tour—sublime mountain views and luxuriant ferns.

The Dandenong Ranges in Victoria, however, were beginning to provide competition. European interest in these ranges was sparse before the 1850s, apart from a few exploratory and surveying excursions. The name 'Dandenong' (spelt variously) was not settled upon until the mid-1850s, when the names 'Western Port Range' and 'Corhanwarrabul' were no longer used. J. S. Prout, ever the prolific watercolourist, painted the *Dandenong Ranges, Victoria* on an excursion to Victoria in 1846–47, and decades later this depiction was widely circulated in E. C. Booth's *Australia Illustrated* (1873–76). Compared to other Victorian mountain ranges—and to the Blue Mountains, Tasmania's mountains and even Mount Lofty—the Dandenong Ranges were considerably lower in height, and this may have been why they did not initially attract the sentimental attention given to mountainous terrain seen as sublime.

But soon European settlement became established in the foothills, and word spread of valleys filled with tall, slender tree ferns. In 1853, government botanist in Victoria, Ferdinand von Mueller (director of Melbourne's botanical gardens, 1857–73) made an excursion to the Dandenongs to survey the region's botany, and marvel at these tree ferns. A published account of this excursion written by John Walters, botanist at Melbourne's botanical gardens, described the 'stately forms of the tree ferns' creating an exotic landscape, 'a sight I shall never forget'. That ferns could be so tall and broad surely conveyed, he said, 'an idea of something like part of a tropical landscape'. He also noted the abundance of small ferns, helping to make this scene a 'fairy retreat'. Even if brief, Walters' description of the gully of tree ferns helped establish the scene as culturally significant, as had happened with tree fern valleys in Van Diemen's Land. Rather than provide botanical descriptions of a specimen, he described it as an experience, and one worth repeating. Mueller was also impressed, years after his own first visit, recommending a visit to Ferntree

Gully to see the 'magnificent displays of tree ferns bathed in vapour from innumerable springs or torrents … [leaving] on the lover of nature the remembrance of their inexpressible beauty'.[18]

A few years later, after Walters' and Mueller's first visit, and probably as a consequence of their enthusiasm, Eugen von Guérard and Nicholas Chevalier accompanied a party of ladies and gentlemen to the Dandenongs to see a gully of tree ferns. Both painted scenes of the impressive tree ferns. But it was the widespread exhibition of Guérard's *Ferntree Gully* (1857), as Tim Bonyhady has documented, that initiated public recognition of the area and contributed to debate about the exemplary quality of colonial scenery. The area came to be known as Ferntree Gully as a consequence of this painting. Despite the use of the phrase 'fern tree gully' to describe any such gully in the Australian colonies—Chevalier painted *Fern Tree Gully in the Australian Alps* (1862)—the phrase had, by the 1860s, become synonymous with this Dandenong gully, at least to those who lived in Melbourne.

Guérard included a lithograph of his painting in *Australian Landscapes* (1867), describing the gully as 'one of the most characteristic and beautiful features of the mountain scenery of Australia'. By the late 1860s it was, according to Guérard, a 'favourite resort for summer tourists' that could be a one-day excursion from Melbourne, with the highlight being a picnic in Ferntree Gully amid the ferns, the 'jewels of nature's scenery', as one guidebook called them, although according to Hingston's *Guide for Excursionists from Melbourne* (1868) not many people knew about the gullies of tree ferns in the Dandenongs despite their proximity to Melbourne.

This changed in 1869 when the city of Melbourne organised an official excursion for hundreds of invited guests to Ferntree Gully to celebrate the visit of the British Navy's Flying Squad. The excursion had been well publicised: crowds of flag-waving children cheered the convoy as it made its way out of Melbourne and on to the Dandenongs. Subsequently, various aspects of the excursion were reported—with gossipy observations about ladies accompanying members of the squadron on the return journey—and included reactions to the scenery encountered in the gullies. The *Illustrated Australian News* reporter appreciated the attractiveness of the scenery in the Dandenongs generally, 'but where the fern-trees were, the effect was exquisite' due to the different shades of green, the arched canopy of tree fronds joined together at 'ever-varying angles', allowing the sun to peep through at different points. This description with its suggestion that the scene was like a sparkling emerald, continued to promote the idea of these gullies, where tree ferns grew profusely, as full of 'nature's jewels'.

Whether these gullies reminded onlookers of fairy retreats or exquisite jewels, the particular compliment was directed to the scene as a whole: the effect was

MOUNT MACEDON'S TREE FERN GULLIES, *like those in the Victorian Dandenongs, were threatened by saw-milling activities, although, ironically, it was the tramways and tracks maintained by the timber industry that helped open the region's attractions to tourists. This engraving depicts an 1869 picnic party with evidence of forest logging (at bottom right). (Robert Bruce,* A Christmas Party on Mount Macedon, *1869?)*

created by a mass of tree ferns rather than individual specimens. Cut down all but a few tree ferns, pick off fronds here and there, and the particular effect would be lost. In the early 1860s, there was considerable public argument for the protection of Ferntree Gully and the surrounding area, in view of timber-getters establishing themselves in these gullies. Yet the colonial government did little to ensure their protection. It ignored the surveyor's 1862 recommendation to create Ferntree Gully as Victoria's first reserve preserved for scenic reasons. There was some environmental hope when the authorities declared 26 500 acres of the Dandenongs a State Forest in 1867. The aim of the reservation was initially to try to regulate the local timber-felling industries, but was extended to the protection of tree fern gullies. In 1870 the authorities set out the rules and regulations governing the use of the forest, establishing as an offence the removal of 'ferns, trees or fronds of fern trees' (or any native shrub) without permission. Although these regulations stayed on the books for the rest of the nineteenth century, they were rarely enforced, and the area they applied to quickly shrank—in the first ten years, by 10 000 acres, and by 1894, by more than another 10 000 acres. As the land was largely reclaimed for small mixed farms, vegetation was cleared, land-holders often illegally selling uprooted tree ferns to city-dwellers. Mueller in a passing comment in his report on the 1866–67 Intercolonial Exhibition had recommended them as 'ideal garden ornaments'. By the 1890s gardening books were giving instructions on how to plant and maintain tree ferns. Mrs Boldrewood recommended tree ferns as beautiful with 'their straight stems and graceful spreading heads', explaining how to use them as decorative features in the suburban home and garden.

In the following years, as some suburban gardens gained a small grove of tree ferns, many of the Dandenong's acclaimed gullies were denuded of their tree ferns, although there remained the 412 acres of Ferntree Gully reserved in 1882 for public recreation and the protection of the tree ferns. As Tim Bonyhady demonstrates, by the late 1880s arguments were put forward to preserve this area as a national park. This never occurred, although the Melbourne press referred to the area as a national park in the late 1880s. There were local protests against settlement in the early 1890s, and protesters appealed to Victorians to 'at once come forward and assist to protect this, their own exceptional heritage, the great National Park, with its giant sassafras and fern gullies'. The reclaimed land for settlement was part of a government scheme to provide crown land to the unemployed to help them become, at the very least, self-sufficient, if not economically productive. As Michael Jones suggests in *Prolific in God's Gift. A Social History of Knox and the Dandenongs* (1983), the local protesters may generally have been ill-disposed to the idea of large amounts of productive land tied up in the Dandenong State Forest (also a concern of protesters against the proposal to declare a large reserve around the Yallingup Caves in Western Australia), and perhaps even unsympathetic to the idea that fern gullies should be preserved as part of the colony's natural heritage for the enjoyment of city-dwellers. But the alternative, the threat of an invasion of poor people, was worse. The settlement scheme was largely a failure, and within years, cleared land plots with ramshackle structures were being sold to some city-dwellers keen to have a holiday retreat.

In 1888 guidebooks were still directing visitors to the Dandenongs to view the tree ferns, ranging in height to thirty feet (9 metres), for the 'beauty of the scene'. But by the turn of the century, the landscape around Ferntree Gully and Sassafras Gully was starting to take on its modern appearance of holiday retreats set in pleasant gardens filled with exotics. Contemporary guidebooks directed tourists to Sherbrooke Forest for the lyrebirds and Ferntree Gully for 'fern glades' amid the 'gigantic eucalypts'—leftovers from the land clearances. Visitors were still directed to see exquisite scenes created by dappled light through interlacing fern fronds, but were no longer able to admire their previously praised extent.[19]

The story of the gigantic eucalypts—the wide-trunked mountain ash reaching hundreds of feet high—in the Dandenongs (and other parts of Victoria and Tasmania) is not unrelated to that of tree ferns. For one, their dense growth, great heights and profuse foliage at the very top of their trunks helped create perfect shady conditions for tree ferns. As a natural attraction worth viewing they had their followers, as did the karri, the tall eucalypts in south-western Western Australia. But aside from naming a few favourite trees in Victoria, and preserving a tall stringybark in Tasmania for the enjoyment of the people, those who argued for the preservation of these forests as remarkable features of Australian scenery (among various reasons) never succeeded. The government line in all colonies was that trees were an important economic resource, and where possible, to be protected and regulated as a renewable resource, but not as a natural wonder, although visitors were welcomed in state forests to admire these tall trees while they still stood. Yet as we have seen, arguments for the preservation of other types of natural attractions in Australia, such as mountain landscapes, caves and even tree ferns, often did succeed insofar as rudimentary steps were put in place, which at the very least officially recognised these sights as wonderful and important public assets even if they were subsequently partially destroyed. This never happened to Australia's tall trees even though elsewhere in the world a sentimental appreciation of tall trees did exist, sufficient to establish them as sights to be preserved for the people's enjoyment for all time.

In North America in the second half of the nineteenth century there was a growing appreciation for tall trees, most famously the Mariposa grove of 'Big Trees' in Yosemite. As John Sears argues in *Sacred Places* (1989), for decades there had been a debate about the natural beauty of trees and their effect on human sentiment and importance to American scenery. When the Mariposa 'Big Trees' first came to the attention of Europeans in the 1850s, they were almost immediately proclaimed a valuable cultural asset, a part of American national identity, to the extent that the grove (and Yosemite Valley) were reserved for public use in the 1860s, to try to forestall the sort of commercial development notorious at Niagara Falls.[20] In

Australia, the creation of the Dandenong State Forest in 1867 led to the introduction of government regulations on the felling of trees—a permit was needed—but whereas under these regulations tree ferns were to be protected for their aesthetic value, cutting down eucalypts was allowed for their economic value, but regulated to help promote them as a renewable resource.

In Australia economic concerns largely prevailed. Still, there was appreciation for the magnificence of these trees, especially in terms of size and as rivals to the American Big Trees. After Mueller's and Walters' tour of the Dandenongs in 1853, Walters had written of 'some of the finest timber trees which it is possible to have any idea of … clear of branches and as clean as a walking stick' for well over 100 feet (30 metres) high. His comments referred to their economic value as timber, but helped establish as unique the sight of tall broad tree trunks, branchless for more than the height of some of the tallest buildings then existing. Mueller later wrote of the 'grand picture to see a mass of enormously tall trees of this kind, with stems of mast-like straightness and clear whiteness, so close together in the forest as to allow them space only toward their summit to send their scanty branches and sparse foliage to the free light'. Despite such accolades these towering eucalypts were not preserved for the enjoyment of colonists. Tree-felling was encouraged and the disastrous practice of stripping bark off living trees for huts and such continued. Dead trees—including waste left by tree-fellers—created substantial fuel for devastating bushfires that swept through tracts of land.

This triumph of commercial imperatives conceals the sentimental attachment to Victoria's tall forests held by some colonists. Bonyhady has explained in detail that

WESTERN AUSTRALIA'S GIANT KARRI *was praised in the nineteenth century as a 'grand noble tree', and was the timber of choice for planking, beams and street-paving. There was no public interest in preserving these forests for their scenery. Now, the forestry industry co-exists with a tourist industry that encourages visitors to see old-growth forests. (Archibald James Campbell*, Karri Forest, Western Australia, *post 1870.)*

there were strongly expressed if ultimately ineffectual voices in support of preserving these forest giants. Mueller pleaded to preserve Victoria's native forests 'as a heritage given to us' which, if wisely used, might be maintained forever, singling out the mountain ash as 'among the wonders of the world'. When the preservation of the mountain ash became the subject of a hotly contested political debate in the late 1880s, those proposing the preservation of the trees, including members of the parliamentary Opposition and journalists, failed to change government policy on granting saw-millers greater access to the Black Spur forest, north-east of Melbourne, hence giving them licence to cut down the region's mountain ash. They did articulate the justification for preserving the mountain ash in terms recognisable to a public versed in the language and meaning of wonder, and they challenged a prevailing notion that forests without saw-mills were wastelands. Forest giants were, on the contrary, things of beauty that would enrich the human imagination. They were wonderful because of their great height and great age: some proclaimed them living vestiges of a primeval age. So, if they were the tallest and oldest trees in the world why weren't they preserved?

This claim was at the crux of the preservation issue: were they really the tallest and oldest? Throughout this period their height and age were often queried because of the difficulties in measuring standing trees, and in establishing a tree's age accurately. Mueller participated in the debate of how tall these trees were, convinced that they were taller than the Mariposa Big Trees. According to him, the American trees were about 310 feet (95 metres) tall, but he had collected anecdotal evidence of ones in the Dandenongs reaching 500 feet (154 metres), finally determining the tallest measured was 420 feet (129 metres), but arguing there were taller

OBSESSION WITH HEIGHT *often underpinned nineteenth-century discussion about the Australian mountain ash as a natural wonder. Was it the tallest tree in the world? This 1870s photograph compares the difference in height between a man, a horse and a mountain ash. (Brookes' Photographic Union photographer,* Mountain Ash, *1891.)*

specimens still standing. (This 'tallest tree' was measured after it had been felled and before it was taken to the saw-mill, but its destruction created subsequent difficulties in confirming these reports.) To give some idea of height he wrote: 'A standard of comparison we possess … [is] the pyramid of Cheops, 480 feet, which if raised in our ranges would be overshadowed probably by eucalyptus trees.'[21] (These measurements were later shown to be highly questionable and, finally, wrong. Now, mountain ash is described as achieving heights of 100 metres, which is 10 metres shorter than the Californian Redwood, and some 60 metres shorter than the most optimistic estimates of the tree's height in the nineteenth century.)

The basis for the worldwide significance of the mountain ash as an object of wonder was that they were taller and older than the Californian Big Trees. The doubt cast on the tall tree's vital statistics in all likelihood dampened political enthusiasm for their preservation. The tree fern gullies—despite the fact that great swathes were made through them to take economic advantage of the land—were recommended for a beauty colonial Australians could, unconditionally, be proud of, along with other characteristically Australian scenery—sublime views from mountain ridges, slender waterfalls of great height, and striking lake scenery. The place of giant trees within this Australian imaginative framework was on less certain scientific ground, their magnificence continually overshadowed by the possibility of California's big trees being taller and older.

With the destruction of the Dandenong mountain ash forests also came the demise of its tree fern gullies. The felling of its trees meant the inevitable destruction of the very conditions necessary for tree ferns. Despite significant support from some sectors for the protection of tree ferns, these tree fern groves were doomed from the moment of the first swing of the tree-feller's axe. But the failure of the tree fern protection lobby did not in itself signify the end of a fern-appreciation era—a period lasting from the 1820s, with the publication of the first accounts of the beauty of tree ferns, until World War I, when many drawing rooms were decorated with potted ferns, and all types of ferns adorned the backyard. While tempers raged over the need for protection of the tree-fern clad forests of Victoria and Tasmania, attention had now also turned to the delights of Australia's smaller ferns, the extent of which had intrigued Robert Brown at the beginning of the nineteenth century.

In Britain, the fern craze reached its zenith with the commercial availability of exotic ferns, and was characterised not only by the publication of many books about ferns appealing to a popular market, but also by the appearance of fern-filled wardian cases—self-contained ecosystems providing a protected, moist environment suitable for growing exotic varieties—in middle-class drawing rooms, and for the more ambitious, fern-filled glass houses.[22] By the 1860s more than 650 exotic species were available in Britain from almost thirty countries in the Pacific, Asia, the Americas and Africa, including the 'magnificent specimens' from Australia and New Zealand.[23] They were cheaper to buy than orchids, but still represented a slice of paradise. ('Orchid fever' was confined to the wealthy.) But whereas Britain's fern craze was based largely on acquiring the 'exotic' for display in the home, the Australian interest was about also appreciating local varieties, and associated with this was a certain amount of pride. The botanist William Woolls, an Australian fern enthusiast, argued that once people saw Australian varieties, especially the tree ferns, they would be aware of the 'comparative insignificance of English ferns'.[24] By the 1860s there were pleasant ferneries where visitors could wander in one or two of the established plant nurseries, such as Baptist's Nursery in Surry Hills, Sydney, with its 'large commodious span-roofed fernery … [with ferns] staged about … in conservatory fashion'.[25] Instructions were published for Australians to create their own ferny retreat at home. One of the earliest manuals appeared in 1866 when Samuel Hannaford published a 'complete list of indigenous ferns and instructions for their cultivation' in his general account of Tasmanian native plants.[26]

Part of this new-found pride in Australian ferns was a consequence of the work of an active community of local botanists, in which some government-appointed botanists, such as Ferdinand von Mueller, took an interest. Previously, much of what they collected had been sent off to British botanical gardens and societies, where it was classified and became part of general botanical knowledge, although individual colonists did maintain their own extensive private collections. Mueller created Melbourne's botanical gardens as a colonial collecting and classifying centre, erecting a herbarium and donating his own considerable collection of Australian botany. Many colonial botanists (men and women) sent specimens and information to help with his project of classifying Australian botany systematically, which publicly began with the first issue of *Fragmenta Phytographiae Australiae*, a quarterly periodical about Australian botany, the magazines of each two-year period published as a single volume between 1858 and 1882. Mueller initiated *Fragmenta* to publish his botanical descriptions and, thus, avoid the long wait for European publication.[27] The 1866 volume concentrated on Australian ferns. Like Sir William Hooker's book about fern species, *Species Filicum,* Mueller's was written in Latin and intended for an international scientific audience.[28] But the reference books also prompted wider interest in ferns in the Australian community. William Woolls used them as a basis for several articles and also a book, stating that 'I was impressed with the idea that a popular [account of] our ferns might be acceptable to many persons in these colonies'.[29]

While tree ferns were notable as tourist sights from the 1820s, it was not until the second half of the nineteenth century that small, dainty ferns became an Australian tourist attraction. Their existence in various regions throughout the colonies had been well documented from the late eighteenth century, which ensured botanical interest, and some botanists, including James Backhouse, had mentioned them in passing in general travel accounts. In the last part of the eighteenth century and first half of the nineteenth century, travellers usually described the smaller varieties of ferns in scientific language in Latin, in the second half of the century they did so in English, proclaiming them beautiful in themselves quite apart from any scientific interest.

As interest in the smaller varieties of Australian ferns increased so did literature promoting them as tasteful. The language used was the same as had been used with regard to tree ferns for decades, comparing them to jewels and praising their elegance, delicacy, exquisiteness, gracefulness, quiet beauty, not dissimilar to contemporary compliments describing ladies of good-breeding.[30] In an otherwise straightforward account of Australian ferns, William Woolls remarked how ferns inspired:

> the lover of nature's works to the contemplation of grace and elegance, and to invite him from the toil and bustle of the city to the freedom of the country, to the purity of the mountain air, and to the dark mysterious shades where the sun never penetrates … They shrink, as it were, from vulgar gaze. They are too pure for the outer world.[31]

In his introduction to a systematic listing of Australian ferns, the colonial botanist Frederick Manson Bailey wrote:

> Ferns … have at all times been favorites [*sic*] with the lovers of the beautiful … They are always welcome, and draw forth our admiration … They are eagerly sought after by young and old—by some for the gratification of the present moment, by others for cultivation about their homes and for the purpose of decoration. Indeed, so attractive are these beauties of Flora's Kingdom, that it is almost impossible to find a house where they are not to be met with either living or dead.[32]

By the 1880s many Australian-published gardening books gave instructions on constructing and maintaining a fernery and a bush house (another garden structure in which ferns grew successfully).[33]

As far as travel expectations went, by the 1880s this love of ferns was pervasive, almost a necessity in any Australian mountainous landscape. Mountains initially valued for their sublimity gained further acclaim if they sheltered small fern varieties. In the Blue Mountains, Weeping Rock (part of Wentworth Falls) was praised for its 'pale green fronds' and 'luxuriant ferns'. The mountain ranges surrounding Beechworth in Victoria were said to have thirty to forty fern varieties, so many that boulders were 'fringed with ferns', and Mount Buffalo's

QUEENSLAND'S FERNS, *by the end of the century, were prized by fern lovers, largely because of Queensland botanist Frederick Manson Bailey, above, and his books. Fern Island, opposite, in Brisbane's Botanic Gardens in the 1870s contained local fern varieties and rainforest plants. (Above: P. Poulsen,* Botanist Mr Frederick Manson Bailey, *date unknown. Opposite: Photographer unknown,* Fern Island in the Botanic Gardens, Brisbane, Queensland, *c. 1878.)*

mountain paths were 'clothed with a luxuriant growth of ferns'. The deep gorges of Ben Lomond in Tasmania were covered in ferns. Day-trippers returned from Mount Lofty laden with 'many rare kinds of ferns'. Gippsland's thickly wooded forests had a luxuriant undergrowth of ferns and mosses. The ferns around Fitzroy Falls in what are now called the Southern Highlands in New South Wales were a 'source of wonder and pleasure'. Mount Wilson in the Blue Mountains was gaining a reputation for its ferns.[34] It is not that ferns had suddenly sprouted in these places, but that they were now valued as a spectacle, something to be sought out while touring. By the 1880s the most fern-laden colony was undoubtedly Queensland, and this recognition was the beginning of what—much later in the twentieth century—became rainforest tourism.

Frederick Manson Bailey had determined that Queensland had more ferns than any other Australian colony. Both his *Handbook to the Ferns of Queensland* (1874) and *The Fern World of Australia with Homes of the Queensland Species* (1881) helped bring Queensland ferns to the attention of colonial botanists and fern lovers. Queensland ferns, he explained, grew in all shapes and sizes, including a climbing variety and the long-admired tree fern. They had a number of different habitats—along creek banks, on trees, in between rocks, in forests, scrub or swamp—and might be found throughout the coastal, mountainous and forest regions of Queensland.

What we today call rainforest was called 'scrub' in nineteenth-century Queensland. James Backhouse in the 1830s visited a forest called the Three-Mile Scrub in southern Queensland, with interesting Moreton Bay fig trees that were the homes to fern species and orchid epiphytes, 'gigantic climber' vines strung between the tree tops, and jasmine growing profusely. He compared the size of one of the tree-clinging fern varieties to a 'full-grown Scotch cabbage' adding that it was 'remarkably beautiful'.[35] By 1870 when Alice Frere published her round-the-world travel account she likened 'scrubs' to 'tropical jungle' describing how:

> 'scrubs' … generally following the course of a 'creek' with tall, dark, glossy-leaved trees, hung with luxuriant creepers, and their stems covered with magnificent "stag's horn" fern. If it were only possible to transplant to England a mile or so of this rich, luxuriant vegetation, the trees with such beautiful leaves … and the ground *carpeted* with the Adiantum pedatum and other lovely ferns, how delightful it would be![36]

Scrub was a landscape of dark glossy-leaved trees, thick vines, tropical plants like orchids—and ferns. One of the places where these conditions came together near Brisbane was Tambourine Mountain (its name changed to Mount Tamborine around the 1940s). Its cooler climate compared with Brisbane, and its splendid view of the coast and ocean made it a favourite resort for tourists by the end of the nineteenth century. Its main appeal was as a 'rich mountain garden' where tree ferns were protected by tall forests, and acacias, wildflowers, orchids, mosses and vines abounded. Above was its 'luxuriantly covered' summit with many types of ferns, and creeks and rills forming 'lovely waterfalls' that emptied into 'fairyland pools' fringed by feathery ferns. This was 'fernland'. In a series on the 'picturesque spots' of Queensland, George Craig praised Tambourine Mountain for its 'quiet spirit of peace on this primeval tableland of "maiden hair", eucalyptus, and enchanting waterfall'.[37] Mountain, forest, fern and water had come together to create a perfect, Australian landscape.

The pursuit of scientific knowledge and the creation of certain natural features as attractions often went together. The very act of acquiring botanical knowledge involved travelling, observing, looking for new and interesting botanical specimens, and a curiosity about the meanings of these discoveries—and these were also aspects of nineteenth-century touring. The botanical characteristics of a new genus were expressed in dry, scientific terms, but travel writing was the means to express the wonder associated with such discoveries and to describe what was seen as inherent beauty or other aesthetic characteristic. Although the nature of scientific enquiry has changed, eco-tourism, for example, still relies on this nexus between scientific discovery and explanation—*why* tourists want to see particular natural attractions, even *how* they express their responses. Tourist trips to the Barrier Reef are an example. Most people enjoy the experience of seeing for themselves a sea turtle in its natural environment carefully searching for food in coral gardens, or the shell of a giant clam closing when its deep-blue lips are tickled. Yet one of the reasons why tourists want to see sea turtles and giant clams in their natural environment rather than, say, in an aquarium, is because scientific studies have demonstrated the environmental significance of ecology—the interrelatedness of animals with their environment—and the importance of preserving a region's ecology. Scientists have told us that the beauty of the sea turtle and the clam partly arises from seeing them in their natural environment (and that we should obey environmental regulations to help preserve this beauty).

In the nineteenth century, scientific observation and explanation were integrally related to the appeal of certain natural attractions. The wonder of giant eucalypts, elegant tree ferns, and the smaller, dainty fern varieties, involved science and sentiment coming together and contributing to an Australian imaginative framework.

THE EYE OF
THE BEHOLDER

*In which perspective is shown to be important
to the changing appreciation of scenery*

In 1853 a young Louisa Atkinson tried her hand at nature writing with a series of articles published in the short-lived weekly, the *Illustrated Sydney News*. 'In these busy times, and in the universal pursuit of wealth which characterises the state of things among us, the beauties of nature are in danger of being overlooked', she wrote in her first column.

Perhaps a few remarks on our natural history, in a simple and popular style may be acceptable. So numerous are the writers who have illustrated the beauties of England that ignorance of them, on the part of anyone who can read, must be voluntary. Australia, a land of many wonders, claims a similar attention.

A few years later she and her mother moved to Kurrajong, a small township nestled amid the northern ridges of the Blue Mountains. There, she developed her interest in the colony's natural wonders by organising small parties of ladies and gentlemen to explore this part of the Blue Mountains on horse and foot, sometimes camping out overnight. She sketched and collected anything of interest, especially specimens small enough to fit into her shoulder bag. Back at her mother's house, Fernhurst, she wrote numerous articles based on these explorations, which were published in the *Sydney Morning Herald* and the *Sydney Mail*, and which initiated many interested responses from readers. Louisa Atkinson was a favourite correspondent of colonists because she described the scenery and natural history of her own surroundings.[1]

From around 1860 travel writing about the Blue Mountains started to include detailed references to smaller ferns, largely as a consequence of the work of Louisa Atkinson, who also sent many of her specimens to Ferdinand von Mueller to help with the classification of Australian ferns. In her nature study articles about the Blue Mountains Louisa Atkinson almost always referred to the natural vegetation as luxuriant, green and fresh and would describe the various species of ferns and other plants that she came across. To her, the Blue Mountains were filled with ferns, of all shapes and sizes, many tiny, others over thirty feet (9 metres) high. On one tour she collected twenty-six distinct varieties; she described what she saw in detail, even providing the Latin names of species (although this was done, she explained, with the help of her botanist friend, William Woolls). Ferns were everywhere: alongside roads, protruding from sandstone crevices, as well as in their usual habitat, the moist dells, where, she explained, conditions were unfavourable to weeds and grasses that could overwhelm the smaller varieties of fern. Ferns helped make a scene beautiful: 'the words luxuriant, fresh, green—all the epithets which can be piled together to express a superabundance of beauty in tint and form are in constant use'. The beauty of a scene enriched with ferns had to do with their appearance—their colour, various tints of green, and their shape, feathery and light. For Atkinson, there was 'something so cheerful and simple about this tribe of plants'.[2]

Throughout the nineteenth century there was a strong belief that upper middle-class women were motivated by a taste for delicate beauty, not only in their dress and surrounding objects, but also in the scenery they sought. This preference contrasted with the acceptable masculine propensity to seek the sublime and manifestations of it that hinted at such terrible strength as to threaten even the most manly.[3] Men still studied the beautiful and women experienced the sublime (although early in the nineteenth century there was some evidence that there were observed differences in response based on gender): however, a particular field of enquiry was marked out as feminine, where women could forge their own routes of discovery, and in doing so, continue to define themselves as feminine.

As we have seen fern collecting had become a masculine pursuit, and continued to be even as women joined the ranks.[4] But where men's assessment of beauty had largely been directed to tree ferns, their tall, erect stems crowned with green glory, women were now writing of settings beautiful for their small fern varieties. Women had long been admirers of landscapes filled with Australian wildflowers. Their interest in the smaller fern varieties as a landscape feature was part of this historical tradition. The Blue Mountains provides an interesting example of this change, showing how a mountainous landscape initially admired for its sublime qualities came to be noted also for its smaller fern varieties, and how women's botanical observations contributed to this change.

LOUISA ATKINSON *painted this 1850s study of some of the delicate* Doodia *species when she lived in the Blue Mountains. (Louisa Atkinson, [Ferns], c. 1860.)*

Dicksonia antarctica

LOUISA ATKINSON *depicted a Blue Mountains tree fern that lacked the elegant crown of fronds so admired by nineteenth-century gentlemen travellers. (Louisa Atkinson, Dicksonia antarctica, c. 1860.)*

Until the second half of the nineteenth century ferns were not a major feature of Blue Mountains scenery as painted by artists or described in travel writing. The travel writer Louisa Meredith in the 1840s had commented on the 'moist greenness' around the stream leading to the waterfall she had admired, but she had not elaborated any further. One reason for the absence of any mention of ferns in early Blue Mountains' travel literature was, simply, that most of the tracks off the Bathurst Road led to views of vast expanses, ravines and waterfalls. Few went down into the gullies where deep shade provided ideal conditions for the growth of ferns. Gentlemen travellers with botanical interests who did descend into these regions reported on the large tree ferns, ignoring the smaller varieties of ferns—as Alan Cunningham had done on his trip to the same region in the early 1820s that Louisa Atkinson later explored. Cunningham's account of Blue Mountains' botany was mostly in scientific Latin, but his enthusiasm for the region's tree ferns was expressed in English, using adjectives familiar in travel writing.[5] His reference to their 'stupendous size' indicated that they could not be easily missed and fitted the general image of the Blue Mountains as sublime, with the eye directed towards large objects or distant views. There was, however, no similar admiration for the variety of dainty ferns that, later, came to form a significant part of Blue Mountains' travel description.

Early explorers and gentlemen tourists did, on occasion, describe the region's floral species, usually by noting botanical details and type of soil, the type of information useful in assessing agricultural potential, rather than describing plants in the context of their immediate surroundings and their relationship to other plants.[6] French botanist Jules d'Urville and naturalist René Lesson observed on their journey an area where 'the surface layer is composed of a detritus of sandstone and maintains Proteaceae and the pretty *Lambertia speciosa*'.[7] Some gentlemen travellers did describe plants that had become attractions in themselves and could be viewed on a journey over the mountains, the waratah, for instance, not easily missed with its very large flower and tall stem. But rarely did they describe details such as colour and how they contributed to the scenery. For example, one writer remarked that, 'the vegetation [near Wentworth Falls] becomes dwarfish, and the tall ironbark

John Lewin, Telopea speciosissima, 1803–1808.

trees of Springwood, are now changed for stunted eucalyptus of box and ash, and several varieties of the honeysuckle (*Banksia integrifolia*), and now and then the telopea or waratah'. Even a professional naturalist, George Bennett, travelling over the mountains in the early 1830s mentioned nothing more inspiring than some waratahs, 'fragrant' acacia, a few 'beautiful flowering shrubs' and commented that plants on the upper portions of the ridges were 'stunted'.[8] James Backhouse described his journey during which he noted the sublime scenery in the upper mountains (near Blackheath and Wentworth Falls) with little reference to its botany. Earlier in his journey while on the lower slopes (around Springwood) he had noticed the blossoms and the birds that drank their nectar, commenting that these scenes 'enlivened the solitude'. The crucial point, though, is that his account continued the prevailing descriptions of the upper mountains as sublime and affording extensive views, ignoring any beauty there of blossom or bird.

In contrast, the part played by vegetation generally (not only ferns) in contributing to some of the best scenery in the upper mountains was established early in women's descriptions. The private correspondence of a young married woman travelling with her family to Bathurst in 1822:

> You will, perhaps, imagine, as I had done, that the mountains are perfectly barren. For forty miles they are barren of herbage for cattle, but as far as the eye can reach, even from the summit of the highest, every hill and dale is covered with wood, lofty trees, and small shrubs, the colours so beautiful that the highest circles in England would prize them.[9]

Louisa Meredith similarly remarked upon the foliage in the highest altitude. Even after a two-year drought she was able to observe how 'amongst these lofty mountains and in their shady recesses the trees and shrubs grew in unchecked luxuriance, and yielded me many a new and beautiful flower'. She continued by describing species she found particularly striking.[10]

This taste for the beautiful meant that some early women travellers identified and praised different features of a landscape long sought after for other qualities, their observations and descriptions gradually building new ways to behold what lay before visitors.

As we have seen, the nature of nineteenth-century travel description was never static, with travellers searching out new ways of looking at old scenery, living examples of George Evans' exclamation 'I see no end to travelling'. But the nineteenth century was a time when certain cultural expectations and duties arose as a consequence of a person's social position and gender. Being a 'gentleman', or being a 'lady', affected most aspects of a person's existence, including how they negotiated acts of cultural production such as travel writing where choices had to be made about what to describe. In this sense, feminine perspective was an important feature of nineteenth-century travel, providing another way of observing landscape in all its variety.

The search for wonder, a cultivated interest in nature, and the ability to describe a scene's noteworthiness underpinned this feminine perspective, just as they did more generally. A good example of feminine perspective in action is how the Blue Mountains came to be reinterpreted not only for grand vistas or ferns, but also for gentle cascades. By the turn of the twentieth century one of the dominant tourist images of the Blue Mountains was the scenic quality of its water as 'white and misty, as the driven snow', 'like the veil of a bride', like 'crystal', even, 'playing laughingly over the stones'. The idea of the Blue Mountains as beautiful because of delicate water features had not been present in the accounts of either explorers or early gentlemen tourists. But the beautifying effects of water were described by at least one woman traveller, who passed through the region in 1839.

Mrs Charles Meredith prepared for her return to Sydney from Bathurst in December 1839. She had spent a productive month in the district, observing facets of local society as well as the surrounding scenery and intriguing flora and fauna. Her journey from Sydney over the Blue Mountains had unsettled her, an experience of 'most dreary, desolate grandeur'. But, whereas the purpose of her forward journey had been to reach Bathurst with time for only a passing interest in the countryside, the return journey was to be more leisurely, to include short excursions off the main mountains route to observe the splendid scenery described by an increasing number of travellers.

Louisa Meredith was an established author in England, who had arrived in New South Wales from England about a month before. She had pondered the possibility of writing an account of colonial life from a 'lady's point of view', one based on her own experiences and written in the form of a diary, a style de rigueur and favoured by prominent English publishers of the time. The purpose of the short excursions was to see the local sights, describe them in her daily jottings, and later, shape these jottings into prose with sufficient attention to detail for the power of her narrative alone to carry readers to a noteworthy sight without them having to leave their armchairs.

She had heard about the view from the Weatherboard, where travellers looked down from a great height upon an expansive sea of trees and rocky ridges, and so her party took a detour down a well-trodden track to the edge of a cliff. The sight was indeed novel, 'one of the most stupendous scenes I ever beheld bursting unexpectedly upon us', she later wrote, and was disappointed she could not stay longer to explore this 'grand and interesting spot'. But she not only encountered stupendous scenery. She also delighted in the discovery of a pleasant brook at the head of a tremendous precipice. This she had not expected. She had been looking forward to an extensive view, intrigued to see for herself such grandeur, as many had claimed. She did not expect water to be part of the scene, and while some of her party continued to clamber over rocks to search for the best lookout, she turned to explore the delights of her first Australian mountain stream. She subsequently wrote up these jottings of her New South Wales travels: *Notes and Sketches of New South Wales During a Residence in that Colony from 1839 to 1844* was published by John Murray, the English publisher of numerous travel books, and was re-issued many times.[11] Of that mountain stream, she wrote:

> After an early breakfast the following morning, we set forth on foot to visit a waterfall. Entering a little valley with low hills on either side, we soon

reached the borders of a bright brook that, as it gurgled and glittered over its rocky bed, spoke to me of many a lovely valley and verdant meadow at home, where instead of being, as here, precious as a font in the desert, such a stream would be but one among the thousands that gladden the teeming earth. After our dry and parching journey, it was delightful to walk close beside it—to be quite sure that it was water—and when wetted feet did not suffice, to stoop and dabble in it—and scoop it up in tightly-clasped hands to drink—and to step over on its large dry stones, with no very great objection to a splash if one's foot slipped ... [Upon reaching the] brink of a tremendous precipice ... [o]n our left, the bright waters of the mountain stream poured over the rocks in one smooth, glassy, unbroken torrent.[12]

No equal description of this scene by a gentleman travel writer at that time is available. Not until the 1880s, when some of Mrs Meredith's elements were beginning to be established as given in Blue Mountains' travel descriptions, did men's travel accounts include similarly sensuous detail about the mountains' water features in descriptions that portrayed the physical sensations of water gently stimulating human sight, sound, touch and even taste. The mountains might be sublime, but as Louisa Meredith had observed, there were nooks and crannies, even vistas, that were made beautiful by water.

But for most of the nineteenth century, the region's waterfalls as described by men seemed there merely as a minor addition to the sublime character of the mountain scene, noted for their scantiness, not for any beauty they might have. Nineteenth-century accounts of the Blue Mountains by men and women reveal a division of descriptive interest: the men were to discover and describe their sublime characteristics, the women to uncover their beauty.

Early explorers had noted their failure to find adequate water in the Blue Mountains and this had helped contribute to the region's image as 'barren'. Nor, it seems, were these remarks dependent on the season and whether or not there was a drought, although it must be remembered that weather in the mountains is unpredictable. George Bass complained of a 'devouring thirst' caused by lack of water, and the scarcity of fresh water was mentioned in later accounts, including David Mann's description of 'pools of stagnant water' and Barrallier's conclusion that there was not 'so barren a desert in any part of Africa as these Mountains are'.[13]

Water was essential to the survival of explorers and its scarcity indicated real threat. In addition water courses were an important aid to mapping the land: rivers were eagerly followed and placement of pools of water carefully examined. Botanist and explorer George Caley wrote of entering a 'deep and dark valley ... destitute of a rill; but water was ... lodged in small lakes or holes' and following these he hoped to find 'a suitable route across the ridge'.[14] The earliest colonial accounts of the mountains suggested expectations of a mighty river providing an accessible route to the interior and fertile soil for the cultivation of colonial crops. Phillip commented

Louisa Anne Meredith, View from the Centre of an Immense Mountain Amphitheatre on the Summit of the Blue Mountains—Near the Weatherboard Inn, NSW, *1839.*

that 'from the rising of the mountains, I did not doubt but that a large river would be found'. His proposal was that European explorers follow Aborigines inland because he assumed Aborigines would live along such a river.[15] Pools of water dispersed haphazardly over the region were a poor substitute.

By the early 1810s brief recordings of the presence of water had become standard, indicating its drinking quality and the suitability for feed of surrounding herbage. Blaxland noted an area near today's Wentworth Falls as having a 'well-watered swamp', and Cox described the same area as having a 'rivulet of fine spring water'. Another swamp a little further on was praised for its 'beautiful stream of water' and its 'abundance of excellent water'. But such comment was rare in descriptions of what was still presented as rocky and sandy country with most mountain swamps criticised for their 'inadequate swamp grass' and scarcity of water.[16] Indeed, the image of the mountains as generally waterless, apart from one or two slender waterfalls, was general in travel accounts for decades:

> One warning may be given to prevent disappointment on the part of the visitor. Australia is a dry country, and the waterfalls have no body of water. They are lofty, but except under quite special circumstances are thin and scanty, not to be compared to such falls as the Schaffhausen, on the Rhine … [T]o most the falls upon the Blue Mountains are only what Darwin calls tiny rills, trickling over the edge of a precipice.[17]

The same waterfall described by Louisa Meredith was viewed by members of Macquarie's tour party in 1815, one writing in his journal that 'the height of the fall was great, but there being very little water, the stream was very inconsiderable'.[18] The waterfall was not described in any account actually published at the time, nor were other waterfalls in the area noted by earlier explorers. Francis Barrallier crossed some rapids (the early nineteenth-century meaning of the word 'waterfall'). His description of river beds so full of 'sharp-edged stones' that his and his men's shoes were torn to shreds hardly presented a desirable image.[19]

Subsequently, waterfalls as described by gentlemen travellers emphasised the great distances they fell, an admirable feature because it contributed to the sublime qualities of a scene. The volume of water was considered small, because of expectations that waterfalls were wide and thundering, in the manner, say, of Niagara Falls (a destination on the American grand tour from the late 1820s).[20] But describing the great height of the falls and the surrounding masses of rock became a convention of travel descriptions for this region for the rest of the century. The general pattern of description went something like this: disappointment in the small volume of water falling—'it would be easy to make as good a one with a tea-kettle' was one remark—but great satisfaction in observing what was described as the 'awful abyss', or the 'immense caldron [*sic*]', or the 'chasm of unknown depth, perhaps two thousand feet perpendicular', or combinations of these and other like phrases.[21] Similar observations were made about the scenery some distance on at Govett's Leap, near Blackheath, which, from the 1830s, was often a diversion on the route over the mountains.

From early on male artists had found the Blue Mountains a suitable subject for painting, but they paid little attention to the major waterfalls, seeing them (if at all) as only one feature of the surrounding sublime scenery. Most paintings of the upper Blue Mountains in the first half of the nineteenth century did not include waterfalls: they were views into the distance often framed by rocky outcrops and sheer cliff drops or, sometimes, by the Sydney–Bathurst road.[22]

The few paintings that did show the falls presented them as part of the surrounding sublime mountain scenery. One was the work of a young artist, Augustus Earle, who, as part of a world tour, had arrived in Sydney in 1825 eager for the unusual.[23] He chose the waterfall and its surrounds at today's Wentworth Falls for his small oil painting, *Waterfall in Australia* (c. 1830). The painting depicts his party, precariously close to the rocky edges, as they peer into the valley below, while Earle, apparently unworried (unlike his companions) by his proximity to the abyss, gazes at an Aboriginal man striking a pose with a spear by the waterfall. To the left of the painting is the waterfall with more water than usually described in written accounts. The painting comprised both the exotic (the Aboriginal man with his

AUGUSTUS EARLE'S 1830 PAINTING OF WENTWORTH FALLS, *above, as sublime with endless ridges and a raging torrent, and W. C. Piguenit's painting of the same waterfall, below, some forty years later with water like a 'shower of silver stars'. (Above: Augustus Earle,* Waterfall in Australia, *c. 1830. Below: W. C. Piguenit,* Weatherboard Falls, *c. 1876.)*

spear) and the sublime (expressed by the terror of the Europeans and the volume of water falling over the edge into the chasm below).[24]

Louisa Meredith's likening of the surrounding land to a 'desert' and her comment about the relief water provided after a 'dry and parching journey' not only reminded her readers of a dominant image of the time, closely associated with masculine accounts of exploration and how waterless much of Australia was, but also provided some justification for her detailed description of water. By contrast, masculine travel writing about Australia had predictably seen calmly flowing water as less significant than either the absence of water, or its appearance as raging torrents, both of which presented challenges to physical and mental endurance. Mrs Meredith's use of 'feminine' observation and her descriptive skills on the details of her surroundings presented an alternative interpretation of the Blue Mountains landscape, one almost impossible for gentlemen travellers to articulate. Given the constraints of masculine intellectual fashions of the time, along with the belief that only the sublime was worth observing and, failing that, any scene of importance could not be less than an extensive view, gentlemen's eyes ranged far and wide to take in the panorama, or fastened on large masses of scenery, or gazed into deep ravines.

Twenty years after Mrs Meredith's descriptions, Louisa Atkinson's writings about the Blue Mountains were filled with accounts of 'numerous small streams' of 'water clear as crystal' that 'trickled', 'dashed', 'tumbled', even 'leaped out of sight' in a mass of white foam, 'distinctly audible'.[25] Her descriptions were not of the major falls, Wentworth Falls and Govett's Leap, but minor falls also located near the Sydney–Bathurst road as well as in the northern ridges of the Blue Mountains. She presented what was still an unusual image (when compared to men's travel accounts) of the mountains as well watered.

By the late 1860s other women travellers were writing about the water that filled the slender falls, which were now being seen for what they were, not what they were not. Alice Frere wrote:

> Grand scarps rose close to us, over which played the lovely fall, not with a
> rush and dash, as is usually the case, but lingeringly and caressingly, as if

loth to leave so fair a scene, and to lose itself in the murky depths below … The water, as it fell, was driven up the face of the rock [by a strong wind], some of it re-falling, like a shower of silver stars, and some of it driven away in mist, forming an almost circular rainbow-frame round the glittering, dancing drops.[26]

In 1876 the artist William Piguenit painted watercolours of the region's waterfalls: in *Weatherboard Falls* (1876) instead of sublime scenery, he depicted the water in a way that evoked (although probably unintentionally) Alice Frere's 'shower of silver stars'.[27]

By this stage other mountainous regions in Australia—previously noted for deep and craggy gullies, precipitous ravines, the panoramas to be viewed from their summits, and in the case of waterfalls and mountain streams, only how they added to the sublime character—were also being reinvented to note the beautiful effect of water. It is difficult to determine whether, as had happened in the case of the Blue Mountains, this was a consequence of published observations by women. But certainly the perspectives pioneered in women's accounts of Blue Mountains scenery, and taken up by artists and gentlemen's accounts, had become the norm in how travellers interpreted mountain scenery elsewhere in Australia.

The Adelaide Hills, and in particular Mount Lofty, had initially been admired both by men and women travellers for the juxtaposition of romantic gullies and majestic rocky valleys from which could be seen a 'stupendous and magnificent scene' almost all the way to the St Vincent's Gulf. Gentlemen travellers noted waterfalls for their sheer drop, and ravines for 'the noise of a brawling torrent' within them, the sort of thing which helped portray a scene as wildly romantic. George French Angas commenting on his three lithographs of the Adelaide Hills wrote of the height of waterfalls on Mount Lofty and their background of perpendicular rock as romantic characteristics attesting to the scene's grandeur. By the 1880s Mount Lofty, a fashionable summer retreat for Adelaide residents, drew comment for its waterfalls—even if most of them had little water over the dry, hot, summer months: summer visitors were urged to imagine the winter glory of fine watery spray dancing over the rocks and reflecting the colours of the rainbow.[28]

LOUISA ATKINSON'S 1860S DRAWING OF A WATERFALL IN THE BLUE MOUNTAINS, *opposite, presents fast-flowing water as if a silken robe draped gently over rocks. By the 1880s, water-filled landscapes were sought after in the Blue Mountains and were a common image when Robert Hunt took this photograph, above, of Mount Victoria's Fairy Bower. (Opposite: Louisa Atkinson,* Long Fall from Below 1ˢᵗ Leap 28th July, *c. 1860. Above: Robert Hunt,* Fairy Bower, Mount Victoria, Blue Mountains, NSW, *1887.)*

Depictions and descriptions of nature by travellers in the late eighteenth and nineteenth centuries helped to shape what people saw. Mountain scenery could be of 'desolate grandeur' or of 'moist greenness' (or other combinations), depending on where a person stood, who they were, what they had read, what they had seen: culture shaped people who shaped nature. Tours of discovery, quests to expand botanical and scientific knowledge, searches for the picturesque, the beautiful and the sublime: the motivation for travels came from a desire, strongly evident from the second half of the eighteenth century and persisting throughout the nineteenth, to seek out natural phenomena, grapple with possible meanings and impose these on an otherwise unknowable land.

But nature also shaped people. The object of these travels, expressed over and over again, was to achieve personal enlightenment, to return a changed person, touched by one's encounters with nature. The pursuit of wonder also became a matter of civic pride, evident in attempts to reserve and provide greater access to places of magnificent and unusual scenery for use and enjoyment by the people. Colonial views of the natural environment not only saw the land in economic terms, with its copious supplies of wood, pasture and minerals, but also as a source of inspiration and enlightenment. Colonists believed in the power of natural attractions as an antidote to modern existence, where the mystery of existence lay hidden. Moves to preserve these natural attractions were democratic in spirit so that all, conceivably, may one day experience for themselves the feeling of wonder at the way nature worked.

Wonder as a state of being has continued into the twenty-first century, and can still be experienced by people travelling to see natural attractions. In some ways, the discovery of the Wollemi pines in a wilderness area of the Blue Mountains in the late twentieth century is very like the fern discoveries made on early botanical excursions to Mount Wellington, or some decades later, the groves of tree ferns in the Dandenongs. In all cases, these finds contributed significantly to botanical knowledge, and in the backwash, helped create interest in Australian mountains as places of great natural beauty and wonder. The pursuit of wonder as the driving force of travel started in the second half of the eighteenth century and evolved throughout the nineteenth century. Part of the original artifice no longer exists— the sublime, a feminine perspective, even certain types of landscape once seen as wonderful. But much of it does, and is still recognisable to us today. Our own experiences of wonder are the legacy of this earlier period.

In the Blue Mountains at Wentworth Falls, a local initiative in 1986 to celebrate the sesquicentenary of Charles Darwin's visit was to renovate the track that took early Europeans, including Charles Darwin, to see the local sight. (It is now known as Charles Darwin Walk.) For years I have taken visitors for a bushwalk along the track. We travel alongside a gentle stream (the same stream, I imagine, that endeared the mountains to Louisa Meredith) crossing it whenever the track takes us that way. There's a little bit of gurgling, and some stagnant water. There is nothing much really to look at, at least not in terms of a beautiful or even interesting landscape. It is just a track, and our visitors, I'm sure, wonder why I have taken them there. They look bored, certainly unimpressed by what's around them. What are they thinking? Then I race ahead, up and over two large rocks. I position myself to see their faces when they, too, emerge from behind the rocks. From polite non-involvement with their surroundings, their faces suddenly show delight, their eyes widen to view what's before them, their mouths open to express satisfaction at what they see. We linger here a little, looking down at the grand canyon of the Jamison Valley into a sea of dark green native tree canopies, across at the noble escarpment and hear the nearby waterfall plunging hundreds of metres below. I take in their excitement and each time I remember again the first time I saw this view and think how Charles Darwin must have felt when he wrote of the same outlook, 'this kind of view was to me quite novel, and extremely magnificent'.

NOTES

ABBREVIATIONS

ACH	*Australian Cultural History*
ADB	*Australian Dictionary of Biography*
AT&CJ	*Australian Town and Country Journal*
BFP	*Bathurst Free Press*
CPA	*Cassell's Picturesque Australasia*
DAA	*Dictionary of Australian Artists*
HRA	*Historical Records of Australia*
HRNSW	*Historical Records of New South Wales*
JRAHS	*Journal of the Royal Australian Historical Society*
LA	Legislative Assembly
ML	Mitchell Library
OED	*Oxford English Dictionary*
PAA	*Picturesque Atlas of Australasia*
SM	*Sydney Mail*
SMH	*Sydney Morning Herald*
V&P	*Votes and Proceedings*

Works that are cited only once and in full in the notes are not included in the list of references. Details re articles published in newspapers and other popular serials are included in full in the notes.

WHAT THIS IS ALL ABOUT, *pp. 1–21*

1 'Country towns of Victoria—Fernshaw', Newspaper Cuttings, ML, vol. 274; 'Beautiful Fernshaw', *Argus*, 23 June 1934, p. 9.
2 *Hall's Directory for 1896*, passim.
3 MacDonald, *Tourists' Handbook of Australia*; Cook & Son, *Railway Official Guide Book to Tasmania*; Morris (ed.), *CPA*, vol. I, pp. 147–8; Garran (ed.), *PAA*, pp. 392–4.

4 Smith, *European Vision*.

5 Field, 'Journal of an Excursion across the Blue Mountains', pp. 462–4, 473.

6 Evans, 'Tasmania', pp. 34–47; Proudfoot, 'Botany Bay, Kew, and the Picturesque', pp. 30–45; Carter, *The Road to Botany Bay*, pp. 231–3; Mackay, The Geological Sublime; Smith, *European Vision*, pp. 201–2; Ousby, *The Englishman's England*, pp. 152–4.

7 Buzard, *The Beaten Track*, pp. 156, 216. This point is explored in detail in the following: Adler, 'Origins of Sightseeing'; Andrews, *The Search for the Picturesque*; Carter, *The Road to Botany Bay*; Dodd (ed.), *The Art of Travel*; Knoepflmacher and Tennyson (eds), *Nature and the Victorian Imagination*; Moir, *The Discovery of Britain*; Pratt, *Imperial Eyes*; Sears, *Sacred Places*; Tinniswood, *A History of Country House Visiting*.

8 Smith, *European Vision*, p. ix.

9 Holloway and Errington, *The Discovery of Scotland*; Sir Walter Scott, *The Lady of the Lake*.

10 Pearce, *The Social Psychology of Tourist Behaviour*, passim esp. pp. 30–2.

11 Horne, Favourite Resorts, pp. 268–72.

12 Davidson and Spearritt, *Holiday Business*.

MAKING TOURISM AUSTRALIAN, *pp. 23–59*

1 The discrepancy between the departure dates noted by Banks and Cook in their respective journals is because Cook operated under naval time.

2 Banks in Smith, *European Vision*, p. 14.

3 Beaglehole (ed.), *The Endeavour Journal*, vol. 1, p. 313.

4 Joseph Banks on the *Endeavour* voyage: Smith, *European Vision*, pp. 14–49; Beaglehole (ed.), *The Endeavour Journal*, vol. 1, pp. 28–33, 40, 139 and passim; O'Brian, *Joseph Banks*, pp. 59–141; Salmond, *The Trial of the Cannibal Dog*, pp. 56–85; Fara, *Sex, Botany and Empire*, pp. 19, 88; *ADB*, vol. 1, pp. 52–3. On eighteenth-century tourists see Adler, 'Origins of Sightseeing', pp. 9–22.

5 *OED*, vol. XVIII, p. 306; Rigby, 'Lady Travellers', passim; Anon., 'Ordered Abroad', *Temple Bar*, vol. XXI, September 1867, p. 252; Sears, *Sacred Places*, passim; Leed, *The Mind of the Traveler*, pp. 2, 43, 179–99.

6 Hanbury-Tenison, *The Oxford Book of Exploration*, p. 422 (Evans); Wood, 'Explorations under Governor Phillip', p. 19 (Tench).

7 Andrews, *The Search for the Picturesque*, pp. 109–12, 136–7, 150; Smith, *European Vision*, p. 2.

8 Millar, *Journals of Australian Explorers*, pp. 275–7.

9 Smith, *European Vision*, pp. 1–189, passim; Boorstin, *The Discoverers*, pp. 256–89; Louisa Atkinson, 'A Voice in the Country: Incidents of Australian Travel', *SMH*, 9 November 1863, p. 2; Daley, *Victorian Historical Memorials to Explorers and Discoverers*.

10 Emergence of the notion, 'wilderness': Nicolson, *Mountain Gloom*, chs 2–5; Smith, *European Vision*, pp. vii–viii and passim; Pratt, *Imperial Eyes*, pp. 20, 25, 137–8; Morse Peckham, 'Toward a Theory of Romanticism' (1950), in Peckham, *The Triumph of Romanticism*, pp. 14–24; Thacker, *The Wildness Pleases*, pp. 1–12, 30, 138–41.

11 Proudfoot, 'Opening Towns' p. 70; Hutchings, 'Eugene von Guérard', pp. 114–17.

12 Early notions of the 'sublime': Nicolson, *Mountain Gloom*, p. 313; Burke, *A Philosophical Enquiry*, pp. 58–9; Mackay, The Geological Sublime, pp. 53–62; Battersby, *Gender and Genius*, pp. 74–7, 86.

13 Burke, *A Philosophical Enquiry*, pp. 36, 53–76, 210–22.

14 Andrews, *The Search for the Picturesque*, passim; J. Dixon Hunt, 'Picturesque' in Turner (ed.), *Dictionary of Art*, pp. 740–3; Smith, *European Vision*, pp. 201–2.

15 Macquarie, 'Journal to and from Van Diemen's Land to Sydney in N. S. Wales' in *Journals*, pp. 66, 69–70; Evans, *Geographical … Description*, p. 43; Frankland, *Five Letters*, pp. 8–9, 24; Chapman, *The Diaries and Letters of G. T. W. B. Boyes*, p. 476 fn. 34 (*Times* quote).

16 Evans, *Geographical … Description*, p. 44; *Quarterly Review*, April 1822, p. 105.

17 'Narrative of an Expedition to the Head of the Derwent, and to the Countries bordering the Huon, performed in February and March, 1835, by George Frankland', *Tasmanian Education*, August 1954, pp. 213–14.

18 ibid., p. 216; Burn, *Narrative of the Overland Journey*, p. 13; Brown, 'John Skinner Prout'; Brown and Kolenberg, *Skinner Prout in Australia*; Meredith, *My Home in Tasmania*, p. 263; *Walch's Tasmanian Guide Book*, 1871, pp. 26–9.

19 R. T. Easterby, 'Gippsland', in Morris (ed.), *CPA*, vol. III, pp. 255–68.

20 Angas, *Savage Life and Scenes*, preface; Kerr (ed.), *DAA*, pp. 19–21; Tregenza, *George French Angas*; E. J. R. Morgan, 'George French Angas', *ADB*, vol. 1, pp. 18–19.

21 Angas, *Savage Life and Scenes*, pp. 162–70; Angas, *South Australia Illustrated*, plate XVII.

22 Press, *Julian Tenison-Woods*, 1994; Tenison-Woods, *Geological Observations in South Australia*, pp. 228 (the section on Mount Gambier was first published in the *South Australian Register*, 1 October 1857 as 'South Australian Geology: the Mount Gambier Volcano').

23 Thomas Burr in Linn, *A Diverse Land*, pp. 10–11.

24 *Sydney Mail*, 21 June 1879, p. 972.

25 Buzard, *The Beaten Track*, pp. 109–10, 130–2 and passim; Pimlott, *The Englishman's Holiday*, pp. 69–70; Whithey, *Grand Tours*, pp. 3–104 passim; Hibbert, *The Grand Tour*, pp. 235–7; Porter, *Haunted Journeys*, p. 27.

26 Buzard, *The Beaten Track*, pp. 19–47; Whithey, *Grand Tours*, pp. 50–2, 102–3; Ousby, *The Englishman's England*, pp. 172–3, 179; Andrews, *The Search for the Picturesque*, pp. 153–4.

27 Brendon, *Thomas Cook*, pp. 5–8, 17, 31, 33, 36–55, 85–6; Buzard, *The Beaten Track*, pp. 49–65. There are several earlier historical accounts of Thomas Cook & Son: Rae, *The Business of Travel*, 1891; Pudney, *The Thomas Cook Story*, 1953.

28 Buzard, *The Beaten Track*, pp. 47, 58–65, 91–7; Brendon, *Thomas Cook*, p. 89; Whithey, *Grand Tours*, pp. 162–6.

29 The tour 'Home' (to England) as a sign of social status: Pesman, *Duty Free*, pp. 23–40; Kingston, *Oxford History of Australia*, vol. 3, pp. 181–2; Serville, *Pounds and Pedigrees*, pp. 222, 236.

30 Henry Lawson in Kiernan (ed.), *Henry Lawson*, p. 78.

31 This is based on a 6d tram fare and 1s admission fare per adult. The entertainments included roller-skating, acrobats, contortionists, magicians, and brass bands as well as displays of marine specimens. The cost of admission compared favourably to costs of other entertainments, such as attending a cricket match, or a music hall performance or entertainments at other seaside suburbs, such as Manly or Clontarf. See: Dunne, The Development of Coogee and Other Sydney Seaside Resorts, pp. 101–32, 152.

32 Clara, 'A Little Trip up the Western Line', *AT&CJ*, 9 April 1881, p. 697; Cook & Son, *Excursions*, pp. 4–8.

33 Morris (ed.), *CPA*, vol. II, p. 36; 'Healthy Holiday Haunts on the Hills. Wentworth Falls' c. 1894 in Newspaper Cuttings, ML, vol. 78, p. 185; 'The Highlands and the Metropolis', c. 1890 in Newspaper Cuttings, ML, vol. 77, p. 62; NSW Railways, *Beautiful Pleasure Resorts*, 1893; William Eyre to

E. G. M. Eddy, Chairman Railway Commission, Correspondence, 1890, in Burke, *Images of Popular Leisure*, Appendix 1.

34 Articles about the caves often noted the type of reception by Wilson. See also Dunkley, *Jenolan Caves*, pp. 14–15.

35 *New South Wales Railways Tourists' Guide, Division I*, pp. 12–14.

36 Davidson and Spearritt, *Holiday Business*, pp. 59–63; Cook & Son, *Excursions*; Brendon, *Thomas Cook*, pp. 95–6.

37 Cooper's Hotels, *Souvenir and Guide*; Davidson and Spearritt, *Holiday Business*, pp. 73–6; 'Tourist Bureau and Agents', *Sand's Sydney and Suburban Directory* for the years 1892–1900.

TRAVEL AS CELEBRATION, *pp. 61–97*

1 Laurent and Campbell, *The Eye of Reason*, p. 73.

2 Stockton (ed.), *Blue Mountains Dreaming*; Thomas, *Artificial Horizon*.

3 Brian Fletcher, 'Introduction' in Mann, *The Present Picture of New South Wales 1811*, 1979 and pp. 31–2 (Mann quotes).

4 Leed, *The Mind of the Traveler*, pp. 27–8, 37, 47–8, 80.

5 Bonyhady, *Burke and Wills*, pp. 26–30, 56; Macpherson, *Mount Abundance*; Hodgson, *Reminiscences of Australia*, p. 5; Fitzpatrick, *Australian Explorers*, pp. 10–11; Roderick, 'The Education of an Explorer', pp. 22–38; Watson, 'Exploring Australian Explorers', pp. 54–62; Smith, *European Vision*, pp. 1, 3 and passim; Fitzpatrick, *Australian Explorers*, p. 12.

6 Holman, *A Voyage Round the World*, vol. 4, pp. 445–6; Bartlett, *New Holland*, chs 9–10; Blainey (ed.), *Oceana*, p. 1; Adler, 'Origins of Sightseeing', pp. 9, 21.

7 Smith, *European Vision*, pp. 214ff, 258, 275 and passim; Bartlett, *New Holland*, pp. 157, 187; Hodgson, *Reminiscences of Australia*, p. 174ff; Gerstaecker, *Narrative of a Journey*, vol. II, p. 268; Morison, *Australia As It Is*, p. 46.

8 Holman, *A Voyage Round the World*, pp. 443–5; Morison, *Australia As It Is*, p. 185ff; Townsend, *Rambles and Observations*, p. 34.

9 There is a difference in opinion about whether Guérard was fifty or fifty-one. I have chosen 'fifty' on the basis of his birth year given in the *Australian Dictionary of Biography*, and a statement in Neumayer's account of the expedition, in which he wrote 'M. de Guérard celebrated his 50th birthday on this very day' (p. 77).

10 For biographical details of Guérard's life and accounts of this expedition and the resulting artwork, see: *ADB*, vol. 4, pp. 306–7; Bruce, Comstock and McDonald, *Eugene von Guérard*, pp. xv, 38, 223; Guérard, intro. by M. Tipping, *Australian Landscapes*; Neumayer, *Results of the Magnetic Survey of the Colony of Victoria executed during the Years 1858–1864*, Mannheim, 1869, pp. 67–89; Andrews, *Kosciusko*, pp. 36, 146–59; Bonyhady, *Images in Opposition*, pp. 94–5; Bonyhady, *Colonial Image*, pp. 72–7.

11 Andrews, *Kosciusko*, p. 163.

12 Laurent and Campbell, *The Eye of Reason*, p. 73.

13 Mackaness (ed.), *Fourteen Journeys*, pp. 234–5; Martin, *The Australian Sketchbook*, p. 29.

14 The journal indicates a fourth gentleman was included, possibly a clergyman or the father of one of the party.

15 This section of the chapter is based on an account of a trip to Jenolan Caves: A Correct and Faithful Account of a Journey to the Fish River Caves by the Pickwick Corresponding Club, (unpub. journal),

Local Studies Collection (acc. no. 18/1–3), Blue Mountains City Library, pp. 1–22. Direct quotations: ibid, pp. 2, 22, 29. See also Smith, *From Katoomba to Jenolan Caves*, pp. 26–31.

16 Horne, Favourite Resorts, Appendix 1 (Women's travel-writing about nineteenth century Australia), pp. 322–7.

17 Kingston, 'The Lady and the Australian Girl', pp. 27, 34, 40. John Hirst examines the meaning of 'gentleman' in Hirst, *The Strange Birth of Colonial Democracy*, pp. 106–9.

18 Hill and Hill, *What We Saw in Australia*, pp. 1, 7; North, *Recollections*, vol. 1, pp. 80, 83, 197; vol. 2, p. 330. For an interpretation of North's work, see: Losano, 'A Preference for Vegetables'; Mills, *Discourses of Difference*, pp. 188–9, 212 (n. 7).

19 Mills, 'Discourses of Difference', pp. 135–7, 140 (n. 27).

20 Davidson, *Hints to Lady Travellers*, p. 63.

21 Hill and Hill, *What We Saw in Australia*, p. 2; *Australian Etiquette*, pp. 177–8; Rains, *By Land and Ocean*, preface, pp. 58–61; North, *Recollections*, vol. 2, p. 88; Macpherson, *My Experiences in Australia*, pp. 61, 89, 293; Adams (ed.), *The Letters of Rachel Henning*, p. 73; Horne, *Jenolan Caves*, pp. 8–11; Vellacott (ed.), *Marianne North in Australia*, p. 3; Roe, 'What Rosamond and Florence Hill Saw in Australia', p. 68.

22 Mills, *Discourses of Difference*, p. 84.

23 Davies, *The Story of an Earnest Life*, pp. 121–68.

24 Mills, *Discourses of Difference*, pp. 211–12; Davies, *The Story of an Earnest Life*, pp. 121–68 passim.

25 Havard (ed.), 'Extracts from letters to Sir John Franklin', p. 289, 308; Also, her diary, a collection of pertinent daily jottings about her trip, upon which many of these letters were based: Russell (ed.), *This Errant Lady*. For an analysis of her Egypt travels, see: Russell, 'The Allure of the Nile'.

26 Kent, 'Abstract of the Journal of a Voyage', p. 101; Davies, *The Story of an Earnest Life*, p. 52; Cohen, *Elizabeth Macquarie*, pp. 100, 102, 105, 140; Meredith, *Over the Straits*, 1861, pp. 56, 58–61, 86; Havard (ed.), 'Lady Franklin's Visit', p. 291; Ritchie, *Lachlan Macquarie*, pp. 96, 140.

27 Trollope, *Britannia's Daughters*, pp. 146–7; Foster, *Across New Worlds*, pp. 12–14.

28 On the importance of the regional context of a journey, see: McEwan, 'Paradise or Pandemonium?'.

29 Fitzpatrick, *The Australian Explorers*, pp. 4–9; Cohen, *Elizabeth Macquarie*, p. 102; Macpherson, *My Experiences in Australia*, p. 134; Trollope, *Australia*, p. 33; Blainey (ed.), *Oceana*, p. 64.

30 Meredith, *Over the Straits*, p. 59; Havard (ed.), 'Lady Franklin's Visit', p. 291; Rains, *By Land and Ocean*, p. 57; Trollope, *Australia*, pp. 213–14.

31 Mackaness (ed.), *Fourteen Journeys*, pp. 107–8, 113; Meredith, *Notes and Sketches*, pp. 66–7, 72, 119; Rains, *By Land and Ocean*, p. 61; Trollope, *Australia*, p. 263; Blainey (ed.), *Oceana*, p. 65; Alcock (comp.), *The Family Year-Book*, p. 46; Havard (ed.), 'Lady Franklin's Visit', p. 283; Cohen, *Elizabeth Macquarie*, pp. 98–9; Macpherson, *My Experiences in Australia*, pp. 92–3; Laye, *Social Life and Manners*, p. 178.

INVENTING THE MOUNTAIN RESORT, *pp. 99–139*

1 Stanbury (ed.), *The Blue Mountains*; Low, *Blue Mountains*; Silvey, *Blue Mountains Guesthouses* ; Low and Smith, *Prince of Whips*; 'A Week in Leura (contributed by a Lassie)' in the *Mountaineer*, 30 June and 7 July 1905; Pickwick Corresponding Club, A Correct and Faithful Account of A Journey to the Fish River Caves; Mrs Lance Rawson, *Cookery Book and Household Hints*, 1886; Bruce, Comstock and McDonald, *Eugene von Guerard*, pp. 220–2.

2 H. Peckham, 'Katoomba Awake' in Low and Smith, *Prince of Whips*, p. 67.

3 Abell, 'Holidays and Health'; Webb and Adams, *The Mount Buffalo Story*; Curtis, *Tamborine Mountain History*; *Australian Garden History*, vol. 6, no. 4, January–February 1995 (issue devoted to Mount Macedon); Davidson and Spearritt, *Holiday Business*, pp. 12–18; Bruck (ed. and comp.), *Health Resorts*, pp. 145–8.

4 *Bailliere's New South Wales Gazetteer*, p. 594.

5 *Gibbs, Shallard & Co.'s Illustrated Guide,* 1882; Lorck (ed.), *New South Wales Picturesque Resorts.*

6 'The Waterfall of the Weatherboard', *AT&CJ*, 5 January 1878, p. 25. For train journey times in the 1880s, see: *Skinner's New South Wales Gazetteer*, 1883, p. 48. For detail of delays, see: Low, *Blue Mountains*, p. 24; M. H. Ellis, 'Blue Mountains History', in Rolfe (ed.), *The Blue Mountains*, p. 107.

7 'The Blue Mountains', *Sydney Mail*, 11 September 1869, p. 6; 'The Blue Mountains', *AT&CJ*, 25 January 1879, p. 168. Low, *Blue Mountains*, pp. 18–25; Mackay, The Geological Sublime, pp. 427–57; Kingston, *Oxford History of Australia*, vol. 3, pp. 32–4; Inglis, *Our Australian Cousins*, p. 202; Adams (ed.), *Letters of Rachel Henning*, pp. 65–6.

8 Martin, *Henry Parkes*, pp. 296–7; Stanbury (ed.), *The Blue Mountains*, pp. 100–1; Grainger, *Martin of Martin Place*, pp. 137, 163 (n. 22).

9 Graham Edds & Associates et al., Conservation Plan: Lilianfels, p. 12; Low, *Blue Mountains*, p. 33; R. M. Crawford, *'A Bit of a Rebel': The Life and Work of George Arnold Wood*, Sydney University Press, Sydney, 1975, pp. 114, 149.

10 'The Scenery of Australia. The Blue Mountains', 4 April 1882 in Newspaper Cuttings, ML, vol. 78, p. 194; 'A trip to the Blue Mountains', c. 1880, Newspaper Cuttings, ML, vol. 78, p. 192; Morris (ed.), *CPA*, 1887, vol. 2, p. 36; *Blue Mountain Guide*, pp. 6, 20, 26; advertisements in *Katoomba Times*, 8 June and 26 October 1889. For estimates of construction costs per room of a weatherboard dwelling, see: N. G. Butlin, *Investment in Australian Economic Development, 1861–1900*, Department of Economic History, RSSS, ANU, 2nd edn, 1971; reissued, 1976, p. 277.

11 Burke, Images of Popular Leisure, pp. 19, 31; *Gibbs, Shallard & Co.'s Illustrated Guide*, 1889, p. 192; 'Faulconbridge, Blue Mountains', *AT&CJ*, 10 May 1879, p. 888; 'Over the Mountains to Lithgow', *AT&CJ*, 22 November 1879, p. 983; *Railway Guide of New South Wales*, 1879, pp. 38–41, 48; *Katoomba Times*, 25 May, 8 June, 26 October 1889. Coghlan states that rents for four-roomed cottages in respectable working-class suburbs reasonably close to Sydney Town were about 12s per week, although they could be as low as 8s in some of those suburbs further out or as high as 18s for a four-roomed house with a kitchen and other conveniences: T. A. Coghlan, *Labour and Industry in Australia*, vol. III, Macmillan, Melbourne, 1969 (1st edn, 1918), p. 1627.

12 *Official Post Office Country Directory for 1878–79*, p. 385; *Mount Victoria*, 1984, pp. 24–26; Low, *Blue Mountains*, p. 19.

13 Silvey, 'Ladies of the Blue Mountains', pp. 12–13; Blue Mountains Historical Society, 'History of the Knight Family'; Low, *Blue Mountains*, p. 88; Horne, Favourite Resorts, p. 242; *NSW Post Office Directory* (henceforth *Wise's Directory*), 1886 (under names of each upper mountains township, excluding Leura and Medlow Bath, which weren't then listed).

14 Horne, Favourite Resorts, p. 229; Holt and Spearritt, 'Retreat to the Mountains'; Silvey, *Blue Mountains Guesthouses*, pp. 1, 35, 84–7, 91, 93–4; *Walter Samson and Co's New South Wales National Directory for 1867–68* (see under 'List of Trades'); *Wise's Directory*, 1878 (under Mount Victoria).

15 For example, see: 'On the Mountain. Letters from an Idler. No III', 1882, Newspaper Cuttings, ML, vol. 78, p. 187; CHWH, 'A Trip to the Blue Mountains', c. 1880, Newspaper Cuttings, ML, vol. 78, p. 192.

16 Low, *Blue Mountains*, pp. 36–7; Blue Mountains Historical Society, Wentworth Falls; Morris (ed.),

CPA, vol. II, p. 39; *The Railway Guide of New South Wales*, 1884, p. 44; Russell (comp.), *Pictorial Guide to the Blue Mountains*, 1885, p. 31; *The Blue Mountain Guide*, p. 36; *New South Wales Railway Tourists' Guide, Div. II*, 1889, p. 81; advertisements in the *Katoomba Times*, 15 May 1892, p. 3, and 11 November 1892, p. 1.

17 Kingston, *My Wife, My Daughter and Poor Mary Ann*, pp. 37, 41–3.

18 Late nineteenth-century concerns about sanitation and cleanliness: Kerreen M. Reiger, *The Disenchantment of the Home: Modernizing the Australian Family, 1880–1940*, Oxford University Press, Melbourne, 1985, pp. 41–4; Kingston, *Oxford History of Australia*, vol. 3, pp. 31–2; A. J. C. Mayne, *Fever, Squalor and Vice: Sanitation and Social Policy in Victorian Sydney*, University of Queensland Press, St Lucia, Qld, 1982.

19 *Katoomba Times*, 15 May 1892, p. 3, 11 November 1892, p. 1.

20 Freeland, *The Australian Pub*, 1966, pp. 145–50.

21 Russell, *Pictorial Guide*, pp. 28, 32, 35; *The Blue Mountain Guide*, pp. 28, 38, 42, 44; '"Doing" the Mountains. Some of the old Hands. Hotel Character Sketches', *AT&CJ*, 25 February 1893, p. 40.

22 'Stray Notes of a Week's Ramble on the Western Line', *Sydney Mail*, 2 January 1869, p. 11; 'The Blue Mountains', *Sydney Mail*, 11 September 1869, p. 6; Silvey, *Blue Mountains Guesthouses*, pp. 96–123; Horne, Favourite Resorts, p. 229 (table 1); *Wise's Directory*, 1904 (under all townships except Sydney listed by *Wise's Directory* for that year). Newcastle had 47 and Tamworth 17; *Census of NSW* for 1891 and 1901 (under the respective townships of Katoomba, Blackheath and Mount Victoria).

23 *Katoomba Times*, 25 May 1889, p. 1; *The Blue Mountain Guide*, pp. 8, 18, 22, 40; Battledore, '"Doing" the Blue Mountains. Fashion and Frivolity at the Western End', *AT&CJ*, 4 March 1893, p. 14.

24 Russell (comp.), *Pictorial Guide*, pp. 28, 32, 38; *New South Wales Railway Tourists' Guide. Division II*, 1889, pp. 82–3; 'The Rise of the Summer Boarder', *Sydney Mail*, 12 December 1896, p. 1250.

25 Proportions for New South Wales calculated from population figures, 'Male Population Colonies and State, 1828–1981' and 'Female Population, Colonies and States, 1828–1981', in Vamplew (ed.), *Australians: Historical Statistics*, pp. 29–30. Proportions for the upper Blue Mountains calculated from population figures for townships in the district from the *Census of NSW* for 1891, 1901 and the *Census of the Commonwealth of Australia* for 1911; Horne, Favourite Resorts, p. 233 (table 2). Census figures are not available for Wentworth Falls, Leura or Medlow Bath until 1911 (although they are available for Wentworth Falls in 1891). The breakdown according to sex of Mount Victoria's population for 1891, 1901 and 1911 shows that the proportion of men to women was higher there than in other townships in the upper mountains, and a little higher than the New South Wales average.

26 *Wise's Directory*, 1900 (figures compiled from the entries for upper mountains' townships); Horne, Favourite Resorts, p. 234 (table 3).

27 Martin (ed.), *Letters from Menie*, pp. 145, 148; 'Other Spheres for Women', *Woman's Sphere*, February 1901, p. 50.

28 Horne, Favourite Resorts, pp. 328–31 (appendix 2). Based on statistics in the section on 'Occupation' in *Census of NSW*, 1901.

29 Low and Smith, *The Prince of Whips*, pp. 8–9, 14–31.

30 Horne, Favourite Resorts, p. 240 (table 4), p. 242 (table 5).

31 Low, *Blue Mountains*, p. 36; Burke, Images of Popular Leisure, 1981, p. 30. Proceedings of Progress Associations' meetings were reported in the *Katoomba Times* for this period.

32 D. Walker, *Anxious Nation: Australia and the Rise of Asia, 1850–1939*, University of Queensland Press, St Lucia, Qld, 1999, pp. 141–5; Powell, *Mirrors of the New World*, 1978, pp. 129–43.

33 M. Roe, *Life over Death: Tasmanians and Tuberculosis*, Tasmanian Historical Research Association,

Hobart, 1999; R. Walker, 'The Struggle Against Pulmonary Tuberculosis in Australia, 1788–1950', *Historical Studies*, vol. 20, 1983, pp. 439–61; J. Burridge, Tuberculosis in the Australian Colonies: An Old Disease in a New Society, BA Honours thesis, ANU, 1978; *Official Post Office Country Directory*, p. 267; *New South Wales Tourists' Guide, Div. II*, 1889, p. 83; Inglis, *Our Australian Cousins*, pp. 347–8; Bruck (ed. and comp.), *Guide to the Health Resorts in Australia*, 1888, pp. 23–4, 50, 64; 'The Blue Mountains as a Health Resort: A Medical Man's Experience', *Sydney Mail*, 12 December 1896, p. 1252; *Wise's Directory*, 1894 (under each of the upper mountains' townships); *The Blue Mountain Guide*, p. 12.

34 *Dymock's Guide to Sydney and New South Wales*, p. 127.

35 'The Tourist. Katoomba's New Sight', *Sydney Mail*, 11 February 1893, p. 291; 'Round about the Mountains', *Sydney Mail*, 12 December 1896, p. 1246; 'Holiday Retreats and Summer Resorts of New South Wales. Katoomba and Blackheath', *AT&CJ*, 12 November 1892, p. 19.

36 Cook & Son, *Excursions in New South Wales*, p. 2.

37 Brief mention of the district's climate had been made in the 1889 edition of the *New South Wales Railway Tourists' Guide, Div. II*. For examples of the more detailed references in 1890s material including those quoted in the main text, see the series of brochures published by the New South Wales Railways: e.g. *Summer on the Mountains*, 1893; *A Summer Excursion to the Blue Mountains*, c. 1895; *Beautiful Pleasure Resorts*, 1893.

PUTTING UP THE SIGNPOSTS AND LAYING DOWN THE TRACKS, *pp. 141–173*

1 Public interest: Wright, *The Bureaucrats' Domain*, pp. 5–14 and passim; *Crown Lands Alienation Act 1861* (NSW), section 5. Public control and environmental protection: Bonyhady, *Colonial Earth*, pp. 42–65.

2 Coral Dow, 'What's in a Name? The Lakes National Park', in Hamilton-Smith (ed.), *Celebrating the Parks*, p. 152.

3 Bonyhady, *Colonial Earth*, pp. 107–15.

4 Smith, Historical Report, p. 11; 'Katoomba Waterfall, Blue Mountains, New South Wales', *AT&CJ*, 1 May 1880, p. 840. When the National Park at Port Hacking south of Sydney (later, the Royal National Park) was reserved for public recreation in 1879, the significance was that a large amount of land had finally been successfully reserved for public recreation and enjoyment for all time.

5 Debbie Quarmby, 'The Early Tasmanian National Parks Movement', in Hamilton-Smith (ed.), *Celebrating the Parks*, pp. 159–67; Wrixon quoted in Sanderson, 'The Alienation of the Melbourne Parks', p. 157.

6 Cotton (ed.), *National Park and Reserves*, p. 14; *The National Park of South Australia*, Commissioners of the Park with the State Tourist Bureau, n.d.; P. Jacobs and G. Anderson, 'Battles and Victories in the Victorian Alps', in Hamilton-Smith (ed.), *Celebrating the Parks*, pp. 95–6; Dow, 'What's in a Name?', in Hamilton-Smith (ed.), *Celebrating the Parks*, pp. 151–2; B. Moore, 'Tourists, Scientists and Wilderness Enthusiasts: Early Conservationists of the South West', in de Garis, *Portraits of the South West*, pp. 110–19; Webb and Adams, *Mount Buffalo Story*, pp. 40–1; Bonyhady, *Colonial Earth*, pp. 310–17 (quote p. 320).

7 Hamilton-Smith (ed.), *Celebrating the Parks*, pp. 95–6, 134, 151–2; Lennon, 'Wilson's Promontory in Victoria', pp. 199–200; T. S. Hall, 'Wilson's Promontory as a National Park', *Victorian Naturalist*, vol. 21, no. 9, 1905, pp. 128–31; J. B. Gregory, 'To Wilson's Promontory Overland', *Victorian Naturalist*, vol. 2, no. 1, 1885, pp. 43–5; pt 2, pp. 54–9; pt 3, pp. 87–90; pt 4, pp. 150–4.

8 Smith, Historical Report, pp. 8, 18–20, 27–9; Russell (comp.), *Pictorial Guide*, 1885, p. 30. Katoomba Municipal Council, which was proclaimed in 1889, managed the sights in and around Katoomba and Leura: Burke, Images of Popular Leisure, p. 29.

9 Quincey, *History of Mount Wellington*, p. 85.

10 Mossman and Bannister, *Australia, Visited and Revisited*, pp. 250–1; 'Random Notes by a Wandering Reporter', *Sydney Mail*, 4 March 1871, p. 15; 'Katoomba Falls Scenery', *Sydney Mail*, 29 May 1880, p. 988; *Sydney Mail*, 24 January 1880, p. 161; Smith, Historical Report, pp. 7–38, 74–86.

11 *Australian Garden History* (edited by C. McConville), pp. 5–14; Curtis, *Tamborine Mountain History*; Garran (ed.), *PAA*, pp. 283–5, 444–6.

12 Smith, *Lindeman Pass*, p. 99 (n. 2); Smith, Historical Report, pp. 29–30; Cook & Son, *Railway Official Guide Book to Tasmania*, 1895, p. 121ff; Hill, *Mount Gambier*, pp. 109–17.

13 Smith, *From Katoomba to Jenolan Caves*, pp. 7–9.

14 Griffiths, *Forests of Ash*, pp. 66, 104, 117, 120.

15 Low, *Blue Mountains*, p. 88; Smith, *From Katoomba to Jenolan Caves*, p. 9; Carne, 'Kerosene Shale Deposits of New South Wales', *Katoomba's Scenic Railway* (facs. n.d.), 1st pub. 1933; *New South Wales Railway Tourists' Guide, Div. II*, 1889, p. 21.

16 F. L. Warleigh, 'Fish River Caves', *The Australian*, vol. 1, October 1878, p. 203; Barnard, 'Notes on a Visit to the Jenolan Caves', p. 129; Maori, 'Holiday Trips in New South Wales: The Fish River Caves', *The Australian*, vol. 5, October–January 1880–81, p. 171; Newspaper Cuttings, ML, vol. 78, pp. 21, 24–5, 36–41; Physician, *Seventy Years of Life*, p. 163.

17 Smith, Historical Report, p. 33; Low, *Blue Mountains*, pp. 72, 74; Burke, Images of Popular Leisure, p. 36; Smith, *Lindeman Pass*, pp. 45–7.

18 Smith, Historical Report, p. 34.

19 'The Tourist. Govett's Leap', in Newspaper Cuttings, ML, vol. 78, c. 1895, p. 199; 'The Katoomba Falls', *Sydney Mail*, 8 February 1890, p. 300; 'Holiday Retreats and Summer Resorts of New South Wales. Katoomba and Blackheath', *AT&CJ*, 12 November 1892, p. 19; 'Visit of the Governor to Katoomba', *Sydney Mail*, 23 December 1893, p. 1315; E. D. H., 'Round about the Mountains: Being the Record of Haphazard Tours', *Sydney Mail*, 12 December 1896, p. 1246.

20 Broad, *A Woman's Wanderings*.

21 Smith, Historical Report, pp. 31, 74–86.

22 *BFP*, 28 December 1859, p. 2; Whiting, *BFP*, 11 January 1860, p. 2; Lucas, *SMH*, 5 June 1863, p. 3.

23 Adams (ed.), *Letters of Rachel Henning*, p. 73.

24 Newspaper Cuttings, ML, vol. 78, pp. 36–7B; Cook, *Jenolan Caves*, p. 29; Physician, *Seventy Years of Life*, p. 163; Foster, *Jenolan Caves*, p. 27.

25 Bloomers and feminism: Winkworth, 'Women and the Bicycle', pp. 97, 109–17; Russell, 'Recycling Femininity', *Australian Cultural History*, no. 13, 1994, pp. 35–7.

26 Foster, *Jenolan Caves*, p. 35.

27 This anecdote appeared on the inside front cover of Cooper, *Track from Katoomba to Jenolan Caves*.

28 Cook, *Jenolan Caves*, pp. 60–2.

29 These photographs were commissioned by the New South Wales government and used in some of their subsequent publications including Trickett, *Guide to the Jenolan Caves*, 1905, p. 21.

30 Cook, *Jenolan Caves*, p. 125; Foster, *Jenolan Caves*, pp. 27, 79.

31 F. F., 'Those Wonderful Caves. A Lady's Visit', 1892–93, in Newspaper Cuttings, ML, vol. 78, p. 38; Mrs Stevenson, *Letters from Samoa*, pp. 266–8; Ackermann, *Australia*, pp. 7–8; F. W., 'Jenolan Caves. Underground Wonderland. A Holiday Jaunt', c. 1894–95, in Newspaper Cuttings, ML, vol. 77, p. 4.

The identity of F. W. is unknown. The author, however, does make references to herself as a woman.

32 'A Visit to Katoomba Falls', c. 1880, in Newspaper Cuttings, ML, vol. 78, p. 192.

33 In the early 1900s at least one guidebook stated that the tracks around Wentworth Falls, 'easy of access, even to aged people, wind in and out … through the beautiful valleys': *Wilson's Sydney … and Blue Mountains Guide*, p. 53. However, the image of 'aged people' as a means to rate a track's difficulty was not usual.

34 'A Lassie', 'A Week in Leura', *The Mountaineer*, 7 July 1905.

35 Hall, *A Woman in the Antipodes and in the Far East*, p. 169. For another example of women walking together without men, see Broad, *A Woman's Wanderings*, pp. 116–17.

36 Annie R. Ramsey, 'Hints on Mountain Climbing', c. 1880–90, in Newspaper Cuttings, ML, vol. 78, p. 173. This article appeared in a collection of articles about the Blue Mountains.

WRITING IT ALL UP, *pp. 175–197*

1 Some paragraphs in this section are direct quotations from book reviews in contemporary publications which I have used to help capture the flavour of nineteenth-century reviewing: citation details are in the reference notes, rather than using quotation marks in the text, which would interrupt the flow of this piece. However, in order to keep this piece focused, I have only included one long quotation from the reviewed books themselves, although many nineteenth-century book reviews were laden with them. The reviewed books are real: Hill and Hill, *What We Saw in Australia*; *The Railway Guide of New South Wales*. See also Roe, 'What Rosamond and Florence Hill Saw in Australia', pp. 66–78.

2 This paragraph is an edited quotation from 'Review', *Argus*, 6 July 1863, pp. 5–6.

3 'spinsterly small talk' is an edited quote from a review of *Three Years in Melbourne* (by Clara Aspinall) in *Argus*, 17 January 1863, p. 5.

4 This paragraph is based on a review of *What We Saw in Australia*, and includes direct quotation ('remarkable valley, one of the lions of New South Wales', which itself is a quotation from the book): W. H. D. Adams, 'Miss Bird and Others'.

5 This sentence is a direct quotation: 'An Excursionist Guide-book', *Argus*, 26 October 1868, p. 7.

6 Raymond (comp.), *New South Wales Calendar and Directory 1832*, pp. 1–45, 108, 125. The directory was compiled by the postmaster of New South Wales with the assistance of other government departments. It measured about 18 cm by 11 cm, the size of a slim novel.

7 There were many gazetteers and directories published from the 1830s, some of which are listed in Joy Hughes, *New South Wales Directories 1828–1950: A Bibliography*, University of New South Wales Press, Kensington, NSW, 1987.

8 Buzard, *The Beaten Track*, pp. 65–79; Vaughan, *The English Guidebook*. John Vaughan's discussion of the history of the English guidebook provides examples of what was published between 1780 and 1870, but has little analysis of its changes over this period.

9 John Murray III, *Handbook for Travellers on the Continent*, John Murray, London, 1836. By 1838 Murray had published handbooks for southern Germany and Switzerland, and by mid-century, for Spain, northern Italy, France, southern Italy, as well as updated the earlier handbooks on the Continent and published tourists' phrasebooks: Buzard, *The Beaten Track*, pp. 66–8, 71–5. John Murray also continued to publish general travel accounts (or travel adventure) including Meredith, *Notes and Sketches of New South Wales*; Karl Baedeker first published a guidebook with some practical information in 1835, but a few years later he began to publish handbooks inspired, he acknowledged,

by John Murray's new publications: Vaughan, *The English Guidebook*, p. 47; Buzard, *The Beaten Track*, pp. 71–2.

10 Vaughan, *The English Guidebook*, pp. 40–1; Buzard, *The Beaten Track*, pp. 156–65.

11 Baird, *The Emigrant's Guide*, preface (quoted); Maclehose, *Strangers' Guide in New South Wales for 1839*; Mackenzie, *The Emigrant's Guide*; Townsend, *Rambles and Observations in New South Wales*; Mossman and Banister, *Australia, Visited and Revisited* .

12 *Stranger's Guide to Sydney*. This guidebook went into several editions. The Mitchell Library holds copies of editions published in 1858, 1861 and 1862.

13 There is very little information available about the life of James William Waugh. For an interesting account of his plans for a bookselling business, see: Correspondence, James W. Waugh to Mother, Sydney, 21 May 1857 in Waugh Family (John Waugh) Papers 1834–59, ML MSS A827, pp. 67–70. See also: *Waugh's Australian Almanac*, James William Waugh, Sydney, 1858; *Waugh's Country Directory*.

14 Hingston (comp.), *Guide for Excursionists from Melbourne*; *Guide for Excursionists from the Mainland to Tasmania*, Melbourne, 1869; *Walch's Tasmanian Guide Book*; *The Railway Guide of New South Wales*; *Gibbs, Shallard & Co.'s Illustrated Guide to Sydney* 1879; Worsnop, *The South Australian Tourist's Guide*; *Through Tasmania: Haywood's Visitor's and Colonist's Guide: when to go, how to get there, and what it will cost*, Hobart, 1885; *Visitors' Handy Guide to Sydney and Port Jackson*; *Fuller's Sydney Hand-book*, C.E. Fuller, Parramatta, NSW, 1879; Russell (comp.), *Pictorial Guide, Blue Mountain Guide*; *New South Wales Railways Tourists' Guide, Div. II*; Cook, *The Jenolan Caves*; *Horrock's Handy Guide*; Foster, *The Jenolan Caves*; *Dymock's Guide to Sydney and New South Wales*; Trickett, *Guide to the Jenolan Caves*; *Tourist's Guide to Pleasant Places Convenient to Railways*, 1900.

15 Pratt, *Imperial Eyes*, pp. 20, 39, 77–85.

16 William Dymock: *ADB*, vol. 8, pp. 394–5. The work of Gibbs, Shallard & Co.: Walker, *The Newspaper Press*, p. 226.

17 Samuel Cook: Walker, *The Newspaper Press*, p. 80. For the statement quoted in the text, see: Cook, *The Jenolan Caves*, preface.

18 Stewart, 'Journalism and the World of the Writer', pp. 178–93. Stewart argues that both country and metropolitan newspapers were places where writers, who in Britain might ordinarily have expected to publish books, could publish their work. Inglis, 'Questions About Newspapers', pp. 120–7; Morrison, 'Reading Victoria's Newspapers 1838–1901', pp. 128–40. For a general history of the newspaper press in nineteenth-century New South Wales, particularly how it was organised, see: Walker, *The Newspaper Press*.

19 Inglis, 'Questions about Newspapers', pp. 123–6. There were also 'weeklies' published in other colonies, including Victoria, South Australia and Queensland. See: Stewart, 'Journalism and the World of the Writer', pp. 183–4; Morrison, 'Reading Victoria's Newspapers', pp. 134–5.

20 Weeklies also published articles about travel beyond their own colonial boundaries: 'Account of a Trip through the Middle Islands of New Zealand', *Sydney Mail*, 13 October 1860; 'My Holiday Trip to Victoria and Tasmania', *AT&CJ* (a series published in 14 parts starting on 29 January 1870, p. 10).

21 'Rambles in the Suburbs by a Stroller' appeared in the *Sydney Mail* as a fairly regular column between July and November, i.e. 14, 21 and 28 July; 4 and 25 August; 1 and 22 September; 20 October; 3 November 1860.

22 'Alpine Sketches', *SM*, 15 December 1860; Aramis, 'A Visit to Shoalhaven', *SM*, 9 May 1863, p. 5; 'The Orange Groves and Orchards Around Parramatta', *AT&CJ*, 29 January 1870, p. 11; 'A Flying Trip to Bourke. Jottings by the Way', *AT&CJ*, 5 February 1870, p. 23.

23 Inglis, 'Questions about Newspapers', p. 125. Illustrations in newspapers: Walker, *The Newspaper Press*, pp. 225–9. Daily newspapers very occasionally used line drawings in the late nineteenth century, but started using photographs, if only sparingly, in the early twentieth century.

24 'A Trip up the Hawkesbury. (By a Correspondent)', *SM*, 2 February 1861, p. 1.

25 'In the Blue Mountains. Wentworth Falls', *AT&CJ*, 10 August 1889, p. 28.

26 W. W., 'An Excursion to the Hawkesbury Between Windsor and Wiseman's Ferry', *SM*, 16 September 1865, p. 6; 'Kiama and its Harbour Works', *AT&CJ*, 23 September 1876, p. 501; 'A Tour to the South, by our Special Correspondent, no. 2—Wollongong and its Vicinity', *AT&CJ*, 26 August 1871, p. 272; W. D. W., 'The Tourist: In and Around Parramatta', *SM*, 13 October 1888, p. 768; *SMH*, 25 May 1889.

27 *BFP*, 28 December 1859, p. 2; 'Up the Hawkesbury', *SM*, 11 December 1869.

28 W. W., 'An Excursion to the Hawkesbury Between Windsor and Wiseman's Ferry', *SM*, 16 September 1865, p. 6; *Bathurst Advocate*, 30 December 1848, p. 2.

29 'Up the MacDonald River. By a Correspondent', *SM*, 1 June 1878, p. 756; 'Towns and Villages of New South Wales: Newcastle', *AT&CJ*, 8 January 1870, p. 29.

30 Foster, *The Jenolan Caves*, p. 87.

31 Thomas, *The Artificial Horizon*, pp. 52–7, 131–2.

32 Schama, *Landscape and Memory*, pp. 10–12.

HOW MOUNTAINS BECAME SUBLIME, *pp. 199–225*

1 Wood, 'Explorations', p. 16.

2 Nicolson, *Mountain Gloom and Mountain Glory*, pp. 113–43, 158ff, 225–70; Thacker, *The Wildness Pleases*, p. 4.

3 Barrallier, *Journal*, pp. 10–14.

4 Thomas, *The Artificial Horizon*, pp. 6, 51, 89–90; Stockton, *Blue Mountains Dreaming*, pp. 55–62.

5 Blaxland, G., 'Gregory Blaxland's Narrative', p. 31; Richards (ed.), *Blaxland–Lawson–Wentworth*, pp. 111–13, 173–4; Mackaness (ed.), *Fourteen Journeys*, pp. 1–12. The expedition's dominance in twentieth-century histories of Australian exploration: Cunningham, *Blue Mountains*, pp. 13–29; Thomas, *The Artificial Horizon*. Only Blaxland's journal was published in his lifetime, first in 1823.

6 Smith, *European Vision*, p. 2; Williams, *Notes on the Underground*, pp. 23, 28–31.

7 Karskens, An Historical Study, pp. 7, 4–26; Proudfoot, 'Opening Towns', p. 68.

8 Cohen, *Elizabeth Macquarie*, pp. 100, 102, 140; Karskens, An Historical Study, p. 50; Mackaness (ed.), *Fourteen Journeys*, pp. 78, 88 (Antill), 105, 108 (Hawkins), 70–5 (XYZ); Havard, 'Some Early French Visitors', pp. 263–82 (Lesson); Meredith, *Notes and Sketches*, pp. 70–5.

9 The Macquarie journey over the Blue Mountains: Governor Lachlan Macquarie, 'Tour over the Western or Blue Mountains', *Sydney Gazette*, 10 June 1815; Mackaness (ed.), *Fourteen Journeys*, pp. 74–90; Macquarie, *Journals of His Tours*, pp. 89–110; Ellis, *Lachlan Macquarie*, pp. 269–74; Ritchie, *Lachlan Macquarie*, p. 143.

10 Governor Lachlan Macquarie, 'Tour over the Western or Blue Mountains', *Sydney Gazette*, 10 June 1815. Reprinted in: *Naval Chronicle*, vol. XXXV, January–June 1816; *Colonial Journal*, vol. 1, January–July 1816; *New Monthly Magazine and Universal Register*, vol. V, no. 25, 1 February 1816.

11 Macquarie, *Journals of His Tours*, p. 91.

12 ibid., pp. 68–70; Ritchie, *Lachlan Macquarie*, pp. 98–188.

13 Pratt, *Imperial Eyes*, pp. 178–81; Ruskin, *Modern Painters*, ch. XX.

14 Martin, *The Australian Sketchbook*, p. 8; Strzelecki in Andrews, *Kosciusko*, pp. 17–18, 87–96; Balfour, *A Sketch of New South Wales*, p. 42; Burn, 'Sir John and Lady Franklin and Party', p. 20.

15 William Wordsworth, *A Description of the Scenery of the Lake in the North of England*, Oxford, 1991 (first published as an essay in 1810, then as a book in 1822, then reprinted time and again).

16 Bicknell, *British Hills and Mountains*, pp. 29–30, 33–4, 37–9; Holloway and Errington, *The Discovery of Scotland*, pp. 89–91, 103–6; Ousby, *The Englishman's England*, pp. 144, 172, 181–4; Andrews, *The Search for the Picturesque*, pp. 109–12, pp. 136–7, 150; Pianzola, *Paysages Romantiques*, pp. 5–6; Ring, *How the English Made the Alps*; Ousby *The Englishman's England*, p. 146; Moir, *The Discovery of Britain*, pp. 134–6, 141ff, 149–54. From the mid-nineteenth century there was much English interest in climbing mountains on the continent. An Alpine Club was formed, expedition accounts published and illustrations drawn of climbers ascending steep, icey mountain peaks with the help of ice picks and ropes: David Robertson, 'Mid-Victorians amongst the Alps' in Knoepflmacher and Tennyson (eds), *Nature and the Victorian Imagination*, pp. 113–36.

17 Nicholas, *Darwin in Australia*, pp. v–17, 7 (Fitzroy), 22 (Darwin). Laurent and Campbell, *The Eye of Reason*, passim.

18 Darwin, *Journal of Researches*, p. 398.

19 Mackaness (ed.), *Fourteen Journeys*, p. 232.

20 Field, 'Journal of an excursion across the Blue Mountains of New South Wales, 1822', in Mackaness (ed.), *Fourteen Journeys*, p. 124. Field's journal of his tour was published in the *London Magazine* in 1823 and in a collection of articles, Barron Field (ed.), *Geographical Memoirs on New South Wales*; Bennett, *Wanderings in New South Wales*, pp. 96–100.

21 Darwin quoted in descriptions of the Blue Mountains: Guérard, *Australian Landscapes*, p. 56; Booth, *Australia*, p. 132; *Gibbs, Shallard, & Co.'s Illustrated Guide*, pp. 102, 104; Morris (ed.), *CPA*, pp. 41–3; *New South Wales Railways Tourists' Guide Div II*, p. 19.

22 Evans, *Geographical … Description of Van Diemen's Land*, p. 35, 44; review of Evans in *Quarterly Review*, April 1822, pp. 99–109; Curr, *Van Diemen's Land*, p. 31.

23 *ADB*, vol. 1, p. 410 (Frankland); 'Rough Notes of a Journal of Expedition to the Westward (from Bothwell to the Frenchman's Cap), by W. S. Sharland, Esquire, Assistant Surveyor AD 1832', pp. 4–5 in Gould's Reports, ML, State Library of New South Wales.

24 G. H. Stancombe et al. (eds), *The Diaries of John Helder Wedge 1824–35*, Royal Society of Tasmania, 1962, p. 64.

25 Glover and Tasmanian mountains: Hendrik Kolenberg, 'Hobart's 1832 Glover Sketchbook', *Art Bulletin of Tasmania*, 1984, pp. 1–9; McPhee, *The Art of John Glover*, p. 32ff; *Hobart Town Courier*, 9 April 1831; *Times* quoted in P. Chapman, *The Diaries and Letters of G. T. W. B. Boyes*, p. 476 (n. 34).

26 'Narrative of an Expedition to the Head of the Derwent, and to the Countries bordering the Huon, performed in February and March, 1835, by George Frankland', *Tasmanian Education*, August 1954, pp. 213–15.

27 Burn in *Colonial Magazine*, May–August 1841, p. 164.

28 Kerr (ed.), *DAA*, p. 646; *Prout's Dioramic Views*; 'Review of J. S. Prout, *Tasmania Illustrated*', *SMH*, 12 March 1846, p. 2.

29 Mount Wellington: Breton, *Excursions*, p. 364; 'Excursion to Mount Wellington', *Hobart Town Courier*, 22 December 1837, p. 2; Meredith, *My Home in Tasmania*, p. 27.

30 Angas, *Savage Life and Scenes*, pp. 41–2; Angas, *South Australia Illustrated*, plate X.

31 Garran (ed.), *PAA*, vol. 2, pp. 277–8; Hingston (comp.), *Guide for Excursionists*, pp. 85–92.

32 The name 'snowy mountains' was used to distinguish this region a couple of decades before Strzelecki

ascended what is now known as Mount Kosciuszko. As early as 1820 on expeditions to search for the Murrumbidgee, colonists noted the 'snowy mountains' in the south-west. It was a literal term referring to the presence of snow, and its use continued. In *A Voyage round the World*, James Holman wrote how 'the view of the snowy mountains … abundantly repays the traveller for the inconveniences [of the] trip to the Murrumbidgee'. Their official colonial naming occurred in 1831. Hamilton Hume in a letter to the *Sydney Morning Herald* registered his surprise at the sight of the mountains: 'to the utmost degree magnificent:—Mountains of an immense height, and some of them covered with snow … They were named the White Mountains, or Australian Alps'. Although the literal reference to their snowy summits persevered for a few years—sometimes as snowy mountains, sometimes as Snow Mountains, and occasionally as the Snow Mountain Range—by 1834 published accounts referred to them as the 'Australian Alps'. This name persevered well into the twentieth century, until the phrase 'Snowy Mountains' again came into common use in post-war Australia.

33 Andrews, *Kosciusko*, p. 24.

34 Strzelecki, *Physical Description*, pp. 55–62; Holman, *A Voyage Round the World*, p. 448; Andrews, *Kosciusko*, pp. 32–3 (Hume), 56–61.

35 Garran (ed.), *PAA*, p. 51.

36 Morris (ed.), *CPA*, vol. III, p. 1.

37 Smith, *Australian Painting*, p. 60; Bonyhady, *Images in Opposition*, pp. 84–6

HOW LIMESTONE CAVES BECAME WONDERFUL, *pp. 227–251*

1 I have fictionalised the first scene where Webb announces to the reading group his intentions to go bush, but elements of the scene are based on historical accounts. Webb did belong to a reading group (he was honorary secretary of the Swan River Reading Club in 1841), and he wrote an account of his excursion to the Maidin Cave. The rest of the account is based on journals and accounts of excursions to the caves in 1841 as detailed below and in following footnotes. Webb's biographical details: Rica Eriksen (ed.), *Bicentennial Dictionary of Western Australians pre-1829 to 1888*, UWA Press, 1988, p. 3240. Account of excursion: George J. Webb, 'Journal kept during an Excursion to the Caves of "Maiden"', *Swan River News and Western Australian Chronicle*, 1 September 1847. See also: Journal of John Septimus Roe during a Journey with Governor Hutt from Perth to the Caves of Madin [*sic*], Field Book 1 (unpub.), transcript, J. S. Battye Library PR8679/YAN; Ian Elliot, The Discovery and Exploration of the Yanchep Caves (unpub. paper), read before the Royal Western Australian Historical Society, 25 February 1977, J. S. Battye Library.

2 This dialogue is based on a similar statement in his published account: see above.

3 J. S. Roe, 'Journal of an Excursion by His Excellency the Governor and the Surveyor General to the Caves of Maidin', *Inquirer*, 3 November 1841.

4 These paragraphs and quotations are drawn from Webb's account (see n. 1).

5 Ousby, *The Englishman's England*, pp. 132–8; Davidson and Spearritt, *Holiday Business*, p. 8.

6 Williams, *Notes on the Underground*, pp. 30–7, 86, 95; Shaw, *History of Cave Science*, pp. 1, 16–34, 244.

7 Jameson, *New Zealand, South Australia and New South Wales*, p. 116; Backhouse, *Visit to the Australian Colonies*, pp. 319–20; Anderson, Wellington Caves: Resource and Management Study (unpub. report), vol. 1, pp. 170–6; Mitchell, *Three Expeditions*, pp. 353–66.

8 Sears, *Sacred Places*, pp. 31–48 (quote on p. 38).

9 Treharne, 'Abercrombie Caves Resort', *Helictite*, vol. 24 (1 & 2), 1986, p. 43; Ellis, *Conrad Martens*, pp. 163–4; Chalker and Nurse, 'The History of Wombeyan Caves', p. 47.

10 Letter to the Editor (signed 'A Constant Reader'), *Bathurst Advocate*, 30 December 1848, p. 2; *BFP*, 30 April 1856, p. 2; Tenison-Woods, *Geological Observations*, p. 321.

11 Tenison-Woods, *Geological Observations*, pp. 319–63.

12 Darwin, *Structure and Distribution of Coral Reefs*, pp. 75–87; Foster, *Jenolan Caves*, p. 95; J. E. Tenison-Woods, 'The Barrier Reef', *Australasian*, 17 March 1866, pp. 8–9; J. E. Tenison-Woods, 'A Trip to a Coral Reef', *Australasian*, 18 October 1879, pp. 486–7; Garran (ed.), *PAA*, vol. 2, pp. 392–4.

13 Shaw, *History of Cave Science*, pp. 200–3.

14 Early geological explanations in travel accounts: Millard, 'Recollections of a Tour', p. 19; *BFP*, 28 December 1859, p. 2; John Lucas, 'A Visit to the Binda Caves', *SMH*, 5 June 1863, p. 3; 'The Binda or Fish River Caves', *AT&CJ*, 14 January 1871, p. 55.

15 'Papers Presented at the Australian Caves History Seminar', *Helictite*, vol. 24 (1& 2), 1986, pp. 36, 43; Middleton, *Oliver Trickett*, pp. 21–7; 'The Yarrangobilly Caves. An Official Report', Newspaper Cuttings, ML, vol. 78, 1889, p. 2.

16 Shaw, *History of Cave Science*, p. 243; Havard, *Jenolan Caves*, p. 29; J. E. Richter, 'The Fish River Caves, Near Sydney, Australia', *Scientific American*, 11 October 1884, vol. 51, no. 15, p. 229; A. Tissandier, *Bulletin Société Spéléologie*, 1895, vol. I, no. 2, pp. 50–6.

17 Wilkinson in Jenolan Caves guidebooks: Cook, *The Jenolan Caves*, p. 170ff; *The Railway Guide of New South Wales* 1886, pp. 144–8; Foster, *The Jenolan Caves*, pp., 25, 34, 90–6.

18 Mackaness (ed.), *Fourteen Journeys*; Adams (ed.), *The Letters of Rachel Henning*, p. 73; Dunkley, *Jenolan Caves*, p. 12 (Whalan).

19 Letter to the Editor, *Bathurst Advocate*, 30 December 1848, p. 2.

20 Horne, *Jenolan Caves*, pp. 8, 13–14, 54–7, 60, 65; Letter to the Editor, *Bathurst Advocate*, 30 December 1848, p. 2; *BFP*, 30 April 1856, p. 2; Millard, 'Recollections of a Tour', p. 19; 'Fish River Creek', *BFP*, 28 December 1859, p. 2; 'The Binda or Fish River Caves', *AT&CJ*, 14 January 1871, p. 55.

21 R. W. Rathbone, 'John Lucas', *ADB*, vol. 5, pp. 107–8.

22 Lucas, *SMH*, 5 June 1863, p. 3.

23 Sears, *Sacred Places*, pp. 29–30, 130–1.

24 Havard, *Jenolan Caves*, passim.

25 ibid., p. 16; Cooper, *Track from Katoomba to Jenolan Caves*, pp. 1–5.

26 Mines Department, Special Bundles, Jenolan Caves 1866–85, AONSW 2/3511–12; Havard, *Jenolan Caves*, pp. 14, 18, 21, 24, 27, 34.

27 Government Geological Surveyor in *Railway Guide*, p. 114; J. B. Youdale, 'The Fish River Caves' in Newspaper Cuttings, ML, vol. 78, 1881, p. 36 (Youdale notes that £500 was spent on outfitting the caves with steps in 1880); C. C. Russell, 'Cave Gossip and a Visit to Jenolan', *Woronora Times*, c. 1892 in Newspaper Cuttings, ML, vol. 78, p. 38; Superintendant of Caves W. S. Leigh, 'Progress Report, January 1893' in Newspaper Cuttings, ML, vol. 77.

28 Middleton, *Oliver Trickett*, pp. 24, 26; Gary Bilton, 'Early History of Yarrangobilly Caves', *Helictite*, vol. 24 (1&2), 1986, pp. 36–8; Chalker and Nurse, 'The History of Wombeyan Caves', pp. 47–50; 'Southern Tourist Districts. Opening up of Wombeyan Caves', Newspaper Cuttings, ML, c. 1896, vol. 78, pp. 47–8; 'The Yarrangobilly Caves', Newspaper Cuttings, ML, 1889, vol. 78, p. 1; Horne, *Jenolan Caves*, pp. 30–48; Grace Karskens, 'Historical and Architectural Development of Caves House Precinct' in Robert Moore Architects and Conservation Consultants, The Caves House Precinct.

29 B. Moore, 'Tourists, Scientists and Wilderness Enthusiasts: Early Conservationists of the South

West' in de Garis, *Portraits of the South West*, pp. 110–19; E. S. Simpson, 'Geological Features of the South-Western Caves District', in Fraser (ed.), *Notes on the Natural History*, pp. 35–6, 41; Ian Elliot, The Discovery and Exploration of the Yanchep Caves (unpub. paper), read before the Royal Western Australian Historical Society, 25 February 1977, J. S. Battye Library.

30 *Western Australia's Wonderland South West Caves*; E. Hamilton-Smith, 'Wilderness Myths and Australian Caves', *Helictite*, vol. 25, no. 2, 1986, p. 71.

31 Foster, *The Jenolan Caves*, pp. 39, 41, 43, 51; Mann, 'Through Jenolan Caves', pp. 426–34; Trickett, *Guide to the Jenolan Caves*, passim; Cook, *Jenolan Caves*, passim.

HOW FERNS BECAME BEAUTIFUL, *pp. 253–279*

1 Cook & Son, *Railway Official Guide Book to Tasmania*.

2 Robert Brown, 'On Woodsia, A New Genus of Ferns' in Brown, *Miscellaneous Botanical Works*, pp. 251–4; Smith, 'A Botanical Essay', pp. 215–64.

3 Brockway, *Science and Colonial Expansion*, p. 74.

4 La Billardière, *Novae Hollandiae Plantarum Specimen*, vol. 2, p. 90ff.

5 'Robert Brown', *Tasmanian Naturalist*, vol. 1, no. 1, December 1925, pp. 15–16; Mabberley, *Jupiter Botanicus*, pp. 117–19.

6 Brown, *The Miscellaneous Botanical Works*, vol. 1, pp. 59–62 (first pub. in M. Flinders, *Voyage to Terra Australis*, 1814). Other examples: Langsdorff et Fischer, *Plantes Recueillis*, Dumont D'Urville, 'De la Distribution des Fougères'.

7 Bunce, *1836 Catalogue of Seeds and Plants*.

8 Allan Cunningham, 'On the Botany of the Blue Mountains', in Field (ed.), *Geographical Memoirs*, pp. 323–65.

9 Lachlan Macquarie, 'Journal of a Tour to the Cow Pastures and Illawarra in January 1822', in Macquarie, *Journals of His Tours*, p. 239.

10 Smith, *European Vision*, pp. 255–6; Breton, *Excursions*, 1833, pp. 71–2; Lady Franklin to Sir John Franklin, April 1839, in Havard, 'Lady's Franklin's Visit to New South Wales 1839', p. 312; Backhouse, *A Narrative*, pp. 422–4; Angas, *Savage Life*, 1847, pp. 239–43.

11 *Prout's Dioramic Views of Australia*.

12 McPhee, *The Art of John Glover*, p. 32.

13 Quincey, *The History of Mount Wellington*, pp. 13–18.

14 Backhouse, *A Narrative*, pp. 34–5.

15 Darwin, *Journal of Researches*, 1839, pp. 535–6; Chapman and Brown, 'Art exhibitions in Tasmania during the nineteenth century—a chronology'.

16 Nicholls (ed.), *Traveller Under Concern*, p. 67.

17 Meredith, *My Home in Tasmania*, pp. 298, 327.

18 J. Walters, 'Botanical Tour of the Dandynoy [*sic*] Ranges, May 6th 1853', *Gardener's Chronicle*, 24 September 1853, pp. 13–14; Coulson, *The Story of the Dandenongs*, pp. 4–10, 34–5; Jones, *Prolific in God's Gifts*, p. 86 (Mueller).

19 Bonyhady, *Colonial Earth*, pp. 105–23; Guérard, *Australian Landscapes*, pp. 68–9; Hingston (comp.), *Guide for Excursionists*, pp. 25–8; Coulson, *Story of the Dandenongs*, pp. 26–53; Jones, *Prolific in God's Gifts*, p. 86 (Mueller), 118–32; Boldrewood, *The Flower Garden in Australia*, p. 101; Anderson, *Victoria's National Parks*, p. 52; *The Visitors' Guide to the Upper Yarra District*, p. 94ff; Victoria Railways, *Picturesque Victoria*, 1908, p. 37–47.

20 Sears, *Sacred Places*, pp. 130, 142–7; Bonyhady, *Colonial Earth*, pp. 260–1.

21 Coulson, *Story of the Dandenongs*, pp. 4–6 (Walters); Jones, *Prolific in God' Gifts*, pp. 78–88, 80–1 (Mueller); G. W. Robinson, 'In the Dandenong Ranges Sixty Years Ago', *Victorian Naturalist*, vol. 28, 1911, pp. 30–2. For the debate around the preservation of Victoria's giant trees and a lively account of the quest to establish how tall and how old were Victoria's mountain ash, see Bonyhady, *Colonial Earth*, pp. 250–9, 262–79. For an environmental history of Victoria's giant trees, see Griffiths, *Forests of Ash*, pp. 12–29.

22 Allen, *The Victorian Fern Craze*, passim.

23 Williams, *Select Ferns and Lycopods*, pp. 2–3, 52–243.

24 Woolls, *A Contribution to the Flora of Australia*, 1867, p. 40.

25 Reprinted from *Horticultural Society Magazine*, in Gelding, *Three Sydney Garden Nurseries*, p. 19.

26 Hannaford, *The Wildflowers of Tasmania*, pp. 175–88; Crittendon, *A History of Australian Gardening Books*, p. 69.

27 Cohn, 'Australian Plants, the Garden and Botany', pp. 16–18.

28 Woolls, 'The Ferns of Australia', p. 189.

29 Woolls, *A Contribution to the Flora of Australia*, preface, pp. 36–85; J. Tenison-Woods, 'The Ferns of Australia', *Australasian*, 14 July 1866, p. 452.

30 Meredith, *My Home in Tasmania*, pp. 94–5; Woolls, *A Contribution to the Flora of Australia*, p. 36; Hannaford, *The Wildflowers of Tasmania*, pp. 132–46.

31 Woolls, 'The Ferns of Australia', pp. 209–10.

32 Bailey, *The Fern World of Australia*, preface.

33 Crittendon, 'Bibliography', *A History of Australian Gardening Books*. For example, William Clarson, *The Flower Garden and Shrubbery*, Massina, Melbourne, 1885; H. A. James, *Handbook of Australian Horticulture*, 1892.

34 *Horrocks' Handy Guide to the Blue Mountains and Caves of New South Wales*; Garran (ed.), *PAA*, vol. 2, pp. 309–10, 524; Morris (ed.), *CPA*, vol. I, p. 225, vol. III, pp. 9–10, 198, 204, 255; P. N. Trebeck, 'Mount Wilson and its Ferns', *Proc. Linnean Society of NSW*, vol. 1, pt 2, 1886, pp. 491–6.

35 Backhouse, *A Narrative*, pp. 361–2.

36 Frere, *The Antipodes and Round the World*, p. 72.

37 Morris (ed.), *CPA*, vol. I, p. 226; G. C. Craig, 'Picturesque Queensland—No. 1 Tambourine Mountain', *The Queensland Review*, 1886, pp. 286–90; John Shirley, 'Tambourine Mountain', in Australasian Association for the Advancement of Science, *Handbook of Excursions*, Brisbane, 1895, pp. 38–40; Eve Curtis, *The Turning Years: A Tamborine Mountain History*, Tamborine, Qld, 1988, pp. 28–30.

THE EYE OF THE BEHOLDER, *pp. 281–301*

1 Louisa Atkinson, 'Notes of the Month, October', *Illustrated Sydney News*, 15 October 1853; Clarke, *Pioneer Writer*, pp. 114–35; Lawson, *The Art of Louisa Atkinson*, pp. 9–20, 53–64; *ADB*, vol. 3, pp. 59–60.

2 L. Atkinson, 'A Voice from the Country', *SMH*, 26 April 1860, p. 2, 9 August 1860, p. 2, 12 February 1863, p. 2; L. Atkinson, 'A Voice from the Country: Mount Tomah', *SMH*, 28 January 1861, p. 2 (quote); L. Atkinson, 'A Voice from the Country: Ferns and their Haunts', *SMH*, 12 February 1863, p. 2 (quote).

3 Battersby, *Gender and Genius*, pp. 74, 76–7.

4 Woolls, *A Contribution to the Flora of Australia*, pp. 45–83, passim.

5 Meredith, *Notes and Sketches*, p. 121; Allan Cunningham, 'On the Botany of the Blue Mountains', in Field (ed.), *Geographical Memoirs*, pp. 323–65.

6 'Appendix—Caley's Description of Plants', in Andrews (ed.), *The Devil's Wilderness*, pp. 110–21. Wentworth in Richards, *Blaxland–Lawson–Wentworth*, p. 112.

7 René Primevère Lesson, 'Journey Across the Blue Mountains', in Havard, 'Some Early French Visitors', p. 270. First published in: Louis Isadore Duperry, *Voyage Autour du Monde, exécuté par Ordre du Roi, sur la Corvette de la Majesté, La Coquille, pendant les Années 1822–5*, Arthus Bertrand, Libraire-Editeur, Paris, 1826.

8 Breton, *Excursions*, p. 89; Bennett, *Wanderings*, pp. 96–105, passim; Backhouse, *A Narrative*, section III.

9 Elizabeth Hawkins, 'Journey from Sydney to Bathurst in 1822', in Mackaness (ed.), *Fourteen Journeys*, pp. 105–6. Other 'ladies' had also travelled across the Blue Mountains, the most famous being Mrs Macquarie, but their accounts have not yet come to light.

10 Meredith, *Notes and Sketches*, pp. 64, 74–5, 80.

11 Swann, 'Mrs Meredith and Miss Atkinson: writers and naturalists', *JRAHS*, vol. 15, pt 1, 1929, pp. 1–13; *ADB*, vol. 5, pp. 239–40; Kerr (ed.), *DAA*, pp. 528–30; Meredith, *Notes and Sketches*, pp. 64–122 (quote p. 122).

12 Meredith, *Notes and Sketches*, pp. 120–1.

13 For the seasons and years during which they travelled, see individual entries in Mackaness (ed.), *Fourteen Journeys*. Journeys referred to in this chapter throughout the period covered all seasons; Stanbury (ed.), *The Blue Mountains*, p. 49 (Bass); Mann, *The Present Picture*, pp. 34–5; Barrallier in *HRA*, vol. 5, p. 588.

14 Andrews (ed.), *The Devil's Wilderness*, p. 43.

15 Tipping (ed.), *Governor Phillip's Letters*, p. 50.

16 Blaxland in Mackaness (ed.), *Fourteen Journeys*, pp. 4–5, 6–7 (Blaxland); Richards (ed.), *Blaxland–Lawson–Wentworth*, pp. 100 (Lawson), 110 (Wentworth); Mackaness (ed.), *Fourteen Journeys*, p. 42 (Cox).

17 Morris (ed.), *CPA*, vol. II, p. 43. Another example of similar sentiments is: Bennett, *Wanderings*, p. 100.

18 Major H. C. Antill, 'Journal of an Excursion over the Blue or Western Mountains of New South Wales to Visit a Tract of New Discovered Country, in Company with His Excellency Governor and Mrs Macquarie and a Party of Gentlemen' was first published in 1914 as part of the Records of the Education Society: Mackaness (ed.), *Fourteen Journeys*, p. 88.

19 Cunningham, *Blue Mountains*, p. 101; Barrallier, *Journal of the Expedition*, p. 36.

20 Niagara Falls: Sears, *Sacred Places*, p. 12; Martin, *The Australian Sketchbook*, pp. 6–7. Victoria Falls (in Africa) was not a major tourist destination until the early twentieth century, only about fifty years after David Livingstone had 'discovered' it for the British in 1856: Hanbury-Tenison, *The Oxford Book of Exploration*, pp. 178–80; Horne, *The Intelligent Tourist*, pp. 17–18, 20.

21 Breton, *Excursions in New South Wales*, p. 82; Mossman and Banister, *Australia*, pp. 250–1; XYZ, 'A Ride to Bathurst, 1827' in Mackaness (ed.), *Fourteen Journeys*, pp. 176–7: Mackaness states that XYZ, author of the article, was Capt. William John Dumaresq. The article was first published as a series of six letters in the *Australian* from 13 March 1827.

22 For example, Augustus Earle, *King's Tableland, Blue Mountains, New South Wales*; Thomas Livingstone Mitchell, *Valley of the Grose*, 1835; John Skinner Prout, *Jamieson's Valley*, 1843; Eugen von Guérard,

View in the Cox'-river [*sic*] *Valley*, 1859.

23 Smith, *European Vision*, pp. 253–4 (Earle). Other examples, E. B. De La Touanne, *Sommet de la Cataracte Bouganville, sur la route de Sidney à Bathurst dans les montagnes bleues*, 1825; John Skinner Prout, *Fall of the Weatherboard*, c. 1843; Eugen von Guérard, *Weatherboard Falls*, 1863.

24 For an account of the 'exotic': Smith, *European Vision*, passim.

25 Atkinson, 'A Voice from the Country', *SMH*, 26 April 1860, p. 2, 9 August 1860, p. 2, 28 January 1861, p. 2, 10 April 1861, p. 8, 20 March 1862, p. 5, 12 February 1863, p. 2.

26 Frere, *The Antipodes*, pp. 64–5.

27 William Piguenit, *Weatherboard Falls*, c. 1876.

28 Watts, *Family Life in South Australia*, p. 82; Hill and Hill, *What We Saw*, pp. 49–50; Rains, *By Land and Ocean*, p. 16; Angas, *Savage Life and Scenes*, pp. 41–2; Angas, *South Australia Illustrated*, 1847, plates X, XXIII, LVII; Mann, *Six Years Residence*, pp. 251, 255–6; Jameson, *New Zealand, South Australia and New South Wales*, pp. 68–9; Backhouse, *A Narrative*, p. 519; B. Armand Wright, 'Mount Lofty', in Morris (ed.), *CPA*, vol. III, pp. 202–4.

REFERENCES

I. ARCHIVES, REPORTS, MANUSCRIPTS AND THESES

Anderson, Grant, Wellington Caves: Resource and Management Study (report), Wellington Shire Council, 1991.

Blue Mountains Historical Society, Wentworth Falls (paper), Blue Mountains Historical Society.

Burke, A., Images of Popular Leisure, BA Hons, Dept of Fine Arts, University of Sydney, 1981.

Dunne, Lawrence J., The Development of Coogee and Other Sydney Seaside Resorts, MA, University of New South Wales, 1988.

Graham Edds & Associates et al., Conservation Plan: Lilianfels, report prepared by Graham Edds & Associates with Lester Tropman & Associates for and on behalf of Mainland Holdings, July 1988, Local Studies Collection, Blue Mountains City Library.

Horne, Julia, Favourite Resorts: Aspects of Tourist Travel in Nineteenth Century New South Wales, PhD, University of New South Wales, 1995.

Karskens, Grace, An Historical and Archaeological Study of Cox's Road and Early Crossings of the Blue Mountains, NSW, paper prepared for the Crown Lands Office, February 1988.

Mackay, Mary Helena, The Geological Sublime: A New Paradigm. An enquiry into an aesthetic convention that informed the representation of landscape in nineteenth century Australia, in reference to how we perceive the Australian landscape today, PhD, University of Sydney, 1990.

Newspaper Cuttings, Mitchell Library, vols 77–78.

Pickwick Corresponding Club, A Correct and Faithful Account of a Journey to the Fish River Caves (diary) 1886, Local Studies Collection, Blue Mountains City Library.

Robert Moore Architects and Conservation Consultants, The Caves House Precinct, Jenolan Caves Reserve: Conservation Plan (Built Environment), report prepared for the Tourism Commission of New South Wales through the NSW Dept of Public Works, Architectural Division, Public Building Branch, 1988.

Smith, Jim, Walking Track Heritage Study, Historical Report, National Parks and Wildlife Service, Blue Mountains District, NSW, 1999.

Waugh Family (John Waugh) Papers 1834–59, ML MSS A827.

2. BOOKS AND ARTICLES

Abell, Lesley, 'Holidays and Health in Nineteenth and Early Twentieth Century South Australia', *Journal of the Historical Society of South Australia*, no. 22, 1994, pp. 83–97.

Ackermann, Jessie, *Australia from a Woman's Point of View*, Cassell Ltd, London, 1913 (republished Cassell Australia, North Ryde, NSW, 1981).

Adams, D. (ed.), *The Letters of Rachel Henning*, Penguin, Melbourne, 1988.

Adams, W. H. D., 'Miss Bird and Others', *Celebrated Women Travellers of the Nineteenth Century*, 1883, in British Biographical Archive, microfiche no. 108.

Adler, Judith, 'Origins of Sightseeing', *Annals of Tourism Research*, vol. 16, no. 1, 1989, pp. 7–29.

Alcock, Peter Cornelius (comp.), *The Family Year-Book and Ladies' Companion for 1875–6*, Peter Cornelius Alcock, Melbourne.

Allen, Alexandra, *Travelling Ladies: Victorian Adventuresses*, Jupiter, London, 1980.

Allen, David E., *The Victorian Fern Craze*, Hutchinson London, 1969.

Anderson, Esther, *Victoria's National Parks: A Centenary History*, State Library of Victoria and Parks Victoria, Melbourne and Kew, 2000.

Andrews, Alan E. J. (ed.), *The Devil's Wilderness: George Caley's Journey to Mount Banks 1804*, Blubber Head Press, Hobart, 1984.

Andrews, Alan E. J., *Kosciusko: The Mountain in History*, Tabletop Press, Canberra, 1991.

Andrews, Malcolm, *The Search for the Picturesque: Landscape Aesthetics and Tourism in Britain 1760–1800*, Solar Press, Aldershot, UK, 1989.

Angas, George French, *Savage Life and Scenes in Australia and New Zealand, being an artist's impression of countries and people at the Antipodes*, Smith, Elder & Co., London, 1847.

Angas, George French, *South Australia Illustrated*, Thomas, McLean, London, 1847.

Australasian Association for the Advancement of Science, *Handbook of Excursions*, Brisbane, 1895.

Australian Dictionary of Biography, vols 1–15, Melbourne University Press, Melbourne, 1966–2000.

Australian Etiquette or the Rules and Usages of the Best Society in the Australasian Colonies, together with their sports, pastimes, games and amusements, D. E. McConnell, Sydney, 1885.

Australian Garden History, vol. 6, no. 4, January–February 1995 (issue devoted to Mount Macedon; edited by C. McConville).

Backhouse, James, *A Narrative of a Visit to the Australian Colonies*, Hamilton, Adams & Co., London, 1843.

Bailey, Fredk. Manson, *The Fern World of Australia with Homes of the Queensland Species*, Brisbane, 1881.

Bailliere's New South Wales Gazetteer and Road Guide containing the most recent and accurate information as to every place in the Colony, F. F. Bailliere, Sydney, 1866.

Baird, James, *The Emigrant's Guide to Australasia*, Virtue, London, 1868.

Balfour, J. O., *A Sketch of New South Wales*, Smith Elder & Co., London, 1845.

Barnard, F. G. A., 'Notes on a Visit to the Jenolan Caves, New South Wales', *Victorian Naturalist*, vol. V, no. 9, January 1889, pp. 121–30.

Barrallier, Francis, *Journal of the Expedition into the Interior of New South Wales 1802*, Marsh Walsh Publishing, Melbourne, 1975.

Bartlett, Thomas, *New Holland: Its Colonization, Productions and Resources, with Observations on the Relations subsisting with Great Britain*, Longman, Brown, Green, & Longman, London, 1843.

Battersby, Christine, *Gender and Genius: Towards a Feminist Aesthetics*, Indiana University Press, Bloomington and Indianapolis, 1989.

Beaglehole, J. C. (ed.), *The Endeavour Journal of Joseph Banks 1768–1771*, Public Library of New South Wales in association with Angus & Robertson, Sydney, 1962.

Bennett, George, *Wanderings in New South Wales, Batavia, Pedir Coast, Singapore, and China; being the Journal of a Naturalist in those countries during 1832, 1833 and 1834*, Richard Bentley, London, 1834.

Bicknell, Peter, *British Hills and Mountains*, Collins, London, 1947.

Blainey, G. (ed.), *Travellers' Tales of Early Australia and New Zealand: Oceana, the Tempestuous Voyage of J. A. Froude, 1884 & 1885*, Methuen Haynes, North Ryde, NSW, 1985 (first edn 1886).

Blaxland, Gregory, 'Gregory Blaxland's Narrative and Journal Relating to the First Expedition Over the Blue Mountains, New South Wales,' *JRAHS*, vol. XXIII, 1937, pt 1.

Blaxland, Gregory, *A Journal of a Tour of Discovery across the Blue Mountains in New South Wales*, London, 1823.

Blue Mountain Guide, Batty & Chalcraft, Sydney, 1887.

Blue Mountains Historical Society, 'History of the Knight Family', *Family History Pamphlet*, Blue Mountains Historical Society.

Boldrewood, Mrs Rolf, *The Flower Garden in Australia*, Mulini Press, Canberra, 1995 (first edn 1893).

Bonyhady, Tim, *Images in Opposition*, Oxford University Press, Melbourne, 1985.

Bonyhady, Tim, *The Colonial Image: Australian Painting 1800–1880*, Australian National Gallery and Ellsyd Press, Sydney, 1987.

Bonyhady, Tim, *Burke and Wills: From Melbourne to Myth*, David Ell Press, Balmain, 1991.

Bonyhady, Tim, *The Colonial Earth*, Melbourne University Press, Melbourne, 2000.

Boorstin, Daniel J., *The Discoverers*, Penguin Books, London, 1986 (first published 1983).

Booth, E. C., *Australia*, Virtue & Co., London, 1873–76.

Brendon, P., *Thomas Cook: 150 Years of Popular Tourism*, Secker & Warburg, London, 1991.

Breton, W. H., *Excursions in New South Wales, Western Australia and Van Diemen's Land*, Richard Bentley, London, 1833.

Broad, Lucy, *A Woman's Wanderings the World Over*, Headley Brothers, London, 1909.

Brockway, Lucile H., *Science and Colonial Expansion: The Role of the British Royal Botanic Gardens*, Academic Press, New York, 1979.

Brown, A. V., 'John Skinner Prout—his Tasmanian Sojourn 1844–46', *Art Bulletin of Tasmania*, 1984, pp. 21–31.

Brown, R., *The Miscellaneous Botanical Works of Robert Brown*, Robert Hardwicke, London, 1866–67.

Brown, Tony and Kolenberg, Hendrik, *Skinner Prout in Australia 1840–48*, Tasmanian Museum and Art Gallery, Hobart, 1986.

Bruce, C., Comstock, E., and McDonald, F., *Eugene von Guerard: A German Romantic in the Antipodes*, Alister Taylor, Martinborough, NZ, 1982.

Bruck, Ludwig (ed. and comp.), *Guide to the Health Resorts in Australia, Tasmania, and New Zealand*, Australasian Medical Gazette, Sydney, 1888.

Bunce, D., *1836 Catalogue of Seeds and Plants, indigenous and exotic, cultivated and on sale at Denmark Hill Nursery, New Town Road*, Mulini Press, Canberra, 1994 (first edn 1836).

Burke, Edmund, *A Philosophical Enquiry into the Origin of our Ideas of the Sublime and Beautiful*, Oxford University Press, Oxford, 1990 (1756).

Burn, David, *Colonial Magazine*, May–August, 1841.

Burn, David, *Narrative of the Overland Journey of Sir John and Lady Franklin and Party from Hobart Town to Macquarie Harbour*, ed. G. Mackaness, George Mackaness, Sydney, 1955 (first published in the *United Services Journal*, June–December, 1843).

Buzard, James, *The Beaten Track: European Tourism, Literature, and the Ways to Culture, 1800–1918*, Clarendon Press, Oxford, 1993.

Carter, Paul, *The Road to Botany Bay: An Essay in Spatial History*, Faber & Faber, London, 1987.

Chalker, M., and Nurse, B., 'The History of Wombeyan Caves, 1828–1985', *Helictite*, vol. 24 (1 & 2), 1986, pp. 47–52.

Chapman, Barbara and Brown, Tony, 'Art Exhibitions in Tasmania During the Nineteenth Century—A Chronology', *Art Bulletin of Tasmania*, 1986, pp. 44–51.

Chapman, Peter, *The Diaries and Letters of G. T. W. B. Boyes 1820–1832*, Oxford University Press, Melbourne, 1985.

Clarke, Patricia, *Pioneer Writer. The Life of Louisa Atkinson, Novelist, Journalist, Naturalist*, Allen & Unwin, Sydney, 1990.

Cohen, Lysbeth, *Elizabeth Macquarie: Her Life and Times*, Wentworth Books, Sydney, 1979.

Cohn, Helen M., *Australian Plants, the Garden and Botany in the Nineteenth Century Periodical*, (*Naturae*, no. 5, May 1995).

Collins, David, *An Account of the English Colony in New South Wales with Remarks on the Dispositions, Customs, Manners, etc., of the Native Inhabitants of that Country* (1798), ed. B. Fletcher, A. H. & A. W. Reed and Royal Historical Society, 1975.

Cook, Samuel, *The Jenolan Caves: An Excursion in Australian Wonderland*, London, 1889.

Cook, Thomas & Son, *Excursions in New South Wales arranged by Thos. Cook & Son*, 1895.

Cook, Thomas & Son, *Railway Official Guide Book to Tasmania*, Rae Bros, Melbourne, 1895.

Cooper, W. M., *Track from Katoomba to Jenolan Caves*, Government Printer, Sydney, 1885.

Cooper's Hotels & Coaches Ltd, *Souvenir and Guide to Blue Mountains, Jenolan Caves, and City and Suburbs*, Cooper's Hotels and Coaches Ltd, c. 1906.

Cotton, B. C. (ed.), *National Park and Reserves: An Account of the National Park and Reserves Situated Near Adelaide, South Australia*, Commissioners of the National Park, Adelaide, 1953.

Coulson, Helen, *The Story of the Dandenongs 1838–1958*, Cheshire, Melbourne, 1959.

Crittendon, V., 'Bibliography', *A History of Australian Gardening Books and a Bibliography, 1806–1950*, Canberra College of Advanced Education Library, Canberra, 1986.

Cunningham, Chris, *The Blue Mountains Rediscovered: Beyond the Myths of Early Australian Exploration*, Kangaroo Press, Kenthurst, NSW, 1996.

Curr, Edward, *An Account of the Colony of Van Diemen's Land Principally Designed for the Use of Emigrants*, Platypus Publications, Hobart, 1967 (facs. 1824).

Curtis, Eve, *The Turning Years: A Tamborine Mountain History*, Tamborine, Qld, 1988.

Daley, Charles with Sir James Barrett, *Victorian Historical Memorials to Explorers and Discoverers*, Victorian Historical Association, 1944.

Darwin, Charles, *Charles Darwin Journal of Researches by Charles Darwin into the Natural History and Geology of the Countries visited during the Voyage of HMS Beagle under the command of Capt. FitzRoy R.M.*, Cambridge University Press, Cambridge, 1961 (first published 1839).

Darwin, Charles, *Journal of Researches into the Geology and Natural History of the Various Countries visited by HMS Beagle*, Henry Colburn, London, 1839.

Darwin, Charles, *On the Structure and Distribution of Coral Reefs*, Ward, London, 1890 (first edn 1842).

Davidson, J., and Spearritt, P., *Holiday Business: Tourism in Australia since 1870*, Melbourne University Press, Melbourne, 2000.

Davidson, Lilias Campbell, *Hints to Lady Travellers at Home and Abroad*, Iliffe & Son, London, 1889.

Davies, Mrs Eliza, *The Story of an Earnest Life: A Woman's Adventures in Australia, and in Two Voyages around the World*, Central Book Concern, Cincinnati, OH, 1881.

Dodd, P. (ed.), *The Art of Travel: Essays on Travel Writing*, Frank Cass, London, 1982.

Dumont D'Urville, J. S. C., 'De la Distribution des Fougères sur la surface du globe terrestre', *Annales des Sciences*, Septembre 1825, 25 pp. (off-print held in Mitchell Library, Sydney).

Dunkley, *Jenolan Caves*, Jenolan Caves Historical and Preservation Society, Sydney, 1986.

Dymock's Guide to Sydney and New South Wales, William Dymock, Sydney, 1897.

Ellis, E., *Conrad Martens: Life and Art*, State Library of New South Wales, Sydney, 1994.

Ellis, M. H., *Lachlan Macquarie*, Angus & Robertson, Sydney, 1978.

Evans, George William, *A Geographical, Historical and Topographical Description of Van Diemen's Land*, John Souter, London, 1822.

Evans, George William, *History and Description of the Present State of Van Diemen's Land containing important hints to Emigrants*, John Souter, London, 1824.

Evans, Michael, 'Tasmania: Landscape and the Past', *Melbourne Historical Journal*, vol. 16, 1984, pp. 34–47.

Fara, Patricia, *Sex, Botany and Empire*, Allen & Unwin, Sydney, 2003.

Field, Barron (ed.), *Geographical Memoirs on New South Wales*, John Murray, London, 1825.

Field, Barron, 'Journal of an Excursion across the Blue Mountains of New South Wales, 1822', *London Magazine*, vol. 8, November, 1823, pp. 461–76.

Fitzpatrick, Kathleen, *Australian Explorers: A Selection from their Writings with an Introduction*, Oxford University Press, Oxford, 1958.

Fitzpatrick, Kathleen, *Sir John Franklin in Tasmania 1837–43*, Melbourne University Press, Melbourne, 1949.

Fleming, Fergus, *Killing Dragons: The Conquest of the Alps*, Atlantic Monthly Press, New York, 2000.

Foster, J. J., *The Jenolan Caves*, Charles Potter Government Printer, Sydney, 1890.

Foster, S., *Across New Worlds: Nineteenth Century Women Travellers and their Writings*, Harvester Wheatsheaf, Hertfordshire, UK, 1990.

Frankland, George, *Five Letters From George Frankland in Van Diemen's Land*, Sullivan's Cove, Adelaide, 1997.

Fraser, M. A. C. (ed.), *Notes on the Natural History of Western Australia*, Perth, 1903.

Freeland, J. M., *The Australian Pub*, Melbourne University Press, Melbourne, 1966.

Frere, Alice M. [aka Mrs Godfrey Clerk], *The Antipodes and Round the World; or, Travels in Australia, New Zealand, Ceylon, China, Japan, and California*, 2nd edn, Hatchfords, London, 1870.

Garis, B. de, *Portraits of the South West: Aborigines, Women and the Environment*, University of Western Australia Press, Perth, 1993.

Garran, Andrew (ed.), *Picturesque Atlas of Australasia*, Picturesque Atlas Publishing Co., Sydney, 1886–88.

Gelding, John, *Three Sydney Garden Nurseries in the 1860s*, Mulini Press, Canberra, 1983.

Gerstaecker, F., *Narrative of a Journey round the world comprising a winter passage across the Andes to Chili, with a visit to the gold regions of California and Australia, the South Sea Islands, Java, &c.*, vol. II, Hurst & Blackett, London, 1853 (Eng. edn).

Gibbs, Shallard & Co.'s Illustrated Guide to Sydney and its Suburbs, and to Favourite Places of Resort in New South Wales, Gibbs, Shallard & Co., Sydney, 1879, 1882, 1889.

Grainger, Elena, *Martin of Martin Place: A Biography of Sir James Martin*, Alpha Books, Sydney, 1970.

Griffiths, Tom, *Forests of Ash: An Environmental History*, Cambridge University Press, Cambridge, 2001.

Guérard, E. von, *Eugene von Guérard's Australian Landscapes*, intro. by Marjorie Tipping, Lansdowne Press, Melbourne, 1975 (facs.; first edn 1867).

Hall, Mary, *A Woman in the Antipodes and in the Far East*, Methuen & Co., London, 1914.

Hall's Country Business, Professional and Pastoral Directory and Gazetteer of New South Wales for 1899–1900, James Best, Sydney, 1900.

Hall's Mercantile Agency, Business, Professional and Pastoral Directory of New South Wales for 1896, James Best, Sydney, 1896.

Hamilton-Smith, E. (ed.), *Celebrating the Parks: Proceedings of the First Australian Symposium on Parks History 16–19 April 1998*, Rethink Consulting, Carlton, Victoria, 1998.

Hanbury-Tenison, Robin (comp.), *The Oxford Book of Exploration*, Oxford University Press, Oxford, 1993.

Handbook of Wm. Howard Smith and Sons' Line of Intercolonial Steamers, Wm. Howard Smith & Sons, 1883.

Hannaford, Samuel, *The Wildflowers of Tasmania or chatty rambles afloat and ashore. Amidst the seaweeds, ferns and flowering plants; with a complete list of indigenous ferns and instructions for their cultivation*, F. F. Bailliere, Melbourne, 1866.

Havard, Olive (ed.), 'Lady Franklin's Visit to New South Wales, 1839. Extracts from letters to Sir John Franklin', *JRAHS*, vol. 29, no. 5, 1943, pp. 280–334.

Havard, Olive and W. L., 'Some Early French Visitors', *JRAHS*, vol. 24, pt IV, 1938, pp. 245–90.

Havard, Ward L., *The Romance of Jenolan Caves*, NSW Department of Leisure, Sport and Tourism, n.d. (facs.; first published 1933).

Hibbert, Christopher, *The Grand Tour*, Methuen, London, 1987.

Hill, Les R., *Mount Gambier: The City Around a Cave*, Investigator Press, 1972.

Hill, Rosamond and Florence, *What We Saw in Australia*, MacMillan & Co., London, 1875.

Hingston, J. (comp.), *Guide for Excursionists from Melbourne*, H. Thomas, Melbourne, 1868.

Hirst, J. B., *The Strange Birth of Colonial Democracy: New South Wales 1848–1884*, Allen & Unwin, Sydney, 1988.

Historical Records of Australia, vol. 5, series 1, Melbourne University Press, Melbourne, 1914–1925

Hodgson, Christopher Pemberton, *Reminiscences of Australia, with Hints on the Squatter's Life*, Simpkin & Marshall, London, 1846.

Holloway, James and Errington, Lindsay, *The Discovery of Scotland: The Appreciation of Scottish Scenery through Two Centuries of Painting*, National Gallery of Scotland, Edinburgh, 1978.

Holman, James, *A Voyage Round the World, including Travels in Africa, Asia, Australasia, America, etc. etc. from 1827 to 1832*, Smith, Elder & Co., London, 1835, vol. 4.

Holt, Patricia and Spearritt, Peter, 'Retreat to the Mountains', in G. Davison (ed.), *Journeys into History*, Weldon Russell, Willoughby, NSW, 1990, pp. 47–59.

Horne, Donald, *The Intelligent Tourist*, McGee Publishing, McMahons Point, NSW, 1992.

Horne, Julia, *Jenolan Caves: When the Tourists Came*, Kingsclear Books, Crows Nest, NSW, 1994.

Horrock's Handy Guide to the Blue Mountains and Caves of New South Wales, John J. Horrocks, Sydney, c. 1885, 1890.

Hutchings, Patrick, 'Eugene von Guérard: A Fitting Vision', *Meridian*, no. 4, 1985, pp. 112–21.

Inglis, James, *Our Australian Cousins*, Macmillan & Co., London, 1880.

Inglis, Ken, 'Questions About Newspapers', *Australian Cultural History*, no. 11, 1992, pp. 120–7.

Jameson, R. G., *New Zealand, South Australia and New South Wales: A Record of Recent Travels in These Colonies*, Smith, Elder and Co., London, 1842.

Jones, Michael, *Prolific in God's Gift: A Social History of Knox and the Dandenongs*, Allen & Unwin, Sydney, 1983.

Kent, Eliza, 'Abstract of the Journal of a Voyage from New South Wales to England by a Lady', *Athenaeum*, July 1808, pp. 8–10; August 1808, pp. 99–103.

Kerr, Joan (ed.), *The Dictionary of Australian Artists*, Oxford University Press, Melbourne, 1992.

Kiernan, Brian (ed.), *Henry Lawson*, University of Queensland Press, St Lucia, Qld, 1976.

Kingston, Beverley, *My Wife, My Daughter, and Poor Mary Ann: Women and Work in Australia*, Thomas Nelson, Melbourne, 1977.

Kingston, Beverley, 'The Lady and the Australian Girl: Some Thoughts on Nationalism and Class', in N. Grieve and A. Burns (eds), *Australian Women: New Feminist Perspectives*, Oxford University Press, Melbourne, 1986.

Kingston, Beverley, *Oxford History of Australia, Volume 3, 1860–1900: Glad, Confident Morning*, Oxford University Press, Melbourne, 1988.

Knoepflmacher, U. C. and Tennyson, G. B. (eds), *Nature and the Victorian Imagination*, University of California Press, Berkeley and Los Angeles, 1977.

La Billardière, J. J., *Novae Hollandiae Plantarum Specimen*, Paris, 1806.

Langsdorff, G. et Fischer, F., *Plantes Recueillis pendant le voyage des Russes autour du monde. Expédition dirigée par M. de Krusenstern*, A. Tubingue, 1810.

Laurent, John, and Campbell, Margaret, *The Eye of Reason: Charles Darwin in Australasia* University of Wollongong Press, Wollongong, NSW, 1987.

Lawson, Elizabeth, *The Natural Art of Louisa Atkinson*, State Library of New South Wales, Sydney, 1995.

Laye, Mrs E. P. R., *Social Life and Manners in Australia being the Notes of Eight Years' Experience, by a Resident*, Longman, Green, Longman & Roberts, London, 1861.

Leed, Eric J., *The Mind of the Traveler: From Gilgamesh to Global Tourism*, Basic Books, New York, 1991.

Lennon, Jane, 'Wilson's Promontory in Victoria: Its Commercial Utilization in the 19th Century', *Victorian Historical Magazine*, vol. 45, no. 4, November 1974, pp. 179–200.

Linn, Rob, *A Diverse Land: A History of the Lower Murray, Lakes and Coorong*, Meningie Historical Society, 1988.

Lorck, Walter (ed.), *New South Wales Picturesque Resorts Convenient to Railways. An illustrated guide to some of the Principal Towns and Districts in New South Wales*, Edward Lee, Sydney, 1907.

Losano, Antonia, 'A Preference for Vegetables: The Travel Writings and Botanical Art of Marianne North', *Women's Studies*, October 1997, vol. 26, no. 5, pp. 423–49.

Low, John, *Pictorial Memories: Blue Mountains*, Atrand, Crows Nest, NSW, 1991.

Low, John and Smith, Jim, *The Prince of Whips: The Life and Works of the Blue Mountains Pioneer Harry Peckman*, Den Fenella Press, Wentworth Falls, NSW, 1993.

Mabberley, D. J., *Jupiter Botanicus: Robert Brown of the British Museum*, British Museum, London, 1985.

McConville, Chris, 'A Forest at the Edge of the City', *Australian Garden History*, vol. 6, no. 4, January–February 1995, pp. 5–9.

MacDonald, Donald, *Tourists' Handbook of Australia*, Howard Smith Co. Ltd, Melbourne 1905.

McEwan, Cheryl, 'Paradise or Pandemonium? West African Landscapes in the Travel Accounts of Victorian Women', *Journal of Historical Geography*, vol. 22, no. 1, 1996, pp. 68–83.

Mackaness, George (ed.), *Fourteen Journeys over the Blue Mountains of New South Wales 1813–1841*, Horwitz-Grahame, Sydney, 1965.

MacKenzie, The Rev. David, *The Emigrant's Guide; or Ten Years' Practical Experience in Australia*, W. S. Orr, London, 1845.

Maclehose, James, *The Picture of Sydney and Strangers' Guide in New South Wales for 1839*, John Ferguson Sydney in association with the RAHS, 1977 (facs.; first edn 1839).

McPhee, John, *The Art of John Glover*, Macmillan, Melbourne, 1980.

Macpherson, Allan, *Mount Abundance: or, the Experiences of a pioneer Squatter in Australia thirty years ago*, Fleet Street Printing Works, London c. 1877.

Macpherson, E., *My Experiences in Australia: Being Recollections of a Visit to the Australian Colonies in 1856–7, by a Lady*, J. F. Hope, London, 1860.

Macquarie, Lachlan, *Journals of His Tours in New South Wales and Van Diemen's Land 1810–1822*, Trustees of the Public Library of New South Wales, Sydney, 1956.

Macquarie, Lachlan, 'Tour over the Western or Blue Mountains', *Sydney Gazette*, 10 June 1815.

Mann, D. D., *The Present Picture of New South Wales*, John Ferguson with the RAHS, Sydney, 1979 (1811).

Mann, F. C. T., 'Through the Jenolan Caves of New South Wales Australia', *Westminster Review* (off-print held by Mitchell Library, State Library of NSW).

Mann, W., *Six Years Residence in the Australian Provinces ending in 1839*, Smith Elder & Co., London, 1839.

Martin, A. W., *Henry Parkes: A Biography*, Melbourne University Press, Melbourne, 1980.

Martin, A. W. (ed.), *Letters from Menie: Sir Henry Parkes and his Daughter*, Melbourne University Press, Melbourne, 1983.

Martin, James, *The Australian Sketchbook*, James Tegg, Sydney, 1838.

Meredith, Louisa, *My Home in Tasmania*, Bunce and Brother, New York, 1853.

Meredith, Louisa, *Notes and Sketches of New South Wales During a Residence in that Colony from 1839 to 1844*, John Murray, London, 1846.

Meredith, Louisa, *Over the Straits: A Visit to Victoria*, Chapman and Hall, London, 1861.

Middleton, Gregory J., *Oliver Trickett: Doyen of Australia's Cave Surveyors 1847–1934*, Sydney Speleological Society with the Jenolan Caves Historical and Preservation Society, Sydney, 1991.

Millar, Ann, *'I see no end to travelling': Journals of Australian Explorers 1813–1876*, Bay Books, Sydney, 1986.

Millard, John G., 'Recollections of a Tour', *Christian Advocate and Wesleyan Record*, vol. 1, no. 1, 21 July 1858.

Mills, Sara, 'Discourses of Difference', *Cultural Studies*, vol. 4, no. 2, May 1990, pp. 128–40.

Mills, Sara, *Discourses of Difference: An Analysis of Women's Travel Writing and Colonialism*, Routledge, London, 1993.

Mitchell, Major T. L., *Three Expeditions into the Interior of Eastern Australia*, T. & W. Boone, London, 1838.

Moir, Esther, *The Discovery of Britain: The English Tourists*, Routledge & Kegan Paul, London 1964.

Morison, G., *Australia As It Is: or Facts and Features, Sketches and Incidents of Australia and Australian Life*, Longmans, Green, London, 1867.

Morris, E. E. (ed.), *Cassell's Picturesque Atlas of Australasia*, Cassell & Co., Melbourne, 1887–88.

Morrison, Elizabeth, 'Reading Victoria's Newspapers 1838–1901', *Australian Cultural History*, no. 11, 1992, pp. 128–40.

Mossman, Samuel, and Banister, Thomas, *Australia, Visited and Revisited: A Narrative of Recent Travels and Old Experiences in Victoria and New South Wales*, Ure Smith in association with the National Trust of Australia, Sydney, 1974 (first published 1853).

Neumayer, Georg, *Results of the Magnetic Survey of the Colony of Victoria executed during the Years 1858–1864*, Mannheim, 1869.

New South Wales Dept of Mines, *Report by Dr R. von Lendenfeld on the Results of his Recent Examination of the Central Part of the Australian Alps*, 21 January 1885.

New South Wales Government Tourist Bureau, *Katoomba Falls Blue Mountains New South Wales*, 1909.

New South Wales Post Office Directory, Wise's Directories, Sydney, 1886–1904.

New South Wales Railways Tourists' Guide. Division I Southern and Illawarra Lines, Charles Potter Government Printer Sydney, 1889.

New South Wales Railway Tourists' Guide. Division II Western and Northern Lines, Charles Potter Government Printer, Sydney, 1889.

Nicholas, F. W. and J. M., *Charles Darwin in Australia*, Cambridge University Press, Melbourne, 2002.

Nicholls, Mary (ed.), *Traveller Under Concern: The Quaker Journals of Frederick Mackie on his Tour of the Australian Colonies 1852–55*, University of Tasmania, Hobart, 1973.

Nicolson, Marjorie Hope, *Mountain Gloom and Mountain Glory: The Development of the Aesthetics of the Infinite*, W. W. Norton, New York, 1959.

North, Marianne, *Recollections of a Happy Life being the Autobiography of Marianne North*, MacMillan & Co., London, 1892.

O'Brian, Patrick, *Joseph Banks: A Life*, Collins Harvill, London, 1988.

Official Post Office Country Directory and Gazetteer of New South Wales, John Sands, Sydney, 1878–86.

Ousby, Ian, *The Englishman's England: Taste, Travel and the Rise of Tourism*, Cambridge University Press, Cambridge, 1990.

Parker, Mary Anne, *A Voyage Round the World*, Hordern House and Australian National Maritime Museum, Sydney, 1991 (facs.; first edn 1795).

Pearce, Philip L., *The Social Psychology of Tourist Behaviour*, Pergamon Press, Oxford, 1982.

Peckham, Morse, *The Triumph of Romanticism: Collected Essays*, University of South Carolina Press, Columbia, 1970.

Pesman, R., *Duty Free: Australian Women Abroad*, Oxford University Press, Melbourne, 1996.

Physician, A., *Seventy Years of Life in the Victorian Era embracing a travelling record in Australia, New Zealand, and America &c.*, T. Fisher Unwin, London, 1893.

Pianzola, Maurice, *Paysages Romantiques*, Genevois Musée d'art et d'histoire, Genève, 1977.

Pimlott, J. A. R., *The Englishman's Holiday: A Social History*, Harvester Press, Hassocks, UK, 1976 (first edn 1947).

Porter, Dennis, *Haunted Journeys: Desire and Transgression in European Travel Writing*, Princeton University Press, Princeton, 1991.

Powell, J. M., *Mirrors of the New World: Images and Image-Makers in the Settlement Process*, Australian National University Press, Press, Canberra, 1978.

Pratt, Mary Louise, *Imperial Eyes: Travel Writing and Transculturation*, Routledge, London, 1992.

Press, Margaret M., *Julian Tenison-Woods: 'Father Founder'*, Collins Dove, Melbourne, 1994.

Proudfoot, Helen, 'Botany Bay, Kew, and the Picturesque: Early Conceptions of the Australian Landscape', *JRAHS*, vol. 65, pt 1, June 1979, pp. 30–45.

Proudfoot, Helen, 'Opening Towns, Public Virtue and the Interior', in James Broadbent and Joy Hughes (eds), *The Age of Macquarie*, Melbourne University Press with the Historic Houses Trust of New South Wales, Melbourne, 1992.

Prout, J. S., *Tasmania Illustrated*, vols 1 and 2, Hobart Town, 1844.

Prout's Dioramic Views of Australia, London, 1850.

Pudney, J., *The Thomas Cook Story*, Non-Fiction Book Club, London, 1953.

Quincey, Elizabeth de, *The History of Mount Wellington: A Tasmanian Sketchbook*, E. de Quincey, Hobart, 1987.

Rae, W. F., *The Business of Travel: A Fifty Years' Record of Progress*, Thos. Cook & Son, London, 1891.

Railway Guide of New South Wales (for the use of tourists, excursionists, and others), Thomas Richards, Government Printer, Sydney, 1879, 1884, 1886, 1889, 1894.

Rains, Fanny, *By Land and Ocean*, Sampson Low, Marston, Searle & Rivington London, 1878.

'Random Notes by a Wandering Reporter', *Sydney Mail*, 4 March 1871.

Raymond, James (comp.), *The New South Wales Calendar and General Post Office Directory 1832*, Public Library of New South Wales, Sydney, 1966 (facs.; first published 1832).

Richards, Joanna Armour (ed.), *Blaxland–Lawson–Wentworth*, Blubber Head Press, Hobart, 1979 (1813).

Rigby, Elizabeth, 'Lady Travellers', *Quarterly Review*, vol. LXXVI, 1845, pp. 98–137.

Ring, Jim, *How the English Made the Alps*, John Murray, London, 2000.

Ritchie, J., *Lachlan Macquarie: A Biography*, Melbourne University Press, Melbourne, 1986.

Roderick, Colin, 'The Education of an Explorer: Ludwig Leichhardt', in J. Tampke and D. Walker, *From Berlin to Burdekin. The German Contribution to the Development of Australian Science, Exploration and Science*, New South Wales University Press, Sydney, 1991, pp. 22–38.

Roe, Jill, 'What Rosamond and Florence Hill Saw in Australia. Or, Women and Philanthropy', *Women and History* (based on a conference held 26 July 1975), History Teachers' Association of New South Wales, n.d.

Rolfe, Patricia (ed.), *The Blue Mountains*, Jacaranda Press, Brisbane, 1964.

Ross, Valerie (ed.), *The Everingham Letterbook. Letters of a First Fleet Convict*, Anvil Press, Wamberal, NSW, 1985.

Ruskin, John, *Modern Painters* (5th edn), Smith Elder & Co., London, 1851 (first published 1843).

Russell, J. E. M (comp.), *The Pictorial Guide to the Blue Mountains of New South Wales and The Districts between Parramatta and Bathurst including the Jenolan Caves*, Gibbs, Shallard & Co., Sydney, 1882, 1885.

Russell, Penny, 'Recycling Femininity: Old Ladies and New Women', *Australian Cultural History*, no. 13, 1994, pp. 31–51.

Russell, Penny, 'The Allure of the Nile: Jane Franklin's Voyage to the Second Cataract, 1834', *Gender and History*, vol. 9, no. 2, August 1997, pp. 222–41.

Russell, Penny (ed.), *This Errant Lady: Jane Franklin's Overland Journey to Port Phillip and Sydney 1839*, National Library of Australia, Canberra, 2002.

Salmond, Anne, *The Trial of the Cannibal Dog: Captain Cook in the South Seas*, Allen Lane, Penguin, London, 2003.

Sanderson, W. A., 'The Alienation of the Melbourne Parks', *Victorian Historical Magazine,* vol. XIV, no. 4, December 1932, pp. 141–65.

Sand's Sydney and Suburban Directory, J. Sands, Sydney, 1892–1990.

Schama, Simon, *Landscape and Memory*, HarperCollins, London, 1995.

Sears, John F., *Sacred Places: American Tourist Attractions in the Nineteenth Century*, Oxford University Press, New York, 1989.

Serville, Paul de, *Pounds and Pedigrees: The Upper Class in Victoria 1850–80*, Oxford University Press, Melbourne, 1991.

Shaw, Trevor R., *History of Cave Science: The Exploration and Study of Limestone Caves, to 1900* (2nd edn), Sydney Speleological Society, Sydney, 1992.

Silvey, Gwen, 'Ladies of the Blue Mountains', *Explorers' Tree*, no. 14, April 1990.

Silvey, Gwen, *Happy Days: Blue Mountains Guesthouses Remembered*, Kingsclear Books, Crows Nest, NSW, 1996.

Skinner's New South Wales Gazetteer, Batson and Atwater, Sydney, 1883.

Smith, Bernard, *Australian Painting 1788–1960*, Oxford University Press, Melbourne, 1962.

Smith, Bernard, *European Vision and the South Pacific*, Oxford University Press, Melbourne, 1989.

Smith, J. E., 'A Botanical Essay on the Genera of Dorsiferous Ferns. Translated from the Latin, published in the fifth Volume of the Memoirs of the Royal Academy of Sciences at Turin, in 1793', in *Tracts Relating to Natural History*, J. E. Smith, London, 1798, pp. 215–64.

Smith, Jim, *From Katoomba to Jenolan Caves: The Six Foot Track 1884–1984*, Second Back Row Press, Katoomba, NSW, 1984.

Smith, Jim, *The Blue Mountains Mystery Track: Lindeman Pass, A History of the Jamison Valley*, Three Sisters Productions, Winmalee, NSW, 1990.

Stanbury, Peter (ed.), *The Blue Mountains: Grand Adventure for All*, Second Back Row Press and the Macleay Museum, University of Sydney, Leura, NSW, and Sydney, 1988.

Stevenson, Mrs M. I., *Letters from Samoa 1891–1895*, Methuen & Co., London, 1906.

Stewart, Ken, 'Journalism and the World of the Writer: The Production of Australian Literature 1855–1915', in Laurie Hergenhan (general ed.), *The Penguin New Literary History of Australia*, Penguin Books, Ringwood, Vic., 1988.

Stockton, E. (ed.), *Blue Mountains Dreaming: The Aboriginal Heritage*, Three Sisters Productions, Winmalee, NSW, 1993.

Stranger's Guide to Sydney, in a Series of Walks; with a map of the City, and Directory of the Various Streets and Public Buildings, James W. Waugh, Sydney, 1858.

Strzelecki, P. E. de, *Physical Description of New South Wales and Van Diemen's Land*, Libraries Board of South Australia, Adelaide, 1967 (facs.; first edn 1845).

Tench, Capt. Watkin, *Sydney's First Four Years being a reprint of a Narrative of the Expedition to Botany Bay and a Complete Account of the Settlement at Port Jackson*, Library of Australian History with the RAHS, Sydney, 1979.

Tenison-Woods, Julian, *Geological Observations in South Australia*, London, 1862 (first published in *South Australian Register*, 29 March 1858.

Thacker, Christopher, *The Wildness Pleases: The Origins of Romanticism*, Croom Helm, London, 1983.

Thomas, Martin, *The Artificial Horizon: Imagining the Blue Mountains*, Melbourne University Press, Melbourne, 2003.

Tinniswood, Adrian, *A History of Country House Visiting: Five Centuries of Tourism and Taste*, Basil Blackwell and the National Trust, Oxford and London, 1989.

Tipping, G. R. (ed.), *The Official Account through Governor Phillip's Letters to Lord Sydney*, G. R. Tipping, Beecroft, NSW, 1988.

Tourist's Guide to Pleasant Places Convenient to Railways, NSW Railway Commissioners, 1900.

Townsend, Joseph Phipps, *Rambles and Observations in New South Wales with Sketches of Men and Manners, Notices of the Aborigines, Glimpses of Scenery and some Hints to Emigrants*, Chapman & Hall, London, 1848.

Tregenza, J., *George French Angas, Artist, Traveller and Naturalist 1822–1886*, Art Gallery Board of South Australia, Adelaide, 1980.

Treharne, M. J., 'An Introduction to Abercrombie Caves Resort', *Helictite*, vol. 24 (1 & 2), 1986, pp. 43–6.

Trickett, Oliver, *Guide to the Jenolan Caves*, Government Printer, Sydney, 1899, 1905.

Trollope, Anthony, *Australia*, eds P. D. Edwards and R. B. Joyce, University of Queensland Press, St Lucia, Qld, 1967 (first published 1873).

Trollope, Joanna, *Britannia's Daughters: Women of the British Empire*, Cresset Women's Voices, London, 1983.

Turner, J. (ed.), *Dictionary of Art*, Macmillan, London, 1996.

Vamplew, W. (ed.), *Australians: Historical Statistics*, Fairfax, Syme & Weldon, Sydney, 1987.

Vaughan, John, *The English Guidebook c. 1780–1870: An Illustrated History*, London, 1974.

Vellacott, Helen (ed.), *Some Recollections of a Happy Life: Marianne North in Australia and New Zealand*, Edward Arnold Australia, Melbourne, 1986.

Victoria Railways, *Picturesque Victoria and how to get there: A Handbook for Tourists containing general information regarding railways, coaches, steamboats, fares etc.*, Melbourne, 1908.

Victorian Railways, *Tourist's Guide: Containing accurate and full particulars of the watering places, scenery, shooting, fishing, sporting, hotel accommodation etc. in Victoria*, Melbourne, 1885.

Visitors' Guide to the Upper Yarra District, the Picturesque Holiday Resorts of the region eastward of Melbourne … What to see and how to see it, Melbourne, 1888.

Visitors' Handy Guide to Sydney and Port Jackson, Turner & Henderson, Sydney, c. 1879.

Walch's Tasmanian Guide Book: A Handbook of Information for all Parts of the Colony, J. Walch & Sons, Hobart, 1871.

Walker, R. B., *The Newspaper Press in New South Wales, 1803–1920*, Sydney University Press, Sydney, 1976.

Walker, Robin, 'The Struggle Against Pulmonary Tuberculosis in Australia 1788–1950', *Historical Studies*, vol. 20, no. 80, April 1983, pp. 439–61.

Walter Samson and Co's New South Wales National Directory for 1867–68, Walter Jameson Meyer, Sydney, 1868.

Watson, Don, 'Exploring Australian Explorers: The Case of Angus McMillan', *Arena*, vol. 52, 1979, pp. 54–62.

Watts, Jane Isabella, *Family Life in South Australia fifty three years ago dating from 1837*, Adelaide, 1890.

Waugh's Country Directory of New South Wales for 1862–3, James William Waugh, Sydney, 1862.

Webb, Dan, and Adams, Bob, *The Mount Buffalo Story 1898–1998*, Melbourne University Press, Melbourne, 1998.

Western Australia's Wonderland South West Caves, Perth, n.d.

Whithey, Lynne, *Grand Tours and Cook's Tours: A History of Leisure Travel 1750 to 1915*, Aurum Press, London, 1998.

Wilkes, Charles, *Narrative of the United States Exploring Expedition during the Years 1838, 1839, 1840, 1841, 1842*, Lea and Blanchard, Philadelphia, 1845.

Williams, Benjamin Samuel, *Select Ferns and Lycopods: British and Exotic. Comprising Descriptions of Nine Hundred Choice Species and Varieties, accompanied by Directions for their Management in the Tropical, Temperate, and Hardy Fernery*, B. S. Williams, London, 1868.

Williams, Rosalind, *Notes on the Underground: An Essay on Technology, Society, and the Imagination*, MIT Press, Cambridge, Mass., 1990.

Wilson's Sydney and Suburbs Street Directory and Blue Mountains Guide 1910–1911, Wilson & Co., Sydney.

Winkworth, Kylie, 'Women and the Bicycle: Fast, Loose and Liberated', *Australian Journal of Art*, vol. 8, 1989/90, pp. 96–121.

Wood, G. A., 'Explorations under Governor Phillip', *JRAHS*, vol. 12, no. 1, pp. 1–25.

Woolls, W., *A Contribution to the Flora of Australia*, F. White, Sydney, 1867.

Woolls, William, 'The Ferns of Australia', *Lectures on the Vegetable Kingdom with special reference to the Flora of Australia*, Sydney, 1879.

Worsnop, Thomas, *The South Australian Tourist's Guide*, Sands & McDougall, Adelaide, 1887.

Wright, R., *The Bureaucrats' Domain: Space and the Public Interest in Victoria 1836–84*, Oxford University Press, Melbourne, 1989.

PICTURE CREDITS

NOTE: The name of the painter Eugen von Guérard has been recorded with various spellings and Guérard himself signed his work in different ways. Throughout this book the Austrian spelling has been preserved; however, in the following list the specific versions of his name used by the institutions holding the artwork has been followed in each case.

p. ii Ernest Brougham Docker, *The Three Sisters, Katoomba, Blue Mountains, NSW*, 7 February 1898, right frame from mounted stereoscopic albumen print. The University of Sydney, Macleay Museum, 82\007\0046.

WHAT THIS IS ALL ABOUT, *pp. 1–21*

pp. viii–1 Robert Havell, *Panoramic View of King George's Sound, Part of the Colony of Swan River* (segment 7), [drawn by Lieut. R. Dale, 63rd Regt; engraved by R. Havell], 1834, aquatint, hand col., 19 × 274.2 cm folded to 19 × 34.4 cm (full panorama), nla.pic–an7404363–7 (reproduced segment). By permission of National Library of Australia; **p. 2** Samuel Calvert, *Holiday Rambles—Fernshaw and the Black Spur*, 1874?, wood engraving, published in *Illustrated Australian News*, 25 March 1874. IAN25/03/74/SUPP53, La Trobe Picture Collection, State Library of Victoria; **p. 6** Engraver unknown, *The Pinnacle of Mount Wellington*, 1873?, wood engraving, published in *Illustrated Australian News*, 27 March 1873. IAN27/03/73/37, La Trobe Picture Collection, State Library of Victoria; **p. 9** Engraver unknown, *Picturesque Queensland—Cairns. The Barron Falls*, 1888?, wood engraving, published in *Australasian Sketcher*, 9 August 1888. A/S09/08/88/124, La Trobe Picture Collection, State Library of Victoria; **p. 10** W. C. Gosse, [Ayers Rock (Uluru)], 1873, sketch: Illustration of Ayers Rock, Central Australia, first published in South Australian Parliamentary Paper No. 48 of 1874 titled W. C. Gosse's Explorations, 1873. SLSA: B3674, Photograph courtesy of the State Library of South Australia; **p. 13** George French Angas, *Lower Falls of Glen Stuart*, c. 1844, lithograph, hand col., from G. F. Angas, *South Australia Illustrated*, London, 1847, plate 23. By permission of the National Library of Australia; **p. 14** C. Winter, *The Entrance to the Gipps Land Lakes*, 1867?, wood engraving, published in *Australian Illustrated News for Home Readers*, 20 June 1867. IAN20/06/67/8, La Trobe Picture Collection, State Library of Victoria; **p. 17** Edwin Augustus Porcher (d. 1878), *Australia, Sandbank on the Great Barrier Reefs*, 3 July 1843, watercolour, 20 × 28.7 cm, nla.pic-an4102921. By permission of National Library of Australia; **p. 19** Robert Havell,

Panoramic View of King George's Sound, Part of the Colony of Swan River (segment 7), [drawn by Lieut. R. Dale, 63rd Regt; engraved by R. Havell], 1834, aquatint, hand col., 19 × 274.2 cm folded to 19 × 34.4 cm (full panorama), nla.pic–an7404363–7 (reproduced segment). By permission of National Library of Australia.

MAKING TOURISM AUSTRALIAN, *pp. 23–59*

pp. 22–3 W. C. Piguenit (1836–1914), *Lake St Clair, the Source of the River Derwent, Tasmania*, 1887, oil on canvas, 53.7 cm x 113 cm. Gift of the artist to the Tasmanian Government and transferred to the Art Gallery, 1889. Collection: Tasmanian Museum and Art Gallery; **p. 24** John Raphael Smith, *Mr Banks*, c. 1773, after the painting by Benjamin West, engraving, mezzotint, 62 × 38 cm. DL Pf. 69, Dixson Library, State Library of New South Wales; **p. 28** Joseph Banks, The Endeavour Journal, August 1768 – July 1771, vols 1–2. Volume 2 opened at 'Some Account of that part of New Holland now called New South Wales', August 1770, vol. 2, pages 256–7. Banks Series, 03.733, ML Safe 1/12–13, Mitchell Library, State Library of New South Wales; **p. 33** Oswald W. B. Brierly, Journal of a Visit to Twofold Bay, Maneroo: and Districts Beyond the Snowy River, Dec. 1842 to Jan. 1843. Opened at 'An Exploring Breakfast' and 'Source of the Kiah', pages 21–2. A 535, pages 21–2, Mitchell Library, State Library of New South Wales; **p. 36** W. Blandowski, *Pattowatto. Granite Boulders (Perrys Haystack) Looking N.W. 47 Miles N by W of Melbourne*, 1855, line engraving, 21.2 × 27.8 cm, from his *Australia Terra Cognita*. PXE 864/f.8, Mitchell Library, State Library of New South Wales; **p. 39** John Glover, *Ullswater, Early Morning*, c. 1824, oil on canvas, 78.5 × 115.5 cm, purchased 1979. Collection: Art Gallery of New South Wales. Photograph: Ray Woodbury for AGNSW; **p. 41** W. C. Piguenit (1836–1914), *Lake St Clair, the Source of the River Derwent, Tasmania*, 1887, oil on canvas, 53.7 cm x 113 cm. Gift of the artist to the Tasmanian Government and transferred to the Art Gallery, 1889. Collection: Tasmanian Museum and Art Gallery; **p. 45** George French Angas (1822–1886), *Self Portrait*, 1849, lithograph. Collection: National Portrait Gallery, Canberra, purchased 1999; **p. 47** George French Angas, *Interior of the Principal Crater of Mount Gambier*, c. 1845, lithograph, hand col., based on sketch by G. F. Angas in 1844, from G. F. Angas, *South Australia Illustrated*, London 1847, plate 46. By permission of the National Library of Australia; **p. 48** George French Angas (1822–1886), [Sand Dunes, The Coorong], 1840s, pencil and wash drawing, 19.8 × 26 cm, nla.pic–an2887993. By permission of National Library of Australia; **p. 49** George French Angas, *Scene on the Coorong*, c. 1844, lithograph, hand col., from G. F. Angas, *South Australia Illustrated*, London, 1847, plate 9. By permission of the National Library of Australia.

TRAVEL AS CELEBRATION, *pp. 61–97*

pp. 60–1 Eugene von Guérard, *North-east View from the Northern Top of Mount Kosciusko*, 1863, oil on canvas, 66.5 × 116.8 cm. National Gallery of Australia, Canberra; **p. 70** T. H. Maguire (1821–1895), [Portrait of John Gould, Ornithologist], 1849, lithograph, 29.3 × 24 cm, nla.pic–an9547887. By permission of National Library of Australia; **p. 73** Eugene von Guérard, *Prof. G. N's. Wagonzelt 18–19 Oct. 1862* [Tent Wagon], 1862, from his Sketchbooks in Australia, vol. 12, page 24. ZDG B16/vol.12/f.24, Dixson Galleries, State Library of New South Wales; **p. 74** Eugene von Guérard, *North-east View from the Northern Top of Mount Kosciusko*, 1863, oil on canvas, 66.5 × 116.8 cm. National Gallery of Australia, Canberra; **p. 78 (above)** Artist unknown, *Descending the Megalong Cleft*, 1886, from A Correct and Faithful Account of a Journey to Fish River Caves by the Pickwick Corresponding Club, 1886, Acc. No. 18/1–3, page 11. Local Studies Collection, Blue Mountains City Library; **p. 78 (below)** Artist unknown, *Cox's River, Drinking,*

1886, from A Correct and Faithful Account of a Journey to Fish River Caves by the Pickwick Corresponding Club, 1886, Acc. No. 18/1–3, page 19. Local Studies Collection, Blue Mountains City Library; **p. 79 (above)** Artist unknown, *First Camp at Little River*, 1886, from A Correct and Faithful Account of a Journey to Fish River Caves by the Pickwick Corresponding Club, 1886, Acc. No. 18/1–3, page 21. Local Studies Collection, Blue Mountains City Library; **p. 79 (below)** Artist unknown, *Ascending a Hill*, 1886, from A Correct and Faithful Account of a Journey to Fish River Caves by the Pickwick Corresponding Club, 1886, Acc. No. 18/1–3, page 27. Local Studies Collection, Blue Mountains City Library; **p. 87** Photographer unknown, *Last Camp*, 1886, from A Correct and Faithful Account of a Journey to Fish River Caves by the Pickwick Corresponding Club, 1886, Acc. No. 18/1–3, page 31. Local Studies Collection, Blue Mountains City Library; **p. 90** Maker unknown, Trafalgar-back carrying chair, c. 1840, used by Lady Franklin during a visit to the West Coast in 1842. Collection: Tasmanian Museum and Art Gallery; **p. 91 (above)** John Andrew Bonar, *Goulburn River Crossing Place Flooded and a Horse Gibbing*, c. 1856, pen and ink drawing, from his Views in New South Wales and Queensland, with sketches made on his voyages between England and Australia in 1854 and 1860. PXA 538/vol.2/f.18a, Mitchell Library, State Library of New South Wales; **p. 91 (below)** Engraver unknown, *Getting Over a Difficulty—Corduroy Road, Beyond Fernshaw*, wood engraving, from [Views east of Melbourne along the Yarra River, 1881], published in *Illustrated Australian News*, 29 January 1881. IAN29/01/81/8, La Trobe Picture Collection, State Library of Victoria; **p. 93** Joseph Gould Medland, *Cabin Scene. Time 9 a.m. Aboard the* William Jardine. *Oct. 31 1844*, pencil drawing, from Tasmanian Sketches. PXC 287, f.16, Mitchell Library, State Library of New South Wales; **p. 96** Engraver unknown, *A Bush Encampment*, 1860, after a sketch by Emma Macpherson in 1856–57, engraving from E. Macpherson, *My Experiences in Australia*, London, 1860, between pages 98–9. From the original, Rare Books & Special Collections Library, University of Sydney, [RB1560.7].

INVENTING THE MOUNTAIN RESORT, *pp. 99–139*

pp. 98–9 Eugène von Guérard (born Austria 1811, worked in Australia 1852–81, died England 1901), *Weatherboard Creek Falls, Jamieson's Valley, New South Wales*, 1862, oil on canvas, 122.1 × 183.3 cm. Presented through The Art Foundation of Victoria by the ANZ Banking Group Limited, Honorary Life Benefactors, 1989, National Gallery of Victoria, Melbourne; **p. 102** Eugène von Guérard (born Austria 1811, worked in Australia 1852–81, died England 1901), *Weatherboard Creek Falls, Jamieson's Valley, New South Wales*, 1862, oil on canvas, 122.1 × 183.3 cm. Presented through The Art Foundation of Victoria by the ANZ Banking Group Limited, Honorary Life Benefactors, 1989, National Gallery of Victoria, Melbourne; **p. 104** Charles Kerry, *Leura Railway Station*, 1936 print from an 1890s negative, gelatin silver photograph, 16.5 × 21.5 cm. H21810, La Trobe Picture Collection, State Library of Victoria; **p. 109** John Paine (1834–1915), [Blue Mountains Waterfall, Wentworth Falls], c. 1881, albumen photograph, 31 × 26 cm, nla.pic–an10691479–22. By permission of National Library of Australia; **p. 114** F. A. Sleap, *A Visit to Sir Henry Parkes at Faulconbridge*, 1881?, published in *Australasian Sketcher*, 19 November 1881, wood engraving. A/S19/11/81/380, La Trobe Picture Collection, State Library of Victoria; **p. 116** Terence McGann, *'Eurilla', Mount Lofty*, [the House 'Eurilla' Showing Garden and Front Approach], c. 1890, photograph, 39.5 × 53.5 cm. SLSA: B 47676, photograph courtesy of the State Library of South Australia; **p. 119** Engraver unknown, *The Governor's Country House* [Mount Macedon, Vic.], 1886?, published in *Australasian Sketcher*, 7 April 1886, wood engraving. A/S07/04/86/56, La Trobe Picture Collection, State Library of Victoria; **p. 122 (above)** Nicholas John Caire, *The Hotel* [M. Jefferson, Watt's Bridge Hotel, Fernshaw], c. 1883, albumen silver photograph, 14.7 × 19.6 cm. H38469, La Trobe Picture Collection,

State Library of Victoria; **p. 122 (below)** Photographer unknown, [The Carrington], c. 1900, published in *The Blue Mountains: Katoomba and Leura* (published by the Katoomba and Leura Tourist Association 1905), page xxxviii, LS919.445/BLU. From the Local Studies Collection, Blue Mountains City Library; **p. 129** Photographer unknown, *'Shirley', Katoomba*, c. 1900, published in *The Blue Mountains: Katoomba and Leura* (published by the Katoomba and Leura Tourist Association 1905), page xxi, LS919.445/BLU. From the Local Studies Collection, Blue Mountains City Library.

PUTTING UP THE SIGNPOSTS AND LAYING DOWN THE TRACKS, *pp. 141–173*

pp. 140–1 Eugene von Guérard, *Ferntree Gully in the Dandenong Ranges*, 1857, oil on canvas, 92 × 138 cm. Gift of Dr Joseph Brown AO OBE, 1975. National Gallery of Australia, Canberra; **p. 146** Eugene von Guérard, *Ferntree Gully in the Dandenong Ranges*, 1857, oil on canvas, 92 × 138 cm. Gift of Dr Joseph Brown AO OBE, 1975. National Gallery of Australia, Canberra; **p. 149** F. A. Sleap, *Sketches on the Coast—Landing Passengers at Wilson's Promontory*, 1884?, published in *Illustrated Australian News*, 14 May 1884, wood engraving. IAN14/05/84/65, La Trobe Picture Collection, State Library of Victoria; **p. 153** Photographer unknown, *Sir Henry Parkes at Faulconbridge, NSW*, c. 1880s, gelatin silver photograph, 24.3 × 28.8 cm, nla.pic-an23351381. By permission of National Library of Australia; **p. 154** J. W. Beattie (1859–1930), *Track from Crow's Nest, Cataract Gorge, Launceston*, 1890s, albumen photograph, 17.4 × 22.3 cm, nla.pic-an23768270. By permission of National Library of Australia; **p. 158** John Paine, *Shale Mining, Scenic Railway, Blue Mountains, NSW*, c. 1890, photograph, from albumen print, 1884. The University of Sydney, Macleay Museum, 820390425; **p. 159** J. W. Beattie (1859–1930), *Tramway at Geeveston*, 1890s, albumen photograph, 17.4 × 22.3 cm, nla.pic-an23764474. By permission of National Library of Australia; **p. 162** Ernest Brougham Docker, *The Three Sisters, Katoomba, Blue Mountains, NSW*, 7 February 1898, right frame from mounted stereoscopic albumen print. The University of Sydney, Macleay Museum, 82\007\0046; **p. 164 (above)** G. A. Druce, *Track to Linda Falls*, 1900s, White Family Photo collection, PF 1918. From the Local Studies Collection, Blue Mountains City Library; **p. 164 (below)** G. A. Druce, *At Linda Falls*, 1900s, White Family Photo collection, PF 1917. From the Local Studies Collection, Blue Mountains City Library; **p. 171** H. N. Robertson, *A Holiday Ramble in Tasmania—Ascending Mount Wellington*, 1885?, published in *Illustrated Australian News*, 21 January 1885, wood engraving. IAN21/01/85/5, La Trobe Picture Collection, State Library of Victoria; **p. 172** Photographer unknown, *Looking for the Blazed Trees*, 1886, from A Correct and Faithful Account of a Journey to Fish River Caves by the Pickwick Corresponding Club, 1886, Acc. No. 18/1–3, page 47. From the Local Studies Collection, Blue Mountains City Library.

WRITING IT ALL UP, *pp. 175–197*

pp. 174–5 Robert Bruce, *The Zig Zag, Great Western Railway, from the Lithgow Valley, at the Foot of the Blue Mountains, NSW*, 1869?, wood engraving, 22.2 × 37.7 cm, nla.pic–an99119382. By permission of National Library of Australia; **p. 176 (above)** Title page, from Rosamond and Florence Hill, *What We Saw in Australia*, MacMillan & Co., London, 1875. From the original, Rare Books & Special Collections Library, University of Sydney, [RB 1575.21]; **p. 176 (below)** Front cover, from [NSW Railways], *The Railway Guide of New South Wales (for the Use of Tourists, Excursionists, and Others)*, Sydney, 1879. ML 981/N, Mitchell Library, State Library of New South Wales; **p. 181** Robert Bruce, *The Zig Zag, Great Western Railway, from the Lithgow Valley, at the Foot of the Blue Mountains, NSW*, 1869?, wood engraving, 22.2 × 37.7 cm, nla.pic–an99119382. By permission of National Library of Australia; **p. 189** Engraver unknown, *Mount Victoria in its Original State*, c. 1838, from James Maclehose, *The Picture of Sydney and Strangers' Guide in New South Wales for 1838*. From the original, Rare Books & Special Collections Library, University of Sydney, [F2539]; **p. 191** Engraver unknown, *Railway Guide Map Showing Pathways at Leura Falls*, c. 1890, from *Blue Mountains Railway Tourist Guide*, Sydney, 1894, between pages 14 and 15. 981.5/N, Mitchell Library, State Library of New South Wales; **p. 196** Samuel Calvert, *Holiday Rambles— Mount Macedon*, 1874?, published in *Illustrated Australian News*, 25 February 1874, wood engraving. IAN25/02/74/24, La Trobe Picture Collection, State Library of Victoria.

HOW MOUNTAINS BECAME SUBLIME, *pp. 199–225*

pp. 198–9 W. C. Piguenit, *Kosciusko*, 1903, oil on canvas, 179.2 × 261.2 cm, commissioned by the Trustees 1902. Collection: Art Gallery of New South Wales. Photograph: Jenni Carter for AGNSW; **p. 206** John William Lewin, *Spring Wood*, 1815, watercolour, 22.1 × 27 cm. PXE 888/2, Mitchell Library, State Library of New South Wales; **p. 207 (above)** John William Lewin, *Pitt's Amphitheatre*, 1815, watercolour, 24.5 x 29.5 cm. PXE 888/4, Mitchell Library, State Library of New South Wales; **p. 208 (below)** John William Lewin, [Cox's Pass. View of Camp Beside Cox's River], 1815, 21.1 × 25.5 cm. PXE 888/8, Mitchell Library, State Library of New South Wales; **p. 212** Engraver unknown, *Dovedale*, c. 1790, in William Gilpin, *Observations, relative chiefly to picturesque beauty, made in the year 1772, on several parts of England: particularly the mountains, and Lakes of Cumberland, and Westmoreland*, vol. II, London 1792, between pages 226–7. From the original, Rare Books & Special Collections Library, University of Sydney, [G50]; **p. 218** Frederick Grosse, *Ben Lomond, Tasmania*, 1867?, published in *Illustrated Australian News for Home Readers*, 26 October 1867, wood engraving. IAN26/10/67/1, La Trobe Picture Collection, State Library of Victoria; **p. 220** J. W. Beattie (1859–1930), *Rocks on Mount Wellington*, 1880s, lantern slide, 7 cm (dia.), nla.pic-an24930999. By permission of National Library of Australia; **p. 221** Samuel Calvert, *The Heights of Mount Macedon*, 1878?, 23 January 1878, wood engraving. IAN23/01/78/1, La Trobe Picture Collection, State Library of Victoria; **p. 224** W. C. Piguenit, *Kosciusko*, 1903, oil on canvas, 179.2 × 261.2 cm, commissioned by the Trustees 1902. Collection: Art Gallery of New South Wales. Photograph: Jenni Carter for AGNSW.

HOW LIMESTONE CAVES BECAME WONDERFUL, *pp. 227–251*

pp. 226–7 Conrad Martens, *Interior of Burrangalong* [Abercrombie] *Cavern,* 1843–49, oil on canvas, 60.5 × 88.2 cm (framed). DG 163, Dixson Galleries, State Library of New South Wales; **p. 230** Augustus Earle (1793–1838), *Mosman's Cave, Wellington Valley, New South Wales*, no. 5, c. 1826, watercolour, 13.3 × 10.8 cm, nla.pic-an2818416. By permission of National Library of Australia; **p. 234** Thomas L. Mitchell, *Large Cavern at Wellington Valley, New South Wales*, c. 1836, (A. Picken, lithographer), lithograph, in his *Three Expeditions into the interior of Eastern Australia*, London 1839, vol. 2, plate 43. From the original, Rare Books and Special Collections Library, University of Sydney, [F2811]; **p. 237** Conrad Martens, *Interior of Burrangalong (Abercrombie) Cavern*, c. 1843–49, oil on canvas, 60.5 × 88.2 cm (framed). DG 163, Dixson Galleries, State Library of New South Wales; **p. 240** Stephen King, [A Survey Camp on Mosquito Plains, near Naracoorte], 1878, photograph of the sketch. SLSA: B 60262, photograph courtesy of the State Library of South Australia; **p. 245** Engraver unknown, *Grottes de Jenolan—Montagnes Bleues (Australie) Vue du Devil's Coach-house*, c. 1880, wood engraving, after the drawing by Albert Tissandier, published in *La Nature* 13 April 1895. V1B/BLU M/13a, Mitchell Library, State Library of New South Wales; **p. 249** Photographer unknown, *Naracoorte Cave*, c. 1890, photograph. SLSA: B 19670, photograph courtesy of the State Library of South Australia.

HOW FERNS BECAME BEAUTIFUL, *pp. 253–279*

pp. 252–3 Robert Bruce, *A Christmas Party on Mount Macedon*, 1869?, published in *Illustrated Australian News for Home Readers*, 4 January 1869, wood engraving. IAN04/01/69/SUPP/24, La Trobe Picture Collection, State Library of Victoria; **p. 258** Conrad Martens, *Tree Fern*, c. 1835–36, print. PXA 4358, vol. 2, f. 65, Mitchell Library, State Library of New South Wales; **p. 260** John Skinner Prout, [Fern Tree Gully, Possibly Mount Wellington], 1844–48, watercolour and gouache, 37.4 × 27.3 cm. DGD 16/f.8, Dixson Galleries, State Library of New South Wales; **p. 264** Robert Bruce, *A Christmas Party on Mount Macedon*, 1869?, published in *Illustrated Australian News for Home Readers*, 4 January 1869, wood engraving. IAN04/01/69/SUPP/24, La Trobe Picture Collection, State Library of Victoria; **p. 268** Archibald James Campbell (1853–1929), *Karri Forest, Western Australia*, post 1870, sepia toned photograph, 16.7 × 10.7 cm, nla.pic-an24812999. By permission of National Library of Australia; **p. 271** Brookes' Photographic Union photographer, *Mountain Ash*, 1891, albumen silver photograph, 21.5 × 15.7 cm. H42199/46, La Trobe Picture Collection, State Library of Victoria; **p. 276** P. Poulsen, *Botanist Mr Frederick Manson Bailey*, n.d., photograph, image no. 160401. State Library of Queensland; **p. 277** Photographer unknown, *Fern Island in the Botanic Gardens, Brisbane, Queensland*, c. 1878, photograph, image no. 46967. State Library of Queensland.

THE EYE OF THE BEHOLDER, *pp. 281–301*

pp. 280–1 Augustus Earle, *Waterfall in Australia*, c. 1830, oil on canvas, 71 × 83.2 cm, nla.pic-an2273848. By permission of National Library of Australia; **p. 284** Louisa Atkinson, [Ferns], c. 1860, watercolour and pen sketch, 38 × 25.2 cm, from: Ferns 1855–1872 [sketchbook of drawings by Louisa Atkinson]. PXA 4498/f.20, Mitchell Library, State Library of New South Wales; **p. 285** Louisa Atkinson, Dicksonia antarctica, c. 1860, watercolour and pen sketch, 38 × 25.2 cm, from: Ferns 1855–1872 [sketchbook of drawings by Louisa Atkinson]. PXA 4498/f.5, Mitchell Library, State Library of New South Wales; **p. 287** John William Lewin, Telopea speciosissima, 1803–1808, watercolour and pencil sketch, c. 38 × c. 28 cm from Botanical sketches of Australian plants, 1803–1808. PXC 304/206, Mitchell Library, State Library of New South Wales; **p. 292** Louisa Anne Meredith, *View from the Centre of an Immense Mountain Amphitheatre on the Summit of the Blue Mountains—Near the Weatherboard Inn, NSW*, 1839, pencil on white paper drawing, 11.6 × 17.2 cm. W.L. Crowther Library, State Library of Tasmania; **p. 295 (above)** Augustus Earle, *Waterfall in Australia*, c. 1830, oil on canvas, 71 × 83.2 cm, nla.pic-an2273848. By permission of National Library of Australia; **p. 295 (below)** W. C. Piguenit, *Weatherboard Falls*, c. 1876, watercolour. DGD6, f.45, Dixson Galleries, State Library of New South Wales; **p. 298** Louisa Atkinson, *Long Fall from Below 1st Leap 28th July*, c. 1860, watercolour and pen sketch, from Sketchbook of miscellaneous drawings, [Calvert Sketchbook], c. 1855–72. PXA 4500 f.14, Mitchell Library, State Library of New South Wales; **p. 299** Robert Hunt, *Fairy Bower, Mount Victoria, Blue Mountains, NSW*, 24 January 1887, photograph, from silver gelatin negative. The University of Sydney, Macleay Museum, 811060179.

INDEX

This book was designed by Peter Long
The text was typeset by J&M Typesetting
The text was set in 10.5 point Caslon
with 16 points of leading
The text is printed on 130 gsm matt art

This book was edited by Carla Taines

THE
MIEGUNYAH
PRESS